Gentry Politics on the Eve of the Russian Revolution

Gentry Politics on the Eve of the Russian Revolution

The Nationalist Party 1907–1917

Robert Edelman

Rutgers University Press
New Brunswick, New Jersey

Publication of this book was supported by the University of California, San Diego, Faculty Publication Revolving Fund

Library of Congress Cataloging in Publication Data

Edelman, Robert, 1945–
    Gentry politics on the eve of the Russian Revolution

    Bibliography: p.
    Includes index.
    1. Russia—Politics and government—Nicholas II,
1894–1917. 2. Vserossiiskii natsional'nyi soiuz.
3. Russia—Gentry.   I. Title.
DK262.E42   947.08   79–23410
ISBN 0–8135–0885–1

For Page

Contents

Preface		ix
Acknowledgments		xv
Abbreviations		xvii
Map		xviii
I	**The 1905 Revolution and Conservative Politics**	**1**
	The Gentry's Position in a Changing Society	2
	The Problem of Party Formation	6
	The Background of the Revolution of 1905	10
	The Politics of the Transition	19
II	**The Election of 1907**	**30**
	The New Electoral Law	31
	The Makeup of the Third Duma	33
	The Electors	43
	The Nationalists' Stronghold	49
III	**The Rise of the Nationalist Party**	**65**
	The Moderate Right under Octobrist Preeminence	67
	The Realignment of Forces in the Duma and the Ministerial Crisis of 1909	73
	The Birth of the Nationalist Party	86
IV	**A Basis for Power**	**101**
	The National Campaign	102
	The Early Growth of the Nationalist Party	113
	The Western Zemstvo Crisis	116

Political Organization in Western Russia   127
The Zemstvo Elections and Their Aftermath   136

V The Elections to the Fourth Duma   **142**
Preparing for the Elections   143
The Elections of 1912   152

VI The Fourth Duma and the New Crisis   **166**
Confusion and Ambiguity (The First Session)   167
Drift and Division (The Second Session)   176
The Split in Kiev   181
Nationalist Activity outside the Duma   189
Gloom and Doom on the Eve of War   196

VII The War Years: An Epilog   **202**
The First Months of the War   202
The Summer Crisis in the Nation and in the Party   206
The Nationalists Divided and Helpless   224

Selected Bibliography   **235**

Index   **241**

Preface

In the last half-century, historians of modern Europe have concentrated on the growth and ascendancy of those social groups and ideologies that dominate contemporary society. The traditional forces of order have fallen into obscurity, to be brought out and revived by those who might regret the passing of what they see as a better and nobler world. While the political parties and the doctrines of liberals and radicals have received close scrutiny, conservatism remains relatively unstudied. Only in recent years have we seen an attempt to correct the balance. The works of such historians as John Weiss on modern Europe, Eugen Weber on France, Hans-Jurgen Puhle on Germany, Gavin Lewis on Austria, Henry Kissinger on diplomacy, and Hans Rogger on Russia have created a basis for further detailed and critical work on the great variety of conservative groups, parties, and individuals that played and continue to play important roles in modern European politics.

Indeed, this variety has been at the heart of the problem. Richard Pipes, paraphrasing Tolstoy's famous words on happy and unhappy families in *Anna Karenina*, remarked that liberals and radicals sought to advance certain general principles to which they adhered and by which they identified themselves. Conservatives, however, guarded their individuality and mistrusted universal principles; each was conservative in his own way. Thus for the historian seeking to find some meaning and order in events, conservatism can be a frustrating topic of study. One must always resist the tendency merely to catalog groups and individuals. This reason among many others may explain why historians have preferred to concentrate on the left and center of the political spectrum, while ignoring the movements and parties of the right.

In no field is this imbalance more marked than in Russian history. With the exception of Rogger's pioneering efforts on the demagogic and highly untraditional Union of Russian People, there is no work, in any language, on Russia's conservative parties. Since World War II, Western students of Russia have mostly produced intellectual histories of the various components of the revolutionary movement. A desire to comprehend the roots and workings of Bolshevism had much to do with this emphasis, but this great stress on the forces of movement can also be explained in terms of methodological problems. The archival sources, necessary for thorough political and social history, were not open to Western scholars until the mid-1960s, and it took several years for researchers to learn to use these resources effectively. Several good administrative histories have been published in recent years using the voluminous records of the tsarist bureaucracy. Nevertheless, we have only two political histories of the prerevolutionary period based on Soviet archives—Geoffrey Hosking's perceptive study of the government-parliamentary relationship during the period of the constitutional experiment (1907–1914) and Raymond Pearson's innovative account of liberals and moderates during World War I. Yet both these works are "pure" political history. They interpret events from a rather limited perspective that this book seeks to broaden and thereby revise. Indeed, certain institutions and events critical to the political process during 1905 to 1917—the western zemstvo crisis is the most important example—cannot be understood unless we seek data beyond the boundaries of the evidence that Professors Hosking and Pearson have explored. A step in this direction has been taken in a collection of essays on rural politics edited by Leopold Haimson.

Surprisingly, Soviet scholars, who have had access to the archives and who could be expected to seek links between politics and economics, have done little better than their Western counterparts. The leading Soviet specialists on the Duma, V. S. Diakin, E. D. Chermenskii, and A. Ia. Avrekh, have written thorough narrative descriptions of parliamentary politics, but with hastily applied class labels replacing serious analysis of the social base of any party. Other Soviet scholars, most notably A. M. Anfimov, have produced excellent studies of the evolution of gentry landowning, but their works have dealt little with politics. By contrast, Western historians before Hosking, particularly Bernard Pares and Alfred Levin, treated the Duma as a problem of constitutional development. In short, what we know of the Duma parties is written from the perspective of the nation's center, from the Duma itself.

The relationship of the parties to Russia's rapidly evolving social classes remains almost entirely unstudied. Not all parties actually represented specific social groups. In this work, the Nationalist Party will be examined from above and below. This approach has two purposes: first, to demonstrate that the Nationalists, more than any other Duma group, came to represent a distinct constituency, and second, to suggest that a party that actually spoke for an interest group may have been seen as a possible model of political development for different parties representing different interests. Moreover, it is not unreasonable to speculate that had parties of interest developed without the interference of war and revolution, they might very well have replaced the earlier galaxies of national notables and outstanding individuals who grouped themselves around ideologies and who considered themselves to be above class interest.

Writing the history of a political party, with reference to its social base, at a moment when the literature on that social base, the gentry, remains underdeveloped, presents considerable problems. While we know much about the situation of the landed nobility, enough to offer explanations of the political behavior of the Nationalist Party, the gentry's evolution between the emancipation of the serfs in 1861 and the Revolution of 1917 is obviously beyond the scope of a study such as this. Nor is the entire history of the gentry germane to my main concern, the emergence of a political party. I have argued that this party cannot be understood without reference to the social and economic problems of the group of Russian landlords that the Nationalists represented. In the past, this party has been dismissed as the artificial creation of the tsarist government. I have shown in these pages that they did indeed have a base of support in Russian society. Further studies will give us a complete picture of the development of the Russian gentry. I have sought here to contribute to our understanding of the political dimensions of that process.

In the effort to study and explain the emergence and significance of a Russian conservative political party, the scholar must work in largely uncharted territory. As the largest and most successful of the parties of the right, the Russian Nationalists pose special problems for the historian. Unlike the centrist Octobrists or the liberal Kadets, the Nationalists have not been accorded a separate archive of their own in Soviet repositories. Police reports written by infiltrators, spies, and informers, are extensive on the left and center, but they are sparse for the right, an element considered more trustworthy. I was the first Western scholar (and only the second historian, Soviet or foreign) to gain access to the police department's files of intercepted and inspected letters. This source contains communications from citizens of all political persuasions. These files made it possible to locate the Nationalists ideologically and learn something of their thoughts on such matters as political strategy, organizational techniques, and policy initiatives.

Unfortunately, these letters reveal practically nothing that would permit an interpretation of the Nationalists' personalities. Understanding their personalities, or even obtaining a reliable reading on a few prominent individual party members, is made all the more difficult by the fact that, of all the Duma groups, the Nationalists were the one party that lacked an outstanding individual among its leadership. These men were far more given to self-defense than self-examination. In the absence of solid evidence, a scholar cannot responsibly dwell on the Nationalists' psychological motivation or personal styles.

However, one can use these police archives to establish the Nationalists' ideological position and to examine the functional linkages between the rapidly evolving social situation in Russia and the party's activities. This is a sufficiently ambitious task, and it permits one to rely on a considerable body of hard evidence in a variety of rich sources seldom or never investigated previously. The Nationalists' attitudes and collective psychology can be inferred from their day-to-day behavior in the political arenas of the Duma and the provinces. On these matters, the data are convincing and extensive.

In the absence of any secondary literature on the Nationalists, it was necessary to construct an essentially skeletal narrative of events through the systematic reading of the daily press. While the other parties had their organs in St. Petersburg or Moscow, the Nationalists' newspaper was published in Kiev. This proved fortuitous, because it illuminated the world of provincial politics. The Nationalists' responsiveness to events on the local level ultimately enabled them to organize a novel kind of political formation in prerevolutionary Russia. More than any of the other Duma parties, they had a sense of their constituency and a readiness to serve the direct economic and political interests of their supporters. It was their understanding of the connection between the national and the provincial arenas that made the Nationalists function more like a modern political party than any other conservative group in Russia, and the emphasis on this relationship constitutes much of the originality of this study. In particular, the detailed examination of the local elections of 1911 and the Duma campaigns of 1912 proved the most effective way to demonstrate the links between provincial and national politics. Close study of the election processes has been attempted by few students of the period. This particular research is based on the local press and is extensively supplemented by much new archival material, compiled by the police and by provincial governors.

Although the Russian Nationalist Party demonstrated considerable political modernity by succeeding in the representation of a clearly defined group (the Russian noble landlords of the western borderlands), it should not be forgotten that this collection of aristocratic landholders inherited and retained many of the political attitudes of the traditional, patriarchal world that they had so recently dominated. The Russian gentry owed its original wealth and privilege to the all-powerful autocrat, by virtue of bureaucratic and military service. Most of this group remained loyal to the tsar up to the very end. The gentry's adoption of a form of interest politics, novel for the Russian scene, aided the early growth of the Nationalist Party, but this course ultimately proved disastrous, because it placed them squarely between two institutions that eventually became polarized—the Duma and the autocracy.

Acknowledgments

Scholarship is not conducted in a vacuum, and this work is no exception. I have received extensive assistance, advice, and support from many friends, colleagues, and institutions. All have left their imprint on this book. A firm commitment on the part of many people to a process of reciprocity and mutual support made writing this book possible.

My largest debt is to my mentor, Leopold Haimson. His training, support, and diligent criticism are largely responsible for whatever qualities of scholarly rigor, conceptual sophistication, and thoroughness may be found in this work. Arno Mayer was the first to suggest to me that the forces of order required the same careful attention others had given to the forces of movement. He has provided encouragement and assistance at each step along the way. Hans Rogger pioneered the study of the Russian right and encouraged me to follow the lines of inquiry he had first suggested. I value highly the criticisms he has made of several drafts of the manuscript. Geoffrey Hosking's work on the Duma provided the basis for this more specialized study. His precise and helpful readings of the manuscript have improved this work considerably, and his openness to my own interpretive approach has been a model of scholarly understanding.

I owe a special debt to Loren Graham, without whose aid at crucial moments in my career this book would never have been written. My thanks also to my Soviet supervisor and advisor, Evgenii Dmitrievich Chermenskii, whose generosity in sharing the fruits of his massive research and his guidance in the intricacies of archival work in the Soviet Union are largely responsible for my success in obtaining previously unused materials. At points in the text, I have noted our interpretational differences, but those in no way diminish my respect and gratitude.

Harry Scheiber, Ron Suny, and Reginald Zelnik have read the manuscript and made many important suggestions. Page duBois, Temma

Kaplan, and Roy Ritchie examined the introduction and helped make it more comprehensible to the nonspecialist. Saul Steier offered a generous and detailed analysis and criticism of the preface. Alexander Ehrlich, John Hazard, Marc Raeff, and the late Michael Cherniavsky read an earlier version of this work, and all had useful suggestions for revision and expansion. I am also grateful to Ramon Eduardo Ruiz for his encouragement during his chairmanship of the history department at the University of California, San Diego, and to Herbert Mann, the director of Rutgers University Press, for his encouragement, flexibility, and sensitivity. I would also like to note the special intelligence with which Terri LaMothe and Susan Orlovsky aided in the preliminary stages of the manuscript's preparation.

The International Research and Exchange Board supported two research trips to the Soviet Union. It is my hope that this book will demonstrate the value and importance of the exchange in some small way. The Russian Institute of Columbia University provided a junior research fellowship in 1971 and a continuing welcome as a visiting scholar in the years since then. I thank the Regents of the University of California for two research fellowships and the Academic Senate of the University of California, San Diego, for repeated financial assistance. Finally, I must thank the Office of Graduate Studies and Research of the University of California, San Diego, for a grant to aid publication.

I wish to express my gratitude to the staffs of the following archives and libraries: The Central State Archive of the October Revolution in Moscow; the Central State Historical Archive in Leningrad; the Public Records Office in London; the Butler Library of Columbia University; the Slavonic Room of the New York Public Library; the Widener and Lamont libraries of Harvard University; the libraries of the Universities of California at Berkeley, Los Angeles, and San Diego; the Hoover Institute; the British Library; the Bibliothèque de Documentation Internationale Contemporaine in Nanterre, France; the Helsinki University Library; the Lenin Library in Moscow; the Historical Library of Moscow; the Institute for Information on the Social Sciences in Moscow; the library of the Academy of Sciences in Leningrad; and the Saltykov-Shchedrin Public Library in Leningrad.

Finally, my thanks to the editors of the *Russian Review* for permission to use part of my article "The Russian Nationalist Party and the Political Crisis of 1909" (*Russian Review* [January 1975]), and to the editors of Indiana University Press for permission to use part of my essay "The Election to the Third Duma: The Roots of the Nationalist Party" from Leopold Haimson, ed., *The Politics of Rural Russia, 1905–1914.*

Abbreviations

Materialy	*Materialy po agrarno-ekonomicheskoe issledovanie iugo-za-padnogo kraia*
Portrety	*Portrety, biografii, avtografii*
PRO, FO	Public Record Office, Foreign Office Series (England)
Sten. ot.	Gosudarstvennaia duma, *Stenograficheskie otchety*
TsGAOR	Tsentral'nyi gosudarstvennyi arkhiv Oktiabrskoi revoliutsii
TsGIAL	Tsentral'nyi gosudarstvennyi istoricheskii arckhiv v Leningrade
VNS	Obzor deiatl'nosti vserossikogo natsional'nogo soiuva
Vybory	Vybory v tret'iu gosudarstvennuiu duma

The System of transliteration used in this book is Library of Congress, type II, and all dates are according to the Old Style calendar.

The abbreviations TsGAOR and TsGIAL refer to the two central Soviet archives. The numbers following these citations refer to *fond, opis, delo,* and *list.* An exception is the material from the Department of Police (TsGAOR *fond* 102). In these citations the *fond* number is most often followed by the year in parentheses.

I

The 1905 Revolution and Conservative Politics

After the Russian Revolution of 1905, landowning aristocrats had to adjust to a modern world of parliaments and political parties, a world they neither sought nor created. Against their will, they adopted new political tactics to preserve their traditional wealth and privilege. One of the fruits of the 1905 Revolution was the creation of the state Duma, the lower house of Russia's quasi parliament. The Duma was originally designed to be broadly representative, but the third Duma (1907-1912) had been elected under a restrictive electoral law that favored large property holders.

Late in 1909, several hundred Russian conservatives, led by noble landlords from the Empire's western borders, established the Russian Nationalist Party. This new group claimed the second largest number of deputies in the Duma and soon became the base of political support for the leading statesman of this period, the president of the Council of Ministers, Peter Arkadevich Stolypin. More significant, the Nationalists developed new methods and attitudes that aided them in the task of

1

creating a modern political party capable of representing and protecting the interests of conservative landlords in the semiparliamentary system that existed in Russia between the Revolutions of 1905 and 1917.

The Gentry's Position in a Changing Society

The landed nobility's economic and political domination of Russia had been challenged long before the Revolution of 1905 by a variety of modernizing forces. The necessity for such an adjustment to this new situation had been preceded elsewhere in Europe by profound economic and demographic changes, begun as early as the fifteenth century. In particular, an emerging capitalism undermined the corporate societies in which the landed nobility occupied a position of enormous privilege. The primary social groups in premodern societies were legally defined estates of the realm. In an autocracy such as Russia, the character and composition of these social categories were determined largely by each citizen's relation to the powerful state. In this system of social stratification, legal, political, genealogical, cultural, and other considerations of status played a greater role than economics in determining one's place in society.[1] The Russian aristocracy maintained its dominance by serving in the bureaucracy or army. Most aristocrats possessed landed estates, but the work they performed for the tsar, not their ownership of land, gave them status. Despite this situation, agriculture and landed wealth buttressed the entire system. The societies of premodern Europe, including Russia, were agrarian, and the nobility maintained its position partly through its control of the land. Yet, especially in Russia, that control was predicated on continuing service to the state.

The growth of industry and commerce undermined this system in several ways. Most obviously, the emergence of new sources of wealth threatened the predominance of agriculture. Because success could now be achieved outside the old social structure, the categories and principles of the system of legal estates came into question. As economic activity competed with land ownership as the basis for defining social position, modern social classes began to emerge. The work of these new classes was carried on more or less independently of the bureaucratic state structure, and the relative autonomy of the new productive roles provided

1. John R. Gillis, *The Prussian Bureaucracy in Crisis 1840–1860*, (Stanford, 1971), p. 215; Jerome Blum, *The End of the Old Order in Rural Europe* (Princeton, 1978), p. 440.

an eventual basis for the creation of political parties that also operated outside the state's control.[2] Before this parties had been either illegal or, more properly speaking, irrelevant to the political process, especially in autocratic states. The social group most threatened by the emergence of a class society was the landed nobility, which had always justified its dominance in terms of status rather than class. In some nations, most notably England, adjustment had proved possible, but in Russia the aristocracy was closely tied to the state through bureaucratic and military service and only secondarily engaged in such independent activity as management of farming operations.

But the new economic order offered opportunities as well as dangers. As the self-sufficiency of the traditional rural world broke down, the rewards of producing an agricultural surplus were enhanced. The growth of cities increased the demand for farm produce, and advances in transportation facilitated the shipping of grain. Owning an estate now meant owning a source of profit, rather than simply a source of rents. Nobles could now forsake their parasitic roles and become agrarian producers. That they could even contemplate such a course was largely the result of the declining prestige of a bureaucratic career. Nonnobles were finding their way into state service, and the bureaucracy had ceased to be the only elite group in society.[3] By the late nineteenth century, the Russian government found it impossible to resist the need for industrialization. To pay for factories and railroads, Russia was compelled to embark on policies directed by the Minister of Finance, Sergei Witte, that disadvantaged the agrarian sector of the economy. All this activity distanced nobles from a state that had historically been their protector.

However, even the most economically advanced noble landlords did not entirely forsake the attitudes of preindustrial estate society. Their acceptance of the reality of economic competition with other interest groups did not mean that they were above resorting to traditional appeals and practices to serve their ends. But, in the new context, these traditional attitudes took on a different meaning. This was especially true of the Russian landed nobility's relationship with the state. Timeless justifications of an immutable social order now became weapons of immediate political expedience. The state had been the protector of law and order, the symbol of the traditional authority that assured the security of the nobility. Whatever new roles they might adopt, aristocrats had no intention of

2. Joseph LaPolambara and Myron Weiner, "The Origin and Development of Political Parties," in Joseph LaPolambara and Myron Weiner (eds.), *Political Parties and Political Development* (Princeton, 1966), p. 3.

3. Gillis, *The Prussian Bureaucracy*, pp. 217–220.

entirely repudiating older notions of social prestige and influence, especially when those notions could aid them in securing political advantage.

Modernization had created a demand for political participation that
could not be accommodated under the old bureaucratic structures. Both
landed and propertyless aristocrats had fought the creation of the
parliamentary institutions that had been sought by the middle and working
classes. The nobles also opposed the extension of broad suffrage. But
once those institutions were created, conservative landlords were faced
with the task of finding a new political weapon to defend themselves with
in the changed political order. Because the state could no longer defend
and support them at all times, landowning aristocrats had to organize
politically. Pressure groups and interest lobbies were set up to articulate
the nobility's needs, but the form most clearly necessitated by the creation
of parliamentary and semiparliamentary bodies was the political party.

Noble landlords, even those who were economically progressive, did not
approach the task of party formation with great enthusiasm. Parties were
alien to the noble landlords' experience. Under the old order, any kind of
political organization had been illegal. In addition, political parties were
creatures of modernizing societies. Now, however, the Russian nobles
were forced to play by someone else's rules.

Gentry parties faced particularly difficult problems surviving in a
parliamentary system. The need to appeal to voters made it difficult for
them to remain purely class parties. As a result of mass suffrage, their
numbers were simply too small. As Robert Michels has described the
problem,

> A party of the landed gentry which should appeal only to the members of its
> own class and to those of equal economic interests, would not win a single
> seat, would not send a single representative to parliament.[4]

Thus, a gentry party had two alternatives. It could compromise with
other groups in society, or it could agitate for a restriction of the franchise.
Either course involved finding some shared interests or beliefs with
elements outside its own limited circle. In several countries in Europe,
attempts had been made to form alliances with peasants and small
farmers in unions of agrarians. However, this course would dilute the class
character of any party formed by the landed nobility. On the other hand,
the gentry could petition the state to structure the electoral process and
parliamentary institutions to give the gentry far greater power than its
limited numbers would otherwise allow. This approach involved a sacrifice

4. Robert Michels, *Political Parties* (New York, 1915), p. 6.

of political independence. In Russia's case, independence was more often foregone. A conservative party could never be entirely autonomous from the state, which preserved law and order and defended private property. Thus, conservative parties faced a basic conflict between the needs of their immediate constituencies and the necessity to maintain the basic structure of authority. When the state defended their interests, these parties prospered. But, when the state pursued policies that threatened those interests, conservatives were faced with an agonizing choice. Did they defend to the death those social forces they represented, or did they suffer in silence to avoid threatening the institution that was the original source of their wealth and privilege?

Especially in the earliest phase of industrialization, landed interests had to compete with other groups for government support. In assuming a modern class role as agrarian producers, noble landlords were taking their chances in an economy and polity that forced them to take care of themselves. But, even in this new context, there were considerable advantages to be gained by the continuous support of the government. However, the Russian state, headed by traditional figures of authority, could not always concern itself primarily with the gentry's needs. When the demands of the industrial sector took priority, noble landlords had to take a back seat. They did not accept this situation in silence. Conservatives could criticize the government and press for a change in the course of policy, but full-scale opposition remained an uncertain and frightening course. Noble landlords were trained in the habits of obedience, not contention. Their own local authority had the same historic roots as the authority of the crown. Thus, landed nobles were faced with the problem of choosing between the modernizing forces that had created the possibility of their representation in parliaments and the traditional forces that guaranteed that representation through manipulated electoral laws. This proved a difficult, often impossible, choice to make.

In Russia, the state remained an important part of the political equation because it had accorded only limited powers to the representative institutions that it had granted in 1905. Having a large delegation in the Duma did not necessarily mean that a party had increased influence on government decisions. Because the government was not directly responsible to the parliamentary institutions, the parties could not always serve as channels of influence or power. The extension of democratic forms masked other power relations in society. The legislative bodies were not merely window dressing, but much crucial power still resided in state ministries. Groups with specific goals had to approach the state directly. In Russia, both before and after the creation of the Duma, this took the form of direct petitioning of government officials by either individual noble landlords or by the official provincial assemblies of the nobility, which had been created in 1785.

Predictably, these petitions met with better response in some sectors of the bureaucracy than in others. During the 1890s, for example, the gentry often addressed complaints about Witte's industrializing policies to the Ministry of Interior. The competition between agrarian and industrial interests then took the form of a debate within the bureaucracy itself. The gentry was able to influence this discussion through strong personal ties with individual officials, which were often the result of shared educational experiences.

The organization of any national group was forbidden until 1906. After that date, a pressure group of noble landlords (based on the official provincial assemblies of the nobility) did emerge, along with the various political parties that competed for gentry support. The Russian Nationalist Party was the most successful (or, more properly, the least unsuccessful) formation in marshalling the landed nobility in defense of their interests.

The Problem of Party Formation

A central element of the Nationalists' political success was their ability to represent the interests of a distinct constituency. The party's social base was the Russian gentry of the western borderlands. This region was a highly fertile area with extensive commercial agriculture. The relative economic modernity of western Russia does much to explain those elements of political modernity developed by the Nationalists. In particular, they were able to establish close contact between their supporters in the countryside and their deputies in the Duma. For such students of political development as Maurice Duverger, this forging of a nexus between region and center is a crucial step in the evolution of a modern political party. Duverger has argued that before actual political parties were established the predominant forms were cliques, clubs, or unions of notables. It was only when those groupings established organized contact with the localities that one could begin to speak of true political parties.[5] In a vast land such as Russia, whose railroad network was still weak, this kind of communication was difficult to achieve. Of all the conservative

5. Maurice Duverger, *Political Parties: Their Organization and Activity in the Modern State* (New York, 1954), pp. xiii–xxvii.

formations that appeared in Russia before the Revolution of 1917, the Nationalist Party came closest to establishing this necessary contact between the capital and the provinces. The Nationalists' inability to expand this high level of organization outside the western borderland was the reason for their ultimate failure.

The western borderland had a better developed system of railroads than that found in most other parts of Russia (Moscow and St. Petersburg were obvious exceptions). Railroads played an important role in the Nationalists' development, and they always benefitted from close ties with members of the railway administration and the Ministry of Communication. Trains were made available so that party deputies could tour the countryside and organize support. Indeed, the party's deputies played important roles in the establishment of provincial groups. However, between 1907 and 1917, the Nationalists were only able to begin the elaboration of a national and local organization. Although war and revolution prevented the Nationalists from completing their task, their first steps were entirely consistent with the kinds of processes that have led to the formation of fully developed, modern political parties elsewhere.

The close contact between the provincial and national levels was the most novel aspect of the Nationalists' approach to politics. Little else about them would strike the student of political parties as particularly exotic. Their local network maintained intimate ties with their parliamentary group, and eventually the party's Duma members came to work in relative harmony with the Prime Minister, Stolypin. The party used these relationships to advance projects that aided its constituency. While familiar to students of American and West European political parties, this kind of explicit interest politics was new to Russia. Earlier parties such as the Kadets had sought to depict themselves as being above class interest, while the Octobrists and others sought to combine the needs of different social groups. Indeed, one might be tempted to dismiss the Nationalists as simply a special-interest group operating in the guise of a political party. However, this kind of specificity was a common early phase of party development elsewhere.

The existence of the Duma, with its limited franchise, strongly enhanced the attractiveness of a party as an appropriate political vehicle for the particular segment of the gentry represented by the Nationalists. West Russian landlords had few close ties to the tsar or his courtiers, nor were they able to find consistent support within the bureaucracy. Other nobles had already joined the Kadets, Octobrists, and several extreme right-wing parties. It made perfect sense to do likewise. Without the Duma, those who came to form the Nationalists would have had to rely on direct petitions and personal contacts to gain a hearing. If the Duma had continued to exist with a broad franchise, the future Nationalists would have been forced to participate in nonpartisan pressure groups and broadly based right-wing organizations just as they had done between 1905 and 1907. Under the peculiar rules of the Russian system after 1907, however, a political party with a highly constrained social base was a logical choice.

Because the existence of the Duma had convinced the Nationalists of the utility and necessity of forming a party, they considered the Duma a useful and meaningful institution that was well worth preserving. Moreover, it was vital that the Duma retain its legislative rights, for only in such a body could their proposals get the serious attention of the tsar and his ministers. Still, the Nationalists did not wish the Duma to become a true parliament in a genuinely constitutional system. Like Nicholas II, they wanted Russia to remain an autocracy. They had no desire to place formal limits on the tsar. Instead, they dreamed of a Russia ruled over by a true autocrat, an unrestrained monarch who paid attention to their needs as expressed in the Duma.

Thus, the Nationalists faced what proved to be an insurmountable problem. In their ability to represent a definite constituency, they showed a willingness to accept political autonomy and take their chances in the new world of parliaments and political parties. Nonetheless, they also continued to rely on the traditional authority of the autocrat to protect their lands and privileges. The creation of what appeared to be a modern political party that was capable of defending their interests proved to be a successful course of action only in the short run. Ultimately, this approach proved disastrous, because it placed these landowning aristocrats between two institutions that eventually came to oppose each other—the state and the Duma.

Because they were a conservative and aristocratic party, the Nationalists were less concerned than other political groups and parties with the thorough articulation of program and ideology. In fact, conservatives have always tended to be elusive on such matters. Conservative programs are typically distinguished less by what they include than by what they leave out. For example, in a nation that had a crying need for land reform, the failure of a conservative party to mention the question in its program would be as significant as its extensive elaboration by some revolutionary group. Liberals, radicals, revolutionaries, and others who seek to change a particular society have to propose alternatives. Their position requires that they develop some kind of vision of a different future. In Russia, the conservatives' vision of the future was, if not the past, at least not substantially different from the present. Although it was not true in all cases, the preservation of existing social, economic, and political systems was the aim of most conservatives. Thus, except for certain prudent if limited reforms, the program of conservative political groups did not have to be imagined or even spelled out.

Conservatives also tended to be less explicit than liberals and revolutionaries about more complicated questions of ideology. There can be no doubt that conservatives made use of ideas and systems of thought to justify their positions. However, they usually avoided characterizing those ideas as part of any intellectually unified totality. As John Weiss has suggested, conservatives were often skeptical of all ideology, which they considered the province of the left. Instead, they commonly described themselves as realistic, nonideological pragmatists, as solvers of problems rather than spinners of dreams.[6]

However, the massive appeal of liberal and socialist ideas during the last third of the nineteenth century forced the right to develop its own alternative ideologies. Nationalism was probably the most politically successful body of concepts to emerge from the conservative camp in response to the thrust from the left. Loyalty to a culturally and linguistically defined nation was to replace loyalty to a divinely ordered absolutist state. Identification with a specific national group, to which certain admirable human qualities were ascribed, had an enormous emotional and psychological impact on citizens of all classes. Nationalism's political success was largely attributable to the fact that it reinforced the self-esteem of many people at a time when advanced industrial capitalism had destroyed many of the other psychological support mechanisms of traditional society.

Russian nationalism took many cues from its German counterpart. Pan-Germanism, in a variety of forms, had helped to unite Germany on a basis that was attractive to conservatives. Following this example, nationalism in Russia was inevitably mixed with a number of varieties of pan-Slavism or, as it came to be known at the turn of the century,[7] "neo-Slavism." These ideas ranged from visions of a vast, fraternal federation of Serbs, Poles, Ukrainians, Russians, and Bulgarians to complete Russian domination of all Slav nations. Whatever the form of pan-Slavism or Russian nationalism, all these approaches were concerned with the testing of these visions and the national will in the international arena. Before 1914, these nationalist concerns were especially involved with the fate of

6. John Weiss, *Conservatism in Modern Europe, 1770-1945* (London, 1976), pp. 71–75.

7. Hugh Seton-Watson, *The Decline of Imperial Russia, 1855-1914* (New York, 1952), pp. 378–379.

fellow Slavs in the Balkans, and that interest led Russia into repeated confrontations with Austria in an attempt to restore tattered Russian prestige.

The more moderate Octobrist party and the right wing of the liberal Kadets proved far more receptive to these kinds of ideas than the Nationalists did. In fact, according to this particular notion of nationalism, the Russian Nationalist Party was *less* nationalistic than the other parties in the Duma. The Nationalists were not so much a party of nationalism as a party of the dominant Russian nationality in a multinational empire. They sought to achieve the complete domination by the Russians within the Empire, but, by contrast, had little enthusiasm for international affairs. They suspected that any variety of pan-Slavism would force them to cooperate with the Poles, who were the west Russian noble landlords' chief rivals in the highly competitive world of commercial agriculture in the borderlands. The Nationalists were only concerned with those nationalities with whom their constituency had daily contact—Poles and Jews. If the Nationalists had had an autonomous ideological commitment to the ideas of Russian nationalism, their attitudes toward Poles and Jews would have been applied to such other groups as Finns and Armenians who were strangers to the western provinces. However, the Nationalist Party was largely indifferent to such issues.

In short, the Nationalist Party's name is misleading. Such deception is hardly unusual in politics. No one would have expected Germany's National Socialists to join the Third International, nor were the Radicals of France's Third Republic especially progressive. It became a journalistic cliché to call the French Radicals "radishes" (red on the outside but white on the inside). Following the same reasoning, the Russian Nationalists were like eggs (white on the outside and yellow on the inside).

The Background of the Revolution of 1905

Industrialization and Discontent

Twenty years of rapid industrialization had preceded the Revolution of 1905. Even though the tsarist state had initiated this effort in order to support a flagging military structure, it soon found itself ill-equipped to deal with the consequences of its actions. The result was profound and steadily increasing social instability. Tsar Nicholas II's Minister of Finance, Sergei Witte, had orchestrated the programs that had given Russia an average annual growth rate of 8 percent during the 1890s. But industrialization had created new social classes—an industrial bourgeoisie and a proletariat—that simply had no place in Russia's traditional social and political structures. By bringing into being social groups for whom the autocracy's laws and institutions had no place, Witte's policies, which were designed to buttress the state, were instead making it obsolete. At the turn of the century, the Russian Empire, despite its economic progress, found itself in serious political trouble.

The agrarian sector of the economy was severely taxed to pay for the growth of industry. This policy was carried out despite the long-term depression of the international grain market and the rapid increase of the peasant population, which exacerbated their chronic land hunger. Given the already depressed state of the Russian countryside, this policy drove the peasantry to ruin. Disorders broke out in Poltava and Kharkov in 1902. The incidence of violent acts by peasants rose steadily, leading up to massive disturbances in 1905 and 1906. The situation in the towns was no better. Peasants who went to the cities joined a hideously exploited proletariat that was more discontented and better organized than their brothers and sisters in the villages. Massive strike activity had begun with the St. Petersburg textile strikes of 1896 and 1897, and industrial unrest had spread to the south and west after 1900.

However, discontent was not limited to workers and peasants. The number of professionals had increased considerably in the previous decades. Lawyers, professors, journalists, and engineers became more numerous as Russian society grew more urban and complex. In the countryside, the organs of local government (the *zemstvos*) hired great numbers of doctors, statisticians, agronomists, and teachers. All these new elements found it difficult to perform their jobs without bureaucratic interference. In the zemstvos, they joined forces with politically liberal noble landlords, who also resented the authority of the central government. These two groups sought to place limits on the arbitrary powers of the autocracy. Thus, in Russia, increasingly urgent demands for civil liberties and a constitutional regime were advanced by nobles and intellectuals. Members of the middle classes, especially industrialists, remained aloof from liberal politics. This indifference was largely due to their dependence on state support during the early phase of industrialization.

Inevitably, the dissatisfaction at nearly every level of Russian society had political consequences. Although political parties, even conservative ones, were strictly illegal, several parties emerged to channel what came to be called the liberation movement. The Marxist Social Democrats, the populist Socialist Revolutionaries, and liberal Union of Liberation all organized activity aimed at ending tsarist repression. The government harassed, arrested, and exiled its opponents, but made no serious attempt to alleviate the causes of their complaints. In January 1904, the tsar declared war on Japan in the hope that a "short, victorious war" would silence his critics. But the government got an embarrassing, disastrous defeat instead of a quick victory, and disaffection spread to the armed forces. By this point, Russia was a tinderbox. It took the events of "Bloody Sunday," January 9, 1905, to set it off. When peacefully demonstrating workers were massacred in St. Petersburg's Palace Square, the result was an explosion of strikes, demonstrations, disturbances, and petitions that increased with each passing day.

The Tsar's Manifesto

Finally, in October 1905, after nearly a year of political and social turmoil, urban Russia went on strike against the state. In response to the crisis, on October 17, Nicholas followed Witte's advice and reluctantly issued a manifesto designed to meet some of society's demands. Significant changes were promised. There would be a true legislature to be elected by a broad franchise. Civil liberties were to be extended, censorship was to be reduced, and political organization was legalized. It appeared that tsarism had at last set limits on itself. In order for all citizens to understand the precise nature of those limits, a set of Fundamental Laws was promised that would clarify the rules of the new political system. However, Nicholas had agreed to proclaim the manifesto only after he had been assured that Russia would, in fact, remain an autocracy and that the tsar's jealously guarded ancient prerogatives would survive untouched. Indeed, to pacify Nicholas, this principle had been explicitly stated in the manifesto, even though it was an obvious contradiction to the manifesto's intent. When the Fundamental Laws were elaborated during the next months, the government sought to take back many of its promises.

It turned out that the new parliament would consist of two chambers instead of one. The lower house would be the long-promised Duma, elected indirectly but with a broad franchise. The Duma was to be counterbalanced by a revised State Council that was now half appointed and half elected. Its elected members came only from the propertied and educated elements in society. As a result, the upper chamber was a graveyard for most of the legislation that got through the Duma. The lower house was supposed to have extensive control of the budget, but it had no authority over military and court expenses. Either chamber could initiate legislation, and no proposal could become law without the approval of both houses. However, the tsar could veto any project, and, if the Duma turned down a government bill, the tsar could simply decree it to be a law by means of the exceptional power granted in Article 87 of the Fundamental Laws. This power could be exercised only when the parliamentary bodies were not in session, but, as the tsar had the right to dissolve both chambers when he deemed it necessary, it was not difficult to create conditions in which Article 87 could operate. Ministers were still appointed by and were responsible to the tsar, not to the Duma. The ministers' activities were now to be coordinated in a reorganized Council of Ministers that was to be headed by a president who assumed some of the roles of a prime minister. Finally, the principle of autocracy was once again confirmed when the laws were published in May 1906.

No one knew what sort of conclusions to draw from the Fundamental Laws. If there was now a constitution, its character was not clear to anyone. This ambiguity led to a constant tension between the state and society's representatives concerning the limits that the state had placed on itself and on society. This antagonism between the government and the Duma remained a central factor in Russian politics until the Revolution of 1917. As each side changed its sense of what it wanted and what it thought it could get, the struggle was renewed.[8]

An especially significant right that the autocracy had granted was the right to organize politically. Of Russia's traditional legal estates (*soslovia*), the nobility (the *dvoriantsvo*) was the most threatened by this change in the structure of authority. Political parties had been considered as foreign forms that undermined the organic unity of traditional society. Liberals and revolutionaries could organize and risk being arrested or exiled. But for a conservative noble to engage in politics was unseemly and improper. However, that kind of complacency and indifference could no longer be maintained after the Revolution of 1905.

The Noble Estate

The dvoriantsvo faced the challenge of political organization at a moment when its nature was in the process of profound and thorough transformation. Toward the end of the nineteenth century, the homogeneity of the legal estate of state servants, created by Peter the Great and

8. Geoffrey Hosking, *The Russian Constitutional Experiment* (Cambridge, 1973), pp. 1–13; Gilbert Doctorow, "The Fundamental State Laws of 23 April 1906," *Russian Review* (April 1975):32–52.

nurtured by Catherine the Great, was eroding under the impact of the rapid growth of Russian capitalism. New nonnoble elements were beginning to perform many of the bureaucratic tasks previously done only by nobles. Many nobles were leaving the land to seek new careers in the cities or simply to live off the proceeds from the sale of their estates. Aside from a new diversity of activity, nobles also displayed sharp differences in wealth. At the turn of the century, there were slightly more than 100,000 estates owned by nobles. Of these, just about one-quarter were above 500 *desiatiny* or 1,350 acres.[9] (One *desiatin* equals 2.7 acres.) About half the dvorianstvo owned estates of less than 100 desiatiny. In stark contrast, 155 great landowners whose estates averaged 100,000 desiatiny controlled one-third of all noble-owned land.[10]

Still more significant than this growing divergence in levels of wealth among the gentry was the simple fact that nobles were selling or losing their land in massive numbers during the second half of the nineteenth century. Between the two extensive land censuses of 1877 and 1905, noblemen lost approximately 30 percent of their holdings. In 1877, they had owned 73,077,000 desiatiny. By 1905, that figure had been reduced to 52,104,000 desiatiny.[11] Some Soviet scholars have argued that the actual loss of noble-owned land between the emancipation of the serfs in 1861 and the Revolution of 1905 was greater than the 30 percent figure offered by the standard accounts of Robinson and Pavlovsky. While the argument of Soviet specialists that nobles must have lost much land between 1861 and 1877 is obviously logical, the kind of universal data available for 1877 and 1905 is lacking for these earlier years. Studies of certain regions, like that carried on by M. A. Rubach for parts of the Ukraine during the years 1862–1914, have indicated that in even such fertile provinces as Kharkov, Chernigov, and Poltava, nobles lost as much as 60 percent of their land. Similarly, the French scholar, Sylvain Bensidoun, has noted that between 1861 and 1877 nobles in some of the provinces of the Central Agricultural Region lost as much as 45 percent of their land. Given the fact that Robinson's work indicates that the nobles'

9. Terence Emmons, "The Russian Landed Gentry and Politics," *Russian Review* (July 1974):270–271; Iu. B. Soloviev, *Samoderzhavie i dvorianstvo v kontse XIX veka*, p. 205; and A. P. Korelin, "Dvorianstvo v poreformennoi Rossii," *Istoricheskie zapiski*, Vol. 87 (1971):136.

10. L. P. Minarik, *Ekonomicheskaia kharakeristika krupneishikh zemel'nykh sobstvennikov Rossii kontsa XIX–nachala XX veka*, p. 4.

11. Geroid Robinson, *Rural Russia under the Old Regime* (New York, 1932), pp. 131, 268; G. P. Pavlovsky, *Agricultural Russia on the Eve of Revolution* (London, 1930), p. 111. Pavlovsky's estimate of gentry holdings in 1905 is slightly lower than Robinson's. Pavlovsky credits nobles with owning 46,200,000 desiatiny in 1905.

loss of land was greatest in less fertile regions, it is reasonable to assume that the standard accounts give a somewhat understated picture of the extent to which the nobility was losing its grip on the land.[12]

The dvoriantsvo of 1905 was very different from the social group that had emerged as a result of the reforms of Peter the Great at the beginning of the eighteenth century. In search of a bureaucracy to run his modern, Western-style state and army, Peter universalized and formalized the service of the nobility. Later in the eighteenth century, the dvoriantsvo adopted Western culture, and European manners, style, and language became another characteristic of noble status. As a result, ownership of a *pomestia* (landed estate) was only one of the diffuse and varied criteria for determining membership in the aristocracy.[13] Wealth and status were determined by service to the emperor. The dvoriantstvo was a traditional order of loyal servitors and not a modern social class. It certainly could not be called a ruling class, in the strict sense of the term. The nobility did not control the state; this highly privileged, legally defined estate served the autocracy in the new bureaucracy.

The decline of the nobility's economic fortunes was further accelerated by the emancipation of the serfs in 1861. The state compensated landlords for the territory turned over to the peasants, but most nobles were ill equipped to handle the transition to controlling a relatively free labor market and managing a commerical farm. Most Russian landlords actually knew little about agronomy, food processing, or livestock raising. They lacked the necessary capital, and the majority of them still considered service, not farming, to be their true career. Many apparently found it psychologically impossible to accept that their once-total control of peasant lives was now limited. The result was a sharp decline in the dvoriantsvo's economic fortunes during the last third of the nineteenth century. Many noble landlords relinquished their lands. Some sold or mortgaged parts of their holdings, while others simply collected rent from traditional village communes and made no attempt to farm. Some properties went to merchants and other bourgeois elements, but most was sold to peasants.

12. P. N. Pershin, *Agrarnaia revoliutsia v Rossii,* Vol. 1, p. 80; A. M. Anfimov, *Krupnoe pomeshchich'e khoziaistvo evropeiskoi Rossii,* pp. 360–381; M. A. Rubach, "Sotsianl'naia struktura agrarnykh otnoshenii i rassloenie krestianstva v ukrainskoi derevne v 1917g," in *Osobennosti agrarnogo stroia Rossii v period imperializma* (Moscow, 1962), p. 47. On the Central Agricultural Region see Sylvain Bensidoun, *L'Agitation Paysanne en Russie, 1880–1902* (Paris, 1975), p. 73.

13. Marc Raeff, *Origins of the Russian Intelligentsia* (New York, 1966), pp. 8, 9, 37–46; Robert Jones, *The Emancipation of the Russian Nobility* (Princeton, 1975); Arcadius Kahan, "Continuity in Economic Activity and Policy during the Post-Petrine Period in Russia," *Journal of Economic History* (March 1965):61–85.

The rapid increase of the peasant population, from 50 million in 1861 to 79 million in 1905, made both selling and renting attractive alternatives to exploiting the land with one's own resources.[14] The direct management of farms by nobles was further retarded by the relatively low demand of the Russian internal market for an agricultural surplus, a situation exacerbated by the worldwide depression in grain prices (which lasted from 1876 to 1896). The result was not simply the decline but rather the disintegration of the dvoriantsvo as it had been previously known. Noble status and landowning were no longer synonymous. There were now people of noble origin who did not own land, while many new landowners were townspeople or peasants.

Although the common historical description of the Russian nobility in decline is substantially correct, it omits important countervailing trends. As a result of the redirection of the economy, a considerable number of noble landlords did abandon their service careers and return to their estates to make a go of farming. Many noble landlords retained their land and began to orient themselves toward their own estates and to local affairs rather than toward the central government. These members of the dvorianstvo came to resemble a true provincial gentry; that is, they were landowning nobles who participated in local politics. The emergence of this subgroup was made possible by the rapid industrial growth of the late 1880s and 1890s. Although the agrarian sector of the economy was severely taxed to pay for industrial expansion, the growth of industry meant an increase in the size of the towns and, therefore, an increase in the size of the internal market for an agricultural surplus.[15] In 1896, the international grain market revived, enormously enhancing the opportunities for profitable export.[16] Despite a brief dip in grain prices in 1897, favorable prospects now existed for those landlords with sufficient land, money, energy, and talent to become successful gentlemen farmers.

This return to the land differed from noble landlords' earlier vogues for farming, which had been motivated by romantic notions of rural life and liberal Slavophile visions of the dignity of the peasantry. Many landlords now sought to exploit their own lands and to produce by efficient commercial means for the market. This new development meant mechanization, cost accounting, advanced agronomy, and hard work. The traditional and highly primitive three-field system of crop rotation was abandoned in many places in favor of multifield techniques. In fertile

14. Robinson, *Rural Russia under the Old Regime*, p. 94.

15. I. D. Kovalchenko and L. V. Milov, *Vserossiskoi agrarnyi rynok*, pp. 352–379.

16. Alexander Gerschenkron, *Bread and Democracy in Germany* (New York, 1936), p. 78; Pavlovsky, *Agricultural Russia on the Eve of Revolution*, p. 113.

regions, especially the south and southwest, renting to peasants decreased sharply, and land prices rose dramatically as it became more profitable to hold one's land and raise cash crops.[17] Agricultural journals around the turn of the century came to talk of a "managerial revolution," and the periodical press described a similar new wave of interest in commercial agriculture.[18] One commentator, M. Iasnopolskii, writing during 1903 in the monthly, *Mir bozhii*, described a phenomenon others had already noticed.

> A segment of the landed nobility has developed which is buying up the lands of its ruined brothers, rationalizing its own estates, discarding genteel traditions, and gradually losing the characteristics of the so-called "noble type"—a semibureaucrat who lives on rents. Such men have flung off the threadbare uniforms of the service class and have become a landed bourgeoisie in the real sense of the term.[19]

In calling this segment of the nobility a "landed bourgeoisie," Iasnopolskii overlooked the transitional nature of the situation. No portion of the dvorianstvo, no matter how agriculturally progressive, had entirely abandoned traditional notions of honor, service, and family.[20] The nobles continued to feel a sense of social responsibility, a need for some kind of service, that one does not associate with the prototypical behavior of the agricultural entrepreneur. These men and women are better described as a provincial landowning gentry in the best eighteenth-century English sense.

It is extremely difficult to determine the extent of this modernizing trend with any accuracy. Few landlords converted all their holdings to cultivation under modern methods. The most technologically advanced and the most traditional and primitive methods commonly existed side by side. Commerical farming did not necessarily imply a high level of mechanization. Great profits could be made with the extensive use of wage labor. There were also significant regional differences. Typically, those provinces into which market relations had penetrated (mainly in the south and west) were sites of more commercially oriented farming. In addition, agricultural activism was generally confined to that wealthier 25 percent of the dvorianstvo with holdings above 500 desiatiny. However, the very wealthi-

17. Roberta Manning, *The Russian Nobility in Revolution and Counter-Revolution*, p. 20.

18. Ibid., p. 28; Emmons, "The Russian Landed Gentry and Politics," p. 273.

19. M. Iasnopolskii, "Razvitie dvorianskogo zemlevladenia v sovremmennoi Rossii," *Mir bozhii* (December 1903):227.

20. Roberta Manning, "Zemstvo and Revolution: The Onset of the Gentry Reaction," in L. Haimson (ed.), *The Politics of Rural Russia, 1905–1914, p. 50.*

est families, the 155 owners of the most enormous latifundia, did not generally engage in modern agriculture. Their return on rents was so high that there was simply no need to expend energy and capital on new agricultural approaches.[21]

Retirement from service placed the gentlemen-farmers into a social limbo. The change in activity forced a change in self-image on them. The agricultural journals and the conservative press of the day gave much attention to this process. Noble landlords were no longer part of the legal estate of state servitors whose social positions were determined by their relationship to the autocracy. Instead, they were beginning to see themselves as a class of agrarian producers whose position in society was determined by their economic roles.[22] This evolution from a traditional estate to a modern social class was never completed. Rather, it was a possible path of development that different nobles adopted with various degrees of seriousness, depending on individual circumstances and attitudes. At the turn of the century, commentators, excited by the novelty of the new attitudes, stressed the emergence of the new landed class and ignored the extent to which older notions of nobility had been forgotten but not abandoned.

The transitional nature of the gentry's situation was reflected in the mutually contradictory views that these men and women maintained of themselves and of the social group of which they were a part. At times, the more modern conception might be emphasized; at other moments, traditional attitudes might resurface. In the case of the Nationalist Party, a modern class orientation dominated their activity during their rise in the third Duma (1907–1912). When the party ran into difficulties at the beginning of the fourth Duma (1912–1917), old attitudes and conceptions of nobility reemerged.

Despite the uncertainty about the extent of this new trend and the ambiguity of its meaning, there can be no doubt that many noble landlords found themselves in an improved position by 1905. The growth of Russian capitalism had created a new chance for noble landowners. Most nobles were incapable of taking advantage of the new opportunities, and many of those who tried farming failed miserably. However, a sufficient number of landlords succeeded in making the change, and their efforts halted and soon reversed the nobility's general decline. But the old dvorianstvo could not be reconstituted. It was disintegrating into a number of subgroups with different interests and activities. Perhaps the provincial landowning gentry

21. Minarik, *Ekonomicheskaia,* p. 6.
22. Manning, "The Russian Nobility," pp. 24–28.

was most capable of making the transition into the modern world with minimum damage, but for all of its progressiveness in some realms, it too was a prisoner of the past.

The Politics of the Transition

It took some time for these shifts in economic activity and self-image to manifest themselves politically. Before 1905, any overt organization was obviously impossible, and proper nobles felt no need to concern themselves with politics. But the state's support for industrialization had greatly distressed landlords who now sought to defend the agrarian sector that they claimed to represent. During the 1890s, provincial noble assemblies, somnolent for nearly a century, became centers of criticism of the state. Elected marshals of nobility, whose activity was strictly controlled by the bureaucracy, led a muted but nevertheless serious campaign in defense of agrarian interests.

The real arena for the specific articulation of the gentry's concerns was the zemstvos. These local institutions had been created in 1864 as semiautonomous elective bodies charged with the provision of such social services as primary education, health care, road building, and agronomic assistance within each province (*gubernia*) and district (*uezd*). Although the zemstvos were to include representatives of all the estates, property requirements for participation in zemstvo elections gave the landowning nobility control of these assemblies. Despite this, the zemstvos did not develop into centers of reaction and narrow concern for landlord interests.[23] Public service in the zemstvos became an alternative to bureaucratic service for many noble landlords, and, over the years, the zemstvos developed a tradition of antibureaucratic localism, which led a considerable portion of the gentry to flirt with constitutional reforms that might limit the arbitrary power of the central government.

In the 1890s, this movement was given impetus by outrage over the government's handling of the famine of 1891 and by the same agrarian opposition to Witte's programs that had animated the more conservative noble assemblies. Zemstvo liberals from among the gentry and the various professionals working for the zemstvos (the famous Third Element) now began to deal more directly with the needs of the peasantry. They called

23. B. B. Veselovskii, *Istoria zemstva za sorok let*, 4 vols.; Terence Emmons, *The Russian Landed Gentry and the Peasant Emancipation of 186*, p .415; B. B. Veselovskii, *Zemskie liberaly* (St. Petersburg, 1905), p. 7.

for equality of civil rights for all citizens, parliamentary bodies elected by universal suffrage, and, in some cases, alienation of gentry lands. These demands were given wide exposure at a series of national zemstvo congresses beginning in 1901. These annual gatherings were dominated by the liberals, who played important roles in the development of the all-nation crescendo of antigovernment opposition that preceded the Revolution of 1905.[24] In 1903, the zemstvo liberals joined forces with members of the intelligentsia and professional classes to form the Union of Liberation.

Liberals, especially gentry liberals, were always a highly visible minority that dominated a silent, apathetic, conservative majority within the zemstvos. These liberals were not necessarily the same men who had participated in the gentry's recent economic progressivism. Doubtless, many gentry liberals engaged in modern farming, but this movement of zemstvo liberals stressed a far-sighted, often paternalistic concern for the welfare of all citizens. Although they were willing to sacrifice their immediate interests for the sake of progress, the liberals shared the conservatives' aversion to politics and political parties. It had become traditional to view the zemstvos as cultural and economic institutions into which politics did not intrude. Liberals and conservatives alike adhered to historic patterns of deference, and the zemstvos sought to reach all decisions by consensus.[25]

In the western borderland, however, the future Nationalists could not participate in the work of the zemstvos and provincial assemblies. These institutions did not exist in those provinces that were the source of the party's greatest strength. Landlords there had little to do but engage in agriculture once they had left state service. The Nationalists' president, Peter Nikolaevich Balashev, owned an enormous estate in Podol'e. When he retired from service in 1899, he returned to his farm and engaged in agriculture until the elections to the third Duma. Similarly, Alexander Stepanovich Gizhitskii had played an active role in the local politics of Kherson gubernia, but when he moved to his wife's land in Podol'e during 1904, he too found himself with little to do but farm.

Outside the borderland, however, future Nationalists followed the same paths as other members of the gentry. Vladimir Alekseevich Bobrinskii owned 10,000 desiatiny in Tula, just south of Moscow. He was actively involved in zemstvo work and for several years was president of the local

24. B. B. Veselovskii, *K voprosu o klassovykh interesakh v zemstve* (Moscow, 1905), p. 16; Shmuel Galai, *The Liberation Movement in Russia: 1900-1905* (Cambridge, 1973), p. 9.
25. Veselovskii, *K voprosu*, p. 18

zemstvo board. Pavel Nikolaevich Krupenskii had an equally large farm in Bessarabia. His family was the most honored in the province, and he assumed a position of leadership in local politics in both the zemstvo and the noble assemblies. Vladimir Mikhailovich Volkonskii, who later became the vice-president of the Duma, owned a small estate in the central Russian province of Voronezh. These men were typical of the nonborderland Nationalists who joined the party by default. They were active in their local zemstvos, but they had little to do with the national zemstvo congresses.

The Revolution of 1905 put an end to the opposition of the zemstvo congresses. The October manifesto split the movement. The liberal majority, which demanded still further changes, had already joined with opposition groups among the free professions and intelligentsia to form the Constitutional Democratic Party (the Kadets), which played a leading role in the first two Dumas. A conservative minority was satisfied by the tsar's promises. Led by the Slavophile landowner, D. N. Shipov, and Alexander Guchkov (of the famous Moscow textile family), this group was appropriately named the Union of October 17 or, for short, the Octobrists. The new formation's moderate conservative constitutionalism attracted considerable gentry support in the next few years.

The extensive peasant disturbances during 1905 and 1906 dealt a near-fatal blow to zemstvo liberalism. Land and crops were seized, manor houses burned, and peasants refused to work landlords' estates. Almost overnight, the gentry lost interest in making concessions to the peasantry. The previously apathetic and unconcerned majority of zemstvo members was galvanized into action and now took a more active part in zemstvo affairs. In the local elections of 1906 and 1907, they were largely successful in replacing Kadets and liberals with more conservative figures. Liberals had always been among the zemstvos' leaders. It is therefore revealing that the political allegiances of the new zemstvo board presidents showed a sharp shift to the right: Kadets were ousted, and Octobrists and still more conservative men took over. This sharp and dramatic change is shown in Table 1.1.

In most cases, liberals did not revise their views under the impact of the new pressure from the right. Instead, many of them left the zemstvo movement and joined the Kadets who were more concerned with the advancement of constitutionalist principles than with the protection of anyone's interests. The zemstvos were now taken over by a new mass of highly conservative and politically inexperienced noble landlords who finally felt the necessity of organizing to protect their highly threatened property and privileges. As in the case of the zemstvo liberals, there was

Table 1.1. **Political Shifts of Zemstvo Board Presidents**

	1905	*1907*
Kadets	15	1
Progressives[a]	6	3
Octobrists	13	19
Right wing	0	11

Source: B. B. Veselovskii, *Istoria zemstva za sorok let* (St. Petersburg, 1909), 4:49–58.

[a]The term simply signifies a vague political tendency. It does not signify membership in any particular party.

no simple connection between these conservatives and agricultural progressivism, although many such men had modernized their estates.

The old antipathy against politics and political parties had been broken down under the impact of the threat from the left. There now existed a sizeable segment of the provincial gentry that was both conservative and eager for political action. Yet there was still no formation or group that could organize these previously unorganized and unorganizable landlords. The creation of the Duma had raised the possibility of, indeed had virtually necessitated, the creation of a political party of the gentry. However, Russian conservatives were still unsure that a party was the most appropriate form for defending their interests. As a result, none of the conservative groups that emerged between 1905 and 1907 assumed the shape of a modern political party.

Conservative Groups, 1905–1907

Between 1905 and 1907, the first two Dumas met. They were elected under a very broad franchise, and, as a result, the conservative gentry was thoroughly outnumbered by the peasantry. Under these inhospitable conditions, right-wing groups stood little chance of making a major impact. However, a myriad of minor patriotic and monarchist leagues, unions, and associations were formed around a variety of rightist personalities who received considerable but inconsistent support from the police. From this welter of haphazard activity, three organizations emerged that dominated the Russian right from 1905 until 1907—the Union of October, the Union of Russian People, and the Congress of the United Nobility. This last group, a national noble political organization, did not emerge until early 1906. It was composed of delegates from the official provincial assemblies of nobles, many of whom were simply the gubernia marshals of nobility. As a group, the marshals, who occupied official positions confirmed by the Ministry of Interior, were more conservative than the average zemstvo activist. As a result, the Congress, which embraced a range of viewpoints, most often expressed the more reactionary tendencies of the newly aroused conservative movement. It tended to draw support from provinces in which nobles had lost much land. Thus, it was little concerned with modern farming.[26] Many of its members came to join the extreme right fraction in the Duma. V. M. Purishkevich, N. E. Markov II, Count V. F. Dorrer, and the Congress's president, A. A. Bobrinskii, were all members of both the Congress and the right-wing fraction. Such prominent future members of the Nationalist Party as Prince Aleksander Petrovich Urusov and V. A. Bobrinskii also took part.

The Congress met yearly to express opinions on a broad range of matters. It was a powerful pressure group, made still more influential by the close relationships between its members and leading government functionaries. Between 1906 and 1916, despite many recalcitrants among its members, the Congress served as an effective arena for the elaboration of the nobility's new role under the renovated state structure.[27] This group, however, developed no unified ideology and gave voice only to an especially conservative segment of gentry opinion. Because the Congress never became an independent political party with its own local organizations and parliamentary fraction, it represented only a partial step toward the development of an independent noble political party.

The Octobrists occupied the left wing of political opinion among the gentry. Composed primarily of noble landlords and a significant if not sizeable industrial and commercial element, the Union of October was the most liberal noble-based political formation. Its earliest members came from the moderate minority at the zemstvo congresses that met at the time of the revolutionary upsurge of late 1904 and early 1905. Late in October 1905, Witte, long despised by the agrarian nobility, invited the union's future leader, D. N. Shipov, and others to accept cabinet posts. These negotiations soon broke down. Shipov and Guchkov then led a hurried attempt to set up a new party at the November 1905 zemstvo congress. The Octobrists openly accepted the revised state structure

26. I. D. Vaisberg, *Sovet ob'edinn'onogo dvorianstva i ego vlianie na politiku samoderzhavia: 1906-1914*, p. 6.

27. George W. Simmonds, *The Congress of Representatives of the Noble Associations, 1906-1916: A Case Study of Russian Conservatism*, pp. 89-95. See also Geoffrey Hosking and Roberta Manning, "What Was the United Nobility?" in Leonard Haimson (ed.), *The Politics of Rural Russia, 1905-1914*, pp. 142-183.

created by the October manifesto. Unlike the Kadets, they chose to interpret the manifesto as signifying the creation of a constitutional order.[28] They thought a broad, unspecified program would attract the largest number of followers. Accordingly, in the course of their early agitation, the Octobrists simply stressed their support for constitutional monarchy, private property, the legal equality of all citizens, and the indivisibility of the Empire.[29]

The haziness of their program caused trouble for the Octobrists throughout their history, but it did result in the influx of a sizeable and highly diverse group of supporters. The union's original organizational structure was that of a loose league rather than a disciplined political party. In fact, at this stage, the Octobrists seemed little more than an amorphous gathering of local and national notables. In the wake of their failure in the first Duma elections (they succeeded in electing only thirty-eight deputies), this approach was found too weak. In the summer of 1906, Guchkov, the former businessman, began to demand a tighter organizational structure. This conflicted with Shipov's vaguer, moralistic, and consensual approach, which was derived from the political practices of the zemstvos.

During this time, Stolypin declared martial law, which outraged liberal public opinion. Hundreds of genuine and suspected revolutionaries, along with thousands of protesting workers and peasants, were tried and executed by one-day field court-martials. Guchkov supported Stolypin's step; Shipov opposed it. The majority of the party supported Guchkov's position on organization and repression, leading Shipov and several allies to quit the Octobrists and form the Party of Peaceful Renovation (*Partia mirnogo obnovlenia*). Now in control, Guchkov sought to use his ties to Moscow merchants to gain the financial and political support of the city's industrial and commercial interests in order to make a stronger showing in the second Duma. The central committee of the party was strengthened, and an attempt was made to impose greater discipline on its provincial branches, many of which were under intense local pressure from right-wing elements.

The rapid shift to the right in the zemstvos during 1906 forced the Octobrists to heed the fears of conservative nobles and to work with right-wing groups in local coalitions. This led to some gains in the elections to the second Duma. However, the Octobrists were never really in control of

---

28. John Hutchinson, *The Octobrists in Russian Politics, 1905–1917*, p. 24; Ben-Cion Pinchuk, *The Octobrists in the Third Duma*, pp. 8–23.

29. Michael C. Brainerd, *The Union of October 17 and Russian Society, 1905–1917*, p. 2.

the rightward trend in the zemstvos. They were riding the crest of a wave, trying to impose some form and restraint on the movement without ever actually mastering it. In view of the limited Duma representation achieved by large landowners (the result of their small numbers in the total population), the Octobrists' slightly improved showing in the second Duma elections (forty-four seats) scarcely reflected the new tenor of the nobility. Only when Stolypin restricted the franchise in 1907 was there an opportunity for the Octobrists to exercise real influence. Witte had gambled that the peasantry, which was given the largest representation under the December 1905 electoral law, would be a conservative force. That hope had proved unfounded, and the failure of his plans doomed Witte's political career. He was replaced first by an old bureaucrat, Ivan Logginovich Goremykin, and then by the charismatic and forceful Stolypin. The Octobrists became most prominent in partnership with Stolypin during the early stages of the third Duma.

Aside from the United Nobility and the Octobrists, both of which essentially accepted the post-1905 order and limited their appeals to propertied elements, certain archreactionary groups that sought to make use of supraclass appeals emerged on the Russian right. A number of these organizations, which arose during the period of the first two Dumas, resorted to demagogic nationalism and anti-Semitism in order to attract broad support. The best-known of these groups was the Union of Russian People (*Soiuz russkogo naroda*), organized by the Moscow physician, Dr. A. N. Dubrovin. The Union of Russian People openly opposed the changes enacted by the October manifesto. Nevertheless, it came to accept the mass political conditions that the manifesto had created.[30]

The Union of Russian People was always controlled by professional intellectuals and nobles, but it sought to appeal to the entire nation, regardless of social position. It managed to attract a following of lower-class elements, including shop clerks, small businessmen, cab drivers, some workers, and a few peasants to go along with the usual full complement of priests. Throughout 1905 and 1906, the union held public meetings and monarchist demonstrations. The most notable was a deputation to the tsar on December 23, 1905, during which Nicholas accepted the union's badge as a sign of support. Using resentment against the economic dislocations caused by the strike wave of 1905 as well as a violent brand of anti-Semitism, the union entered the campaign for the first Duma with the hope of attracting popular support for the autocracy. They argued that the Duma in no way limited the tsar's prerogatives. They

30. V. I. Gurko, *Features and Figures of the Past* (Stanford, 1939), pp. 433–434.

saw the Duma as a way of avoiding the hated, "cosmopolitan," ministerial-bureaucratic apparatus. Despite opposition to the changes brought about by the October manifesto, the leaders of the Union of Russian People were forced to accept it as an expression of the autocrat's will, and so, unlike any of the rightist organizations that had preceded them on the scene, they accepted the need to engage in full political struggle.[31]

From its inception, involvement in pogroms had been an important element of the union's activities. The use of street thugs to attack and kill Jews was seen as a means to divert enmity from the state by inflaming popular anti-Semitism. The union was one of many groups involved in this sort of activity (all these groups were referred to by the title "Black Hundreds"). From time to time, this violence had the support of police officials, but when it was combined with the increasingly radical antigovern-ment (though not antitsarist) tone of the union's appeals, many more traditional conservatives were repelled. The union's attempts to character-ize itself as a broad, spontaneous movement of support for the holy trinity of traditional Russian values—orthodoxy, autocracy, and nationality—did not necessarily give comfort to those in the privileged strata who stood between the tsar and his supposedly adoring people.

The Union of Russian People claimed a membership of over 600,000, but its rolls had little direct relationship to the number of active members. Moreover, these figures were never translatable into electoral strength in Duma elections. Despite a slight increase in the number of seats, the right was still infinitesimal in the second Duma. The union's failure to produce a broad following for the state and autocracy hastened the disillusionment of ruling circles with it. With the enactment of the restrictive electoral law of June 3, 1907, the Union of Russian People became structurally irrelevant and unnecessary. There was no longer a need for a demagogic, right-wing organization to enlist popular support for the state. However, the union did not wither and die. It had never been entirely the creation of either the government or the police. Because it represented a certain spontaneous feeling among some popular elements, the Union continued to exist in some form throughout the prerevolutionary period. Indeed, in the third Duma, the sizeable extreme right fraction (fifty deputies) contained many members of the Union of Russian People. Yet, over the course of the third Duma, the union decreased in size and influence, split into factions, and lost much of the police support it had enjoyed during

31. Hans Rogger, "The Formation of the Russian Right," *California Slavic Studies*, Vol. 4 (1964):88. See also V. P. Viktorov and A. Chernovskii, *Soiuz russkogo naroda* (Moscow–Leningrad, 1929); V. Levitskii, "Pravye partii," in L. Martov et al. (eds.), *Obshchestvennie dvizheniia v Rossii v nachale XX-go veka*, Vol. 3 (St. Petersburg, 1914), pp. 347–462.

the 1905–1907 period. Most important, the union, despite its reactionary politics, was never representative of traditional noble propertied elements. Its appeals were never restricted to the dvorianstvo, and those nobles in it represented a particularly idiosyncratic tendency among the Russian right.[32]

The Government and the First Two Dumas

The first State Duma, which began its work on April 27, 1906, was far more radical than the framers of the December 1905 electoral law had expected. Because most socialist parties boycotted the elections, the liberal Kadets dominated the new Duma, which they hoped would be the lower house of a parliament organized along British lines. They decided to proceed from the thoroughly incorrect but politically sensible assumption that the tsar had intentionally created a true parliament. The Kadets also strongly supported the compensated expropriation of gentry and state lands to meet the demands of the peasantry. Witte might have been expected to at least discuss these positions, but on the eve of the Duma's opening he was replaced as president of the Council of Ministers by Goremykin, a career bureaucrat and opponent of the notion of government cooperation with society. Goremykin firmly and rigidly opposed all Kadet pretentions. The result was a stalemate that led to the dissolution of the first Duma in July.[33]

While terminating the life of the first Duma, Nicholas also replaced Goremykin with a figure who was destined to become Russia's most important statesman in the period between the revolutions of 1905 and 1917. Peter Arkadevich Stolypin had been the Minister of Interior under Goremykin. Stolypin had made his reputation as the governor of Saratov province, where he had been successful in repressing both sedition and banditry. His severity in that position was combined with great public bravado and considerable personal bravery. After assuming the presidency of the Council of Ministers, Stolypin initiated a massive and harsh repression of all revolutionary activity. Along with the repression, Stolypin put forth a series of proposals for Russia's future development. Most of these had already been advanced by Witte, but Stolypin succeeded in making some of them law. Before the opening of the second Duma, he enacted several elements of the broad agrarian reform that later came to

32. Hans Rogger, "Was There a Russian Fascism?: The Union of Russian People," *Journal of Modern History*, No. 5 (1964):405.

33. Ann Healy, *The Russian Autocracy in Crisis* (Hamden, Conn., 1976), pp. 152–220.

bear his name, through the decree powers of Article 87. The purpose of his reform was to permit peasants who wanted to leave the traditional village commune to become individual small holders. This element of the peasantry was then expected to adopt conservative politics, much like their French counterparts. The new premier also advanced a series of local government and administration reforms that would have ended traditional estate privileges and replaced them with property ownership as the basis for participation in political life. Unlike Goremykin, Stolypin had a program of legislation to place before the Duma and a belief that the existence of the Duma was necessary for the establishment of cooperation between government and society.

Despite this, the second Duma was even less disposed than the first to work with the government. Kadet representation dropped, and the various but ideologically diverse socialist groups controlled the new Duma. But the Octobrists and rightists, with whom Stolypin had some common language, controlled only 50 of the over 500 seats.[34]

Soon the public came to accept dissolution as inevitable. But what would follow the Duma? Would the lower house lose all legislative power and become consultative? Would the whole October manifesto be scrapped in favor of a return to the pre-1905 order? The United Nobility and the newly conservative zemstvo congress had been urging the retention of the Duma as a legislative body, but they now demanded the restriction of the franchise to give power to large property owners. This solution appealed most to Stolypin. His appointment had provoked much dissatisfaction among reactionary circles at court, and he realized that his survival depended on his ability to convince Nicholas that he enjoyed the support of the educated and propertied social elements that would be represented in a new third Duma. At this moment of peril for the regime, the tsar knew that this support could not be refused.

Accordingly, Stolypin assigned his assistant, S. E. Kryzhanovskii, the task of elaborating a new law. Stolypin then seized on a pretext. He accused the Social Democratic Duma deputies of fomenting an insurrection in the St. Petersburg garrison. He demanded that their parliamentary immunity be abrogated and the deputies turned over by the Duma. The Duma refused to accede to this attack on parliamentary immunity, and on June 3, 1907, Stolypin had Nicholas dissolve the second Duma and proclaim the new electoral law according to Article 87.[35]

---

34. Alfred Levin, *The Second Duma*, p. 67.

35. Ibid., pp. 307–339; Gilbert Doctorow, "The Russian Gentry and the Coup d'État of June 3, 1907," *Cahiers du Monde Russe et Soviétique*, No. 1 (1976):43–51.

Stolypin had no doubt that this act violated the letter and spirit of the October manifesto and the Fundamental Laws. No one had intended that Article 87 would be used in such a manner. In effect, the government had carried out a coup d'état. Laws or legislators were powerless to stop it. Only massive disturbances could have induced Stolypin to back down. The premier expected demonstrations of popular indignation and had alerted the army and police. However, the streets remained empty. The revolutionary movement had been thoroughly, if temporarily, repressed. The workers and peasants were exhausted by two years of constant struggle. Liberals in the duma did not wish openly to oppose the government. Their attempt to do so after the dissolution of the first Duma had elicited little popular response. The revolutionary period of 1905 to 1907 had come to an end. The state and its supporters were in firm control. The stage was now set for the election of a third, more conservative Duma in which the gentry would play a leading role. It was in this far more cooperative body that the Nationalist Party coalesced and emerged as a force in national politics.

II

The Election of 1907

The election of deputies to the third Duma took place in a fundamentally different political context. By September 1907, what came to be known as the "Stolypin reaction" had begun. This period of social peace, which Stolypin considered the necessary prerequisite for any thoroughgoing reform, would last until the spring of 1912, when the labor movement revived after striking workers were massacred at the Lena gold fields. For now, however, the resistance of the peasantry had been crushed by the police and the army, but the peasants' demand for the nobles' land remained unsatisfied. Workers faced an industrial bourgeoisie that had been pacified by the October manifesto. Thousands of revolutionaries had been arrested and exiled, and the hopes of the professional classes for achieving political power through the Duma had been crushed with the change in the electoral law. Sedition and revolution had been defeated. With the forces of movement in check, it was now up to Russia's propertied and educated classes to find a basis of cooperation with the autocracy in order to maintain the fundamental structure of society.

The New Electoral Law

Although the franchise was now restricted, the indirect, multistage electoral process was retained. Duma deputies were still picked at meetings of previously chosen electors (*vyborshchiki*) who met in the provincial capitals. Each category (curia) of property owners was allotted a certain number of places in the final assembly. However, large property holders were accorded vastly greater representation than before. Both large and small landowners had been given 31 percent of the vyborshchiki in the first two elections, but now they comprised 50 percent of the provincial assemblies. Peasant representation was reduced. Town voters were divided into two curiae based on wealth. The first (and richer) curia was given more places than the less well-off second curia. In general, the entire process was restricted. The number of vyborshchiki was reduced from 6,164 to 5,252. The Duma was made smaller (from 524 to 422 deputies), and the number of towns directly electing deputies went from twenty-five to seven.[1]

The third Duma afforded adequate representation only to the landed nobility and the wealthiest town dwellers. Large estate holders, in particular, were accorded far more places in the landowners' curia than were owners of small farms. Wealthier landlords elected their vyborshchiki directly, while individual small holders had to go through a series of preliminary meetings. (Communal peasants chose their own representatives.) At this lower level of the process, peasants were easily dominated by the many priests who participated in the elections as representatives of churches that owned land. Within the landowners' curia, the clergy supported the gentry at the final assembly, and control of the landowners' curia usually meant control of the entire electoral gathering. In twenty-seven of the fifty-one gubernias, the landowners were given a majority of the electors. In the other twenty-four, they were only a few vyborshchiki short of a majority, and finding a few allies among the other curiae did not

1. Samuel Harper, *The New Electoral Law for the Russian Duma*; Fiodor Dan, *Novyi izbiratel'nyi zakon* (St. Petersburg, 1907); Alfred Levin, "The Russian Voter in the Elections to the Third Duma," *Slavic Review* (December 1962):660–677; Geoffrey Hosking, *The Russian Constitutional Experiment* (Cambridge, 1973), pp. 45–48; Alfred Levin, *The Third Duma: Elections and Profile*. See also C. Jay Smith, "The Russian Third State Duma," *Russian Review*, No. 3 (1958):201–210; and E. D. Chermenskii, *Bor'ba klassov i partii v-IV-oi gosudarstvennoi dume (1912–1917 gg.)*, Vol. I. Doctoral dissertation, Moscow University (1947), p. 70. On the operation of the electoral process under the old and the new laws, see Leopold Haimson, "Introduction: The Landed Nobility," in Leopold Haimson (ed.), *The Politics of Rural Russia, 1905–1914*, pp. 10–18.

usually prove difficult.[2] Thus, the law succeeded in its intent of giving the gentry dominance of the elections in the countryside.

The structure of the final provincial electoral assembly was of decisive importance. Because the entire assembly chose the Duma members, a tightly disciplined majority, however slight, could elect a full slate of deputies of one persuasion. Although party discipline was not well developed, strong consensual traditions persisted among the gentry. As a result, many gubernias sent delegations composed almost entirely of one political tendency.

The vyborshchiki from the large landowners' curia and the first city curia (the wealthier townsmen) constituted a majority of each gubernia assembly. In theory, if they banded together, large landowners and urban property holders could dominate the final electoral slate. In practice, however, there was an interpenetration of curiae. Merchants and industrialists who owned large blocs of land fell into the landowners' meeting, while nobles possessing houses in the towns were elected to the first city curia.[3]

If large property holders were unable to obtain a majority in the landowners' curia, the clergy was called on to substitute their numbers for missing noblemen. They did not always assume this task with enthusiasm. Usually they exacted the price of a few Duma seats as a reward for their services. Such deals were most often arranged by the governor and the archbishop of the gubernia. The archbishop was then faced with the task of obtaining the acquiescence of his underlings.

Control of the provincial electoral meetings by a conservative, wealthy majority deeply affected the composition of the peasant delegation to the third Duma. Under the electoral law for the previous two Dumas, each gubernia elected one deputy from among the vyborshchiki chosen by the peasantry from their own ranks. Now this choice was taken out of their hands; the peasant representative was chosen by the entire assembly. This made it possible for the assembly majority to elect reliable people who fit conservative stereotypes. Unlike the urban proletariat, the peasants had

2. Harper, *The New Electoral Law*, p. 38.

3. Osoboe deloproizvodstvo po vyboram, *Vybory v tret'iu Gosudarstvennuiu dumu*, (St. Petersburg, 1911). Alfred Levin's "The Russian Voter"; "The Reactionary Tradition in the Elections to the Third Duma," *Oklahoma State University Occasional Papers;* and his recent book on the third Duma are the only works on the elections themselves. A. Ia. Avrekh in *Tsarizm i tret'eiunskaia sistema* and in "Tret'eiunskaia monarkhiia i obrazovanie tret'edumskogo pomeshchich'e-burzhuaznogo bloka," *Vestnik moskovskogo universiteta*, No. 1 (1956):3–70, avoids the problem, offering neither an investigation of the election campaign nor a real analysis of its social significance. Hosking's discussion, *The Russian Constitutional Experiment*, pp. 45–48, is also brief, though more insightful than Avrekh's.

little tradition of solidarity. Workers would agree on one candidate and force him on the assembly. Peasants, on the other hand, competed among themselves for the positions. However, this set of circumstances did not result in a chorus of toadies. Some men severely disappointed their sponsors. But, in general, the Duma peasants sat with the center and the right and supported their patrons on most issues.[4] Thus, neither the clergy nor the peasantry of the third Duma acted independently. Despite important individual exceptions, these men went along with the noble landlords who dominated the third Duma; in no way did the clerical and peasant elements dilute the basic gentry nature of the three conservative parties—the Octobrists, the Nationalists, and the extreme right-wing group (*pravye*).[5]

The Makeup of the Third Duma

Analyzing the elections to the third Duma is a difficult task. The available evidence does not afford a complete picture of all levels of the process. Archival materials on the conduct of the 1907 elections are sparse, and newspaper accounts tend to be incomplete, contradictory, and episodic. Statistics have presented a problem. The only universally accepted figures have been those on the Duma members themselves. Information on the vyborshchiki has been more suspect, but the appearance of previously unused statistical material, prepared by the Ministry of Interior, now affords a more precise picture of this level of the process.[6] One cannot venture with any degree of specificity below the level of the electors, although broad descriptions of social and economic structure are fruitful and necessary.

Aside from these source problems, serious difficulties are raised by the imprecision of political labels. Contemporary observers of the 1907 election did not use the kinds of analytical categories familiar to the student of mid-twentieth century Western European or American politics. Terms used to describe the vyborshchiki were especially vague. Such broad descriptions as "right," "moderate," and "left" had different meanings for different people. Newspapers introduced further variations. Thus, a generally accepted set of terms never did emerge. Choices of descriptive

4. Dan, *Novyi izbiratel'nyi zakon*, p. 30.
5. Smith, "The Russian Third State Duma," p. 202.
6. *Vybory*.

Table 2.1. **Affiliations of Deputies, Center and Right-Wing Groups, Elected to the Third Duma**

Octobrists	110
Moderates	29
Right nonparty	95
Bessarabian center party	8
Union of Russian People	32
Monarchists	33

Source: Golos Moskvy, November 1, 1907.

words and terms of reference expressed the way in which various groups comprehended events. Consequently, uniformity of labels in a period of rapid and elemental change would be clearly unlikely. While the confusion of terminology makes the election process less susceptible to modern analytical techniques, the categories chosen by particular historical actors are significant findings in their own right.

Three conservative fractions emerged in the third Duma—the Octobrists, the Nationalists, and the pravye. Despite differences in their programs and organizational forms, all three groups drew support primarily from the landed nobility.

On the eve of the Duma's convocation, the Octobrist newspaper *Golos Moskvy* broke down the number of deputies elected by center and right-wing groups (see Table 2.1). This classification covered most of the terms used during the campaign. "Right nonparty" is perhaps the best description of that large bloc of deputies who did not publicly define themselves in any way beyond the broad term "right." As deputies came to make formal affiliations, the party divisions, or fractions (*fraktsii*), became more precise. The most commonly cited figures are those given by the leading Soviet specialist on the third Duma, A. Ia. Avrekh (see Table 2.2). Before being merged in 1909, the Nationalists were divided into the moderate right fraction, with seventy-six members, and the National Group, with twenty-one.

On the extreme right of the Duma were the pravye, a disparate collection of reactionaries that possessed little ideological unity or parliamentary discipline.[7] Their most publicized figures were the archreactionary landlords, V. M. Purishkevich of Bessarabia, N. E. Markov II of Kursk, and the Vilna lawyer, G. G. Zamysloviskii. For the most part, they were proponents of a pre-1905 form of autocracy. Accordingly, their attitudes

7. Father Fiodr Nikonovich, *Iz dnevnika chlena gosudarstvennoi dumy ot Vitekskoi gubernii,* p. 11.

Table 2.2. **Political Breakdown of the Third Duma**

Pravye	50
Moderate right and National Group	97
Octobrists and their adherents	154
Progressisty	28
Kadets	54
Muslim group	8
Polish kolo	18
Trudoviki (labor group)	13
Social Democrats	20

Source: A. Ia. Avrekh, *Tsarizm i tret'eiunskaia sistema*, p. 20.

toward popular representation ranged from overt hostility to reluctant acceptance.

Any attempt to define the pravye program quickly falls back on the familiar triad of Autocracy, Orthodoxy, and Nationality. Broadly speaking, anti-Semitism and an obsession with repression of revolutionary activity were common to all pravye.[8] The pravye mistrusted political parties and Duma fractions, which were said to represent special interests. They characterized political questions in broad, general terms of good and evil, subversion versus traditional authority. Loyal to the autocracy, which they said spoke for all Russians, they avoided political causes that might in any way undermine the indivisibility of the Empire. Thus, few pravye deputies ever developed a close relationship with their constituents. On the contrary, they sought to avoid the charge of representing specific local interests. For them, political parties were dangerous, alien organizations that could only fragment the organic unity of the traditional order. These anachronistic attitudes created an uncomfortable relationship between the pravye fraction and the popularly oriented Union of Russian People.[9] Respectable rightists were not pleased with the union, whose tactics such as demagogic mass agitation, often involving street violence, distressed traditional nobles.

The new electoral law was a death knell for the Union of Russian People, which became superfluous with the restriction of the franchise. The need to attract lower-class votes had passed. Counterrevolution with all its connotations of the streets soon fell by the wayside, an ugly reminder of the turbulence of the revolutionary period.[10]

8. G. Iurskii, *Pravye v tret'-ei gosudarstvennoi dume*, p. 3.
9. Levin, "The Reactionary Tradition," p. 4.
10. *Kievlianin*, November 2, 1909.

The union's mass membership, always exaggerated, began to evaporate even before the 1907 election campaign.[11] National figures based on a compilation of provincial governors' reports give some picture of the extent of membership in right-wing groups during 1907. The Union of Russian People was said to have 356,738 members, but numerous governors were quick to point out that their figures were based on reports for 1906, a time when the union was more active. Many branches had either closed down or had ceased to function by 1907. The Octobrists were credited with 14,035 members. The Union of Russian People and the Octobrists were the only two groups that appeared in the reports with any regularity, but the governors noted that many local branches of both groups were either inactive or had ceased to function.[12] Instead, there remained a large section of unaffiliated conservative voters who had not committed themselves to any group.

Despite the sharp distinction between the Duma pravye and the cadres of the union, a social breakdown of the deputies reveals them to be less than the very pinnacle of Russian high society.[13] Of all the center and right-wing fractions, the pravye had the lowest percentage of noble members (23 out of 50). They had more priests (18) than any other fraction, and their clerical deputies proved more independent and erratic than those of other fractions.[14] This pattern was atypical of the other conservative fractions, in which the nobility played a more clearly dominant role.

Not surprisingly, extreme rightists were strong in regions where the local landed nobility felt particularly threatened by the peasantry. For example, Kursk, which suffered severe damage from peasant disturbances during 1905 and 1906, sent ten pravye. Elsewhere, the extreme right fraction was successful in gubernias where Russians were threatened by other nationalities. The presence of a large number of Jews, for instance, usually gave rise to strong pravye support. For example, Kherson gubernia—which included Odessa, whose population was one-third Jewish—sent four pravye. The western provinces were another stronghold: Volynia elected ten pravye, and pravye gained two of Vilna's three Russian seats.[15]

The Nationalists also drew support from the western region. Both the

11. TsGAOR 102. 4-oe dp. (1907), 164. ll. 149–150, 191, 302.

12. TsGAOR 102. 4-oe dp. (1907), 164, 281.

13. S. D. Urusov, *Memoirs of a Russian Governor* (New York, 1908), p. 84

14. N. N. Olshanskii, *Gosudarstvennaia Duma, 3-yi sozyv–Portrety* (St. Petersburg, 1910).

15. *Obzor deiatel'nosti Gosudarstvennoi Dumy*, tretyi sozyv, Chast'l, pp. 72–93.

future Nationalists and the pravye labeled themselves simply as "right" during the election campaign. Such Nationalist leaders as P. N. Balashev, D. N. Chikhachev, A. S. Gizhitskii, N. N. Ladomirskii, F. N. Bezak, and N. K. von Gubbenet, all landlords from the borderland, used this general term.[16] The pravye, however, differed sharply with the future Nationalists on questions of political form. They were opposed to the kind of political party the Nationalists came to build, and they did not share the Nationalists' positive feelings for Stolypin, with whom the new party was to work in close harmony after 1910.

Just to the left of the moderate right fraction sat the Octobrists and their adherents. The Octobrists were the best-organized conservative group at the opening of the third Duma and were soon able to attract the largest number of otherwise unaffiliated deputies into their fraction, which sat in the center of the Duma. It has proven difficult for scholars to correlate the Octobrists' program with their social base. While they are most often characterized as a party of the nobility and the big bourgeoisie, the Octobrists, normally defenders of private property, haphazardly followed a mildly constitutionalist program that occasionally led them to assume positions contrary to the immediate interests of those propertied classes they were supposed to represent.[17] However, the role of the bourgeoisie in the party has apparently been overstressed. Only 15 of 124 Octobrist deputies (third session) can be described as bourgeois.[18] With the exception of those fifteen, the Octobrist deputies had roughly the same social background as the moderate rights.[19] Yet, if this is so, why did the two parties develop different programs, organizational forms, and levels of discipline? The Octobrists represented an attempt by some of Russia's largest industrial and agrarian property holders to reach a political compromise based on principles that outside Russia had historically been associated with the bourgeoisie, but inside Russia had also been supported by gentry liberals in the zemstvos. In this context, those principles were supposed to supersede what might otherwise be divergent interests.

A breakdown of the Union of October by soslovie does give the impression that this party had a multiclass base (see Table 2.3). These

---

16. *Okrainy Rossii*, No. 43, October 27, 1907; No. 47, November 24, 1907.

17. A. Ia. Avrekh, "Stolypinskyi bonapartizm i voprosy voennoi politiki v IIIei Dume," *Voprosy Istorii*, No. 1 (1956):20; "Tret'ia Duma i nachalo krizisa tret'eiunskoi sistemy," *Istoricheskie Zapiski*, No. 53:53; and "Tret'eiunskaia monarkhia," *Istoria SSSR*, Vol. 6 (Moscow, 1968), p. 346.

18. *Portrety*.

19. Avrekh, "Tret'ia duma," p. 54.

Table 2.3. **Octobrist Deputies by Social Estate**

Nobles	80
Peasants	11
Priests	8
Bourgeois	15
Professional men	8
Cossacks	2

Source: Portrety.

deputies characterized themselves as a "constitutionalist center [of the Duma] not striving toward the seizure of government power but at the same time steadfastly maintaining the rights of popular representation within the boundaries specified for it by the Fundamental Laws."[20] This ambiguous constitutionalism attracted noble landlords schooled in the pre-1905 traditions of self-sacrifice and opposition to arbitrary central authority associated with zemstvo liberalism.

Despite the appearance of a multiclass base, the Duma Octobrists were dominated by landowning nobles. The Octobrists had the highest proportion of nobles (64.7 percent) of all the center and right-wing fractions. Because the peasant and clerical elements in the fraction were small, the Duma Octobrists can be characterized as mainly representing that segment of the landed dvorianstvo that received its political education in the zemstvos of central Russia with their quasi-liberal traditions. All zemstvo members were not liberal, but those who were touched by the phenomenon of zemstvo liberalism were motivated by a concern for legality and social justice that led them to adopt positions, particularly concerning the peasantry and the nobility's traditional privileges, that were often in opposition to their immediate interests as landlords. This stance did not mean that they rejected private property, merely that they were not always consistent in its defense.

Given these ambiguities, Octobrist unity was always exceedingly frail. The union's program of moderate constitutionalism was largely derived from the ideas and hopes of its more progressive leadership. Neither the entire Duma fraction nor most provincial Octobrists were inspired by it. Guchkov was constantly subjected to attacks from the union's right wing. As Neville Henderson, a sympathetic British diplomat, observed in 1907:

20. TsGAOR 115.1.34.1. See also Ben-Cion Pinchuk, *The Octobrists in the Third Duma* (Seattle, 1974).

Table 2.4. **Social Estates of Nationalists in the Third Duma (Third Session)**

Nobles	52
Priests	14
Peasants	16
Bourgeois (both merchants)	2
Cossacks	3

Source: Portrety.

> They consist ... of leaders without followers. ... The views of their leaders are personal and do not represent those of the party as a whole. This statement perhaps explains the lack of public support for the Octobrists.[21]

After an interview in 1908 with N. A. Khomiakov, president of the Duma and an Octobrist, Richard Seymour reported to London that

> a split in the Octobrist party had already been foreshadowed and would not be a regrettable eventuality as that party had hitherto only been held together by force of circumstances and its membership were not inspired by any real unity of aims.[22]

Although these statements may be overdrawn, they do demonstrate that the Octobrists were by no means ideally suited to the task of developing into a modern political party of the gentry. They did not seek to represent gentry interests directly, and they had proven ill-suited to the tasks and demands of political organizing.

These brief descriptions bring me to my central concern—those deputies who later came to form the National fraction. Once the forces on the right had coalesced, by early 1908, this amorphous group consisted of some seventy-four deputies calling themselves "moderate rights" and twenty-three members of the National Group. (The numbers varied slightly from session to session.) The party's deputies were elected largely under the broad term "right," and, at this early stage of their development, one can say strikingly little about them. If, for the time being, one ignores the bourgeois wing of the Octobrists, the moderate rights and National Group present substantially the same social picture as the Octobrist fraction. By the third session of the Duma, the Nationalists consisted of eighty-seven deputies from several social estates (see Table 2.4). Of all parties, the Nationalists had the most harmonious relationship with their members

21. PRO, FO 371. 318. 27698 (August 19, 1907).
22. PRO, FO 371. 513. 31810 (September 14, 1908).

from the clergy, and the Nationalist peasants were a carefully selected group. Thus, the nobles maintained complete control of the fraction while comprising a smaller percentage of their Duma delegation (57 percent) than the Octobrist nobles did in theirs.

What is striking about the members of the moderate right fraction is the minimum of preconceptions they brought to the Duma. Not loyal to any party, they were representative of that large element of noble sentiment that felt that the Duma pravye were immoderate and that the Octobrists were enamoured of dangerous constitutional notions and too eager to cooperate with the left. Believers in autocracy, they nevertheless supported representative institutions and prudent reforms. However, this simultaneous loyalty to the traditional monarchy and to the new legislative bodies lasted only as long as the government sought, as Stolypin did, to cooperate with the Duma and educated, propertied society.

The old dvorianstvo prejudice against political parties had changed by 1906. Nobles had fewer fears of acting independently, but at the time of the 1907 election campaign none of the available alternatives offered a sufficient expression of the landlords' needs. Thus, a large number of noble landlords remained uncommitted. Theoretically, the moderate rights could have represented this group, and, in fact, they drew their initial support from this segment of gentry opinion. In this sense, they bear a certain resemblance to the newly elected English country gentry of the late eighteenth century described by Sir Lewis Namier.

> The distinguishing mark of the country gentleman was disinterested independence: he should not be bound either to administration or to any faction in the House, nor to a magnate in his constituency;... he should owe his election to the free choice of the gentlemen of the country.[23]

In a report from Russia prepared for the British Foreign Office in 1908, Bernard Pares noted that

> these [the moderate rights] are country gentlemen who, having [had] no such class unity as the English gentry, took no particular interest in parties until the Reform movement.... The more apathetic of the country gentry now woke to life and expelled the Kadets ... from the zemstvos all over the country.[24]

23. Sir Lewis Namier, "Country Gentlemen in Parliament, 1756–84," *Crossroads of Power* (New York, 1962), p. 31.

24. PRO, FO 371. 30901 (September 5, 1908).

As both parties had roughly similar composition by soslovie, the differences between the Octobrists and Nationalists could be explained in purely intellectual terms. However, within the broad estate category, there was a wide possibility for variation in terms of other considerations—in this case, education, geography, occupation, and landownership—all of which provide a basis for distinguishing the Nationalists from their neighbors to the left.

The two groups differ quite sharply in terms of educational background. Excluding those with military educations (because of its specialized nature), 54 of 124 Octobrists in the third session (45 percent) had received higher education, while only 22 of 89 Nationalists (25 percent) had similar training. This difference may account for the Octobrists' greater receptivity to political programs emphasizing broad principles. In addition, 30 of those 54 Octobrists had attended the elite universities of Moscow and St. Petersburg, which made them part of an educated aristocracy that had been at least touched by the major intellectual currents of the time. In contrast, only six of the university-trained Nationalists had been schooled in the capitals.[25]

However, the most profound point of divergence is geography. Rather than dividing the vote between themselves in each gubernia, the two parties drew their support from different regions. A few provinces elected deputies from both parties, but, as noted earlier, the typical pattern was the domination of a gubernia's whole delegation by one of the conservative groups. Nationalist deputies came primarily from the western borderlands. Thirty-three came from the nine western gubernias originally included in Stolypin's controversial proposal to introduce zemstvos in the borderland. Of these, twenty-seven were from the six southwestern and Bielorussian provinces covered by the final bill—Kiev, Podol'e, Volynia, Minsk, Vitebsk, and Mogilev. Kiev with eight Duma members, and Minsk and Podol'e, with six each, had the largest Nationalist delegations. The three northwestern gubernias—Kovno, Vilna, and Grodno—together returned only six Nationalists. Bessarabia, under the influence of the enormously wealthy Krupenskii family, sent seven deputies, and Kherson sent four. Only eleven future Nationalists came from the capitals or from the central Russian gubernias, and five of these deputies came from Tula, where the families of such leading Nationalists as Vladimir Alekseevich Bobrinskii and Prince Alexander Petrovich Urusov exercised a great influence on the province's nobility. Most of the leadership of the Nationalist Party eventually emerged from the moderate right fraction. The leaders of this fraction—the future

25. *Portrety.*

Table 2.5. **Activities of Octobrist and Nationalist Deputies in the Third Duma**

	Octobrists	*Nationalists*
Agriculture	22	12
Military service	17	15
Zemstvo service	66	27
State service	22	18

Source: Portrety.

president P. N. Balashev, F. N. Bezak, S. M. Bogdanov, and D. N. Chikhachev—were all landlords from the strongholds of Kiev and Podol'e. P. N. Krupenskii and V. A. Bobrinskii were to play leading roles in Duma politics, but in internal party life they carried less weight than the men from the west. The National Group of twenty-three deputies, which sat between the moderate rights and the pravye until the formation of the Nationalist Party, came from roughly the same areas as the moderate rights, but none of its members were from Kiev, Podol'e, or Minsk, areas of the greatest moderate right strength.[26]

The fundamental institutional distinction between the western gubernias and central Russia—the absence of zemstvos—affected the type of activity Duma members had pursued (see Table 2.5). Because many men followed different occupations at different times, there is considerable overlap in the figures, but one basic distinction is clear: the Octobrists grew out of the zemstvo movement, while the Nationalists evolved from a once-strong service tradition and were not committed to any single field of endeavor.

Landholding was more extensive among Octobrist deputies. Eighty-three of them owned tracts larger than 200 desiatiny. Forty-two of the Nationalists owned such tracts, the average holding being 1,686 desiatiny. Those Octobrists who owned land averaged 2,349 desiatiny. These figures give some credence to the view that more economically secure landlords would be willing to forego class interest on occasion, while threatened elements would be concerned less with legality and more with survival. Although it may be absurd to characterize any group whose average holding is over 1,500 desiatiny as threatened, the Nationalists did represent a segment of the nobility that was severely challenged on the most fundamental day-to-day level.[27]

26. Ibid.
27. Ibid.

The Electors

With these differences between Nationalist and Octobrist deputies in mind, we now turn our attention to the electors who actually chose the Duma members. Do the distinctions that appear in the Duma hold up at the next lowest level of the election process? Until now, analyses of the electors have been drawn from incomplete and inconsistent newspaper accounts. These descriptions used a variety of terminologies and often did not corroborate each other. However, statistical breakdowns of the third Duma electors compiled by the Ministry of Interior's *Osoboe deloproizvod-stvo po vyboram* are available. Although the categories used by the ministry's observers are not those that would necessarily occur to the

Table 2.6. **Breakdown of 1907 Electors by Social Estate**

	Vyborshchiki of the landowners' curia (2,542)		All vyborshchiki (5,150)	
	Number	Percentage	Number	Percentage
Dvorianstvo	1,542	61	1,896	37
Clergy	533	22	631	12
Honorary citizens	117	4	316	6
Merchants	121	5	395	8
Petty bourgeois	47	2	320	6
Peasants	0	0	1,244	24
Others	119	4	344	7

Source: *Vybory*, p. 272.

modern political analyst, the government's criteria are sufficiently clear to permit greater clarity about this level of the election process. For purposes of comparison, it is useful to look at some of the national totals on all the electors by soslovie, by government-described political tendency, and by education (see Tables 2.6, 2.7, and 2.8).

Contrasting the election results for areas that returned Nationalists with returns from provinces that elected Octobrists can help to highlight more precise distinctions between the two parties. The six western gubernias that received zemstvos in 1911 and made up the Nationalists' base (Kiev, Podol'e, Volynia, Minsk, Vitebsk, and Mogilev) will be compared, first, with other gubernias that chose future Nationalists (Bessarabia, Tula, and Pskov) and, second, with regions that went heavily Octobrist (Ekaterinoslav, Samara, Chernigov, and Poltava).

The most striking aspect of the comparison is the numerical weakness

Table 2.7. **Political Tendencies of 1907 Electors**

	Landowners		All vyborshchiki	
	Number	Percentage	Number	Percentage
Right	1,569	62	2,432	47
Moderate	585	23	1,046	20
Left	97	8	1,118	22
Unknown	191	7	552	11

Source: Vybory, p. 272.

Table 2.8. **Educational Level of 1907 Electors**

	Landowners		All vyborshchiki	
	Number	Percentage	Number	Percentage
Higher	943	37	1,473	29
Secondary	1,197	47	1,474	29
Primary	402	16	2,201	42

Source: Vybory, p. 272.

Table 2.9. *Soslovie* **of Electors in Nationalist and Octobrist Strongholds**

	Western gubernias (6)	Nationalist gubernias (3)	Octobrist gubernias (4)
Dvorianstvo	195	104	198
Clergy	174	17	44
Honorary citizens	12	5	10
Merchants	5	10	18
Petty bourgeois	15	2	8
Peasants	10	0	6
Others	8	11	10

Source: Vybory.

of the nobility in the landowners' curiae of the western gubernias. Although one would expect them to be dominant, they do not constitute even half of that curia. This poor showing stands in marked contrast to other Nationalist gubernias and to Octobrist strongholds (see Table 2.9). The large number of priests in the west is the most salient feature of this comparison. It clearly demonstrates the severe problems of the Russian landlord element in these gubernias.

Although the distribution of social groups in the Octobrist and Nationalist fractions in the Duma was basically the same, this similarity did not carry over to the vyborshchiki who elected them. According to these statistics, the Nationalists represented an especially weak segment of the landed nobility. The precariousness of their situation made it impossible for them to take politics for granted. They could not be secure in the belief that their wealth and position would assure representation in the Duma. Thus, it was necessary to do what nobles had never done previously— organize politically. Given the institutions, ethnic mix, and economy of the region in which they lived, it is not surprising that the gentry of western Russia evolved a particularly modern form of political organization.

As the statistics reveal, the clergy was to play a special role in the development of this new political machine. Priests were forced to act as surrogates for Russian noble interests, a role with which they were not always happy but which they accepted and fulfilled. Had the priests' position been one of absolute independence, the number of clerics in the Nationalist fraction would probably have been considerably larger than it was. The large number of clerical electors may explain the Nationalists' intense concern with religious questions during the course of the Duma. But the party's ideological predispositions and concern for nationality probably would have assured a strong interest in religious matters under any circumstances. What is really underscored here is the extreme difficulty of the west Russian landlords' position. The Nationalist constituency had to concentrate first and foremost on safeguarding its most immediate interests. Severely threatened, they were far less likely to experiment with such notions as legality and constitutionalism than their counterparts elsewhere.

Because of the absence of zemstvos, the Russian nobles in the west had been more involved in state service and less in public work than had their Octobrist counterparts. Where such bodies did exist in Nationalist areas, the rate of participation in zemstvo work is roughly the same as that encountered in Octobrist regions. Indeed, Nationalist electors from other areas and Octobrist electors have no major differences for any criterion save political tendency.

This similarity of characteristics makes the phenomenon of Nationalist strength outside the west difficult to explain. Logically, the inability of the Octobrists to attract the entire dvorianstvo would create a broad base for a party that eschewed constitutionalism and explicitly defended the nobility's interests. People with such beliefs were, in fact, elected to the Duma, and many of them entered the moderate right fraction. However, their affiliation was more reflective of negative feelings toward the orga- nized alternatives in 1907 than of any positive attraction to the specific kind of political formation then evolving in the west.

Why did some nobles choose Octobrism while others rejected it? Often local traditions played a role. In some gubernias, the eminence of a particular family may have been decisive. Local heroes or generally recognized men of honor could have disproportionate influence. For example, the family of P. N. Krupenskii dominated the local politics of Bessarabia and led that gubernia's Duma delegation into the moderate right fraction. Krupenskii's primary political commitment was not to the specific needs of the borderland Nationalists. Rather, he was obsessed with the creation of a smoothly working conservative center majority in the Duma. Suspicious of the Octobrists, he saw the moderate rights and later the Nationalists as the best basis for a constellation of moderate conservative forces in the lower house. When the Nationalists became a divisive force after the western zemstvo crisis, he split with them.

In Tula, the eminent families of V. A. Bobrinskii and Prince A. P. Urusov were recognized as leaders of the local gentry, and some of them followed their example in joining the Nationalists. Interestingly, both Bobrinskii and Urusov had family ties to the borderland. Other Urusovs owned large estates in the west, and V. A. Bobrinskii was listed as co-owner of the 35,000-desiatin family estate in Kiev gubernia, which he shared with his brothers Lev and the more famous Alexander, who was a pravye deputy.

In the absence of clear social distinctions, the nonborderland nobles who eventually became Nationalists were distinguished from the Octobrists largely by attitudes and ideas. The most important of these was anticonstitutionalism. Men like Krupenskii, Bobrinskii, and Urusov all shared the belief that, despite its newly created institutions, Russia was still an autocracy. Although their own views on the nature of the post-1905 Russian state were vague, it was impossible for them to join the Octobrists, who considered Russia a constitutional monarchy. V. A. Bobrinskii, in particular, was a veteran of the struggles that preceded the Revolution of 1905, and from that experience he gained an intense antiliberalism, tinged with a hatred of "Jewish" Kadets, which all Octobrists did not share.

In general, nonwesterners played a problematic role in the party's development. The idea for the creation of a party came from the borderland. People from outside that region never offered clear reasons for joining the Nationalists. They did not share the westerners' concerns. In most cases, they made their decision for lack of a better alternative. Over time, many of these reluctant Nationalists drifted away, and the party became progressively more homogeneous. Krupenskii, for example, eventually left the party, and others in the Duma followed his course. Such Petersburg intellectuals as M. O. Menshikov, columnist for the conservative daily *Novoe Vremia*, had always been dubious about the idea of a party despite the other views he shared with most Nationalists. By 1912, he and other conservative intellectuals had drifted away from the party's orbit before they could complete the task for which they were best suited— developing a fully elaborated ideology of nationalism.

If there were no sharp distinctions between nonwestern Nationalist and Octobrist electors, what of the contrasts we have drawn between the two Duma fractions? One of the clearest differences was educational level. Forty-five percent of the Octobrists had some higher education as opposed to 25 percent of the Nationalist deputies. However, the picture among the electors is not the same. The national average for members of the landowners' meetings with higher education was 37 percent. In the western gubernias, 35 percent of the landowners' electors had such education. In the other Nationalist regions, the figure is 40 percent, the same as that found in the Octobrist strongholds. Disregarding peasant and clerical deputies from both Duma fractions (their educational opportunities were clearly different), the contrast becomes even more acute. Of the nobles, bourgeois, and professionals among the Octobrist deputies, 50 percent had higher education, while the figure for the Nationalists is 39 percent. When dealing with Duma fractions, we are concerned with groups that definitionally are composed entirely of men from one party. However, a gubernia electoral assembly that supported one or another group was not necessarily a politically homogeneous body. Thus, these figures should simply be seen as indicative of a broad trend. Despite this reservation, the pattern is clear. The Octobrist deputies exhibit a higher educational level than the people who elected them, but the Nationalists, in terms of this criterion, are more typical of their milieu. This finding would appear to reinforce my earlier contention that the Octobrist fraction was less representative of its social base than the Nationalists were.

The composition of the first city curiae repeats the pattern seen in the landowners' assemblies (see Table 2.10). The western gubernias present different results from both the nonwestern Nationalist and the Octobrist provinces, which are again similar in all categories except for political inclination.

The alliance of larger property owners did not operate in the borderland, and fewer nobles were among the town electors. Instead, Jews dominated the city assemblies. Their politics were, not surprisingly, decidedly left-wing. Quite clearly, then, the alliance of electors from the landowners' curiae with those in the first city assembly could not occur in the west, which forced the local Russian gentry deeper into the embrace of the clergy.

Table 2.10. **Makeup of First City Curiae (1907)**

	Western gubernias	*Nationalist areas*	*Octobrist areas*
By soslovie			
Dvorianstvo	14	10	16
Clergy	0	2	2
Honorary citizens	9	6	10
Merchants	25	18	12
Petty bourgeois	21	3	19
Peasants	0	0	1
Other	17	2	1
By nationality			
Russian	17	34	40
Polish	8	0	1
Jewish	63	7	19
By politics			
Right	11	20	10
Moderate	19	11	13
Left	49	10	33
Unknown	8	0	5

Source: Vybory.

The Russian landlord found it hard to deal with Jews, who controlled much of the borderland's commerce. In addition, much of the landed wealth was owned by Poles. Intimidated, Russian landlords raised the demand of "Russia for Russians," but their particular form of nationalism had a highly expediential and pragmatic character. Some more romantic Russian nationalists were willing to subordinate their immediate interests to the national principle or to view nationalism as a supraclass ideology, but the Nationalist Party's principles were nearly always consistent with the most basic, pragmatic interests of its constituents.

The figures for the vyborshchiki amplify the indications, given by the profiles of the Duma fractions, that the Nationalists represented a less secure and historically less well established element of the dvorianstvo. The national divisions in the western borderlands further exacerbated this feeling. Thus, the genesis of the Nationalist Party was primarily a regional phenomenon. Nationalist strength outside the west had a different and far less significant meaning.

Nevertheless, the Nationalists' economic and political insecurity does much to explain the intransigence of their defense of what they perceived to be their immediate interests. With less to sacrifice in the interest of social peace, the Nationalists were far less willing than the Octobrists to engage in compromise. The Nationalists' unswerving support of the Western Zemstvo Act, which introduced zemstvos into the borderland in 1911, is probably the most dramatic instance of this attitude. The campaign for control of local government in the west provided a broad basis for the development of the Nationalist Party. In fact, it was around the demand for zemstvos in the borderland that the Nationalists coalesced during the first years of the third Duma.[28] The western zemstvo issue was not a simple question of extending an institution to a place where it did not exist; it highlighted all of the party's fundamental concerns.

The Nationalists' Stronghold

The Nationalists drew their greatest numbers as well as their leadership from the western borderland. The party received scattered support elsewhere, drawing in part on the bloc of uncommitted dvorianstvo opinion, but the pecularities of the west had a a crucial impact on Nationalist ideology, program, and organizational form.

This flat, fertile region had been Polish since the Middle Ages. After the partitions of Poland late in the eighteenth century, it became part of the Russian Empire, but the area remained dominated economically and culturally by Polish noble landlords. After the Polish rebellion of 1830, still more Polish nobles moved into the area. The government sought to use the terms of the emancipation of the serfs in 1861 to disadvantage the Polish landlords. Elsewhere, the redemption payments given to landlords for the loss of their property far exceeded the market value of the land. In the nine western provinces, however, *pomeshchiki* (landlords) actually got somewhat less than the value of their land. After the Polish rebellion of 1863, the autocracy began an aggressive policy in support of Russian landowning in the region.[29] Many bureaucrats were rewarded with estates in the west, and the balance gradually began to shift. By 1907, Russians of all soslovia held more land in the west than their Polish neighbors did. Most of this land had been given to recently rewarded bureaucrats. These first Russian pomeshchiki had been deeply involved with their service careers and were therefore especially prone to absenteeism. By 1907,

28. Robert Edelman, "The Russian Nationalist Party and the Political Crisis of 1909," *Russian Review* (January 1975):22–45.

29. V. V. Shulgin, *Vybornoe zemstvo v iugo-zapadnom krae*, p. 17.

Table 2.11. **National Composition of the Nine Western Gubernias**

	Total Russians	Poles and Lithuanians	Jews	Germans
Vilna	61.05	25.99	12.71	—
Vitebsk	84.93	3.38	11.69	—
Volynia	73.73	6.16	13.20	5.73
Grodno	71.20	10.08	17.30	0.10
Kiev	85.25	1.93	12.09	—
Kovno	7.27	77.31	13.72	—
Minsk	80.93	3.00	16.00	—
Mogilev	85.93	1.03	12.06	—
Podol'e	84.54	2.30	12.20	—

Source: Mary Schaeffer, *The Political Policies of P. A. Stolypin,* p. 268.

Note: Figures are given in percentages.

however, second- and third-generation descendants, both female and male, had inherited title to these estates, and many of them chose to remain on the land and farm.[30]

For all their recent gains, Russian noble landlords in the west still lived a precarious existence. They were challenged on the land by Poles, who were more aggressive and efficient farmers, and in the commercial life of the towns by Jews, whom they feared and mistrusted. Despite their control of extensive economic resources and property, both Jews and Poles were only small minorities of the total population of the western provinces (see Table 2.11).

The "Total Russian" category in Table 2.11 includes Great Russians, Bielorussians, and Ukrainians. Great Russians numbered only 3 or 4 percent of that total; the peasantry was primarily Ukrainian or Bielorussian. However, during the 1897 census, 31,919 of 145,150 hereditary and personal nobles in the southwest listed Ukrainian as their native language. It would be a mistake, therefore, to overemphasize the extent to which any of these peasants felt estranged from their Russian landlords for reasons of nationalism.[31] As was revealed in the disturbances of 1905 and 1906,

30. *Ibid,* p. 20; Geroid Robinson, *Rural Russia under the Old Regime* (New York, 1932), p. 88. In 1861 Poles held 89 percent of all private land in the southwest. By 1905 that figure had fallen to 47 percent. V. P. Teplytskii, *Reforma 1861 roku i agrarni vidnosini na ukraini* (Kiev, 1959), p. 161.

31. Tsentral'nyi statisticheskii komitet ministerstva vnutrennykh del, *Pervaia vseobshchaia perepis' naselenia Rossiskoi Imperii, 1897 g.* Vol XVI, p. 258, Vol. VIII, p. 248, Vol. XXXII, p. 256.

Ukrainian peasants made no distinctions: they attacked landlords of all nationalities.[32] In addition, they exhibited little, if any, interest in the various Ukrainian nationalist movements or parties that emerged during 1905,[33] even though in some cases those parties considered themselves revolutionary and supported peasant demands.[34]

Similar national movements sprang up in Russian Poland during the years of turmoil. The Polish noble landlords of the western provinces did not participate actively in these groups, but the west Russian gentry lived in fear that they would take part in the fight for Polish liberation. To add further trouble, Jews had been participants in the revolutionary struggle for some time. They had opposed tsarism, both through the major revolutionary parties and in their own organizations, all of which were especially active in the western borderland, which roughly corresponded to the territory of the Pale of Settlement to which Jewish residence was restricted.[35] Thus, national tensions of all sorts ran high in the western provinces. It was a situation from which the west Russian gentry could hardly take comfort.

The Russian landlord was cut off from the peasantry by clearly perceived class divisions and separated from the Polish nobility by equally sharp national barriers. As a result, Russian pomeshchiki came to fasten on any means that might strengthen their position on the land and give them the political power to defend themselves. The first two Duma elections had made these fears real. The 1905 electoral law had been fairly even-handed in its treatment of nationalities, and, as a result, a number of Poles from the borderland had been elected to the Duma. In invoking Russian nationalism, the west Russian gentry appealed to outside authorities for support in their political and economic struggle with Polish landowners. The ethnic composition of the west provided the basis for local Russians' special obsession with nationalist concerns.[36]

This particular distribution of nationalities also explains the fundamen-

32. *Agrarnoe dvizhenie v Rossii v 1905–06 gg., Trudy imperatorskogo vol'nogo ekonomicheskogo obshchestva,* No. 3 (May–June 1908), Vol. 2, p. 193.

33. Michael Palij, *The Anarchism of Nestor Makhno* (Seattle, 1976), pp. 6–9.

34. Ralph Carter Elwood, *Russian Social Democracy in the Underground* (Assen, 1974), pp. 16–19.

35. Hugh Seton-Watson, *The Decline of Imperial Russia, 1855–1914* (New York, 1952), pp. 231–235.

36. A. Ia. Avrekh, "Vopros o zapadnom zemstve i bankrovstvo Stolypina," *Istoricheskie zapiski,* Vol. 70 (1962):61–112; Edward Chmielewski, "Stolypin's Last Crisis," *California Slavic Studies* Vol. 3, (1964):95–126, and *The Polish Question in the Russian State Duma;* A. S. Izgoev, *P. A. Stolypin.* All three writers show a tendency to regard the Nationalists' concern with nationalism as an autonomous factor divorced from questions of class.

Table 2.12. **Land Ownership in 1907 (in Desiatiny)**

	Russians	*Poles*
Kiev	1,540,000	616,000
Podol'e	1,126,000	619,000
Volynia	2,372,000	1,091,000

Source: V. V. Shulgin, *Vybornoe zemstvo v iugo-zapadnom krae,* p. 52.

tal institutional peculiarity of the borderland. The zemstvo reform of 1864 had not been extended to the western provinces, because local government would have been controlled by Polish nobles, who were considered politically untrustworthy after 1863. A law of April 2, 1903, had created appointive zemstvos in Kiev, Podol'e, Volynia, Minsk, Vitebsk, and Mogilev; the members of these assemblies were chosen by the Ministry of Interior. These particular institutions were deemed entirely inadequate by local Russian landlords.[37] The Polish element had been eliminated, but the appointment of members made the ethos of these bodies essentially bureaucratic. Only the gubernia assemblies had any power. On the uezd level, the appointive zemstvos were merely consultative.[38] Therefore, this kind of zemstvo merely aggravated local awareness of Russian landlord absenteeism, which, although diminished with passing generations, still remained a problem.

This bureaucratic solution to the west's problem had been necessitated by the historic domination of landholding and agriculture by Polish landlords who owned more land and were better managers of farms.[39] By 1907, however, the total number of desiatiny privately owned by Russians in the southwest gubernias of Kiev, Podol'e, and Volynia was far greater than that owned by Poles (see Table 2.12). But the traditional pattern of large tracts owned by Poles and smaller tracts owned by Russians, while diminished, still persisted (see Table 2.13). This predominance of large Polish property holdings directly affected the composition of the west's State Council delegation, chosen by special noble assemblies. All the borderland's State Council members were Polish. Had the 1890 zemstvo law been introduced into the borderland without alteration, Polish landlords would have dominated local government as well.

Considering this region's high fertility and its accessibility to the international grain market, control of the land was essential. The gentry

37. Chmielewski, *The Polish Question in the Russian State Duma,* p. 82.
38. Shulgin, *Vybornoe zemstvo,* pp. 25–32.
39. Ibid., p. 50.

Table 2.13. **Patterns of Land Ownership (1907)**

| | Tracts above 200 desiatiny | | Tracts below 200 desiatiny | |
	Russian	Polish	Russian	Polish
Kiev	1,027,663	725,289	2,194,774	24,763
Podol'e	756,040	788,821	1,839,546	33,499
Volynia	1,234,923	1,423,546	2,502,712	83,664

Source: V. V. Shulgin, *Vybornoe zemstvo v iugo-zapadnom krae*, p. 54.

was not willing to relinquish it easily. Land was either farmed by pomesh-chiki themselves or rented on long-term leases to people who could run it profitably. Often renters were light industrial firms involved in food processing. Distilling and sugar beet refining were the most common such enterprises. There were over 300 distilleries on the estates of noble landlords in the southwest. These were not necessarily small operations, and they employed thousands of full-time workers who were not members of peasant communes.[40] Although the distilling of spirits was a significant element of the region's economy, the raising and refining of sugar beets was the most distinguishing characteristic of agriculture in the southwest-ern provinces. Sugar beets were a cash crop; nearly the entire output was marketed. The beets were raised on the larger noble estates, and extensive wage labor was employed.[41] Little mechanization was used. All a landlord required was sufficient numbers of landless or near landless peasants willing to work for starvation wages.[42] As a result of this advantageous situation, the amount of land given over to sugar beets rose rapidly in the second half of the nineteenth century. In 1850, 21,000 desiatiny were planted with sugar beets. By 1900, the figure had risen to over 300,000 desiatiny, and, on the eve of World War I, 507,000 desiatiny were planted with this crop.[43] The expansion of the output in the southwest was similarly swift (see Table 2.14). The figure for 1900 accounted for over 90 percent of all Russian sugar production. With the increase in production came a rise in the number of refineries. In 1830, there were six such plants; by 1900, there were 147 refineries of sugar beets in the southwest, employing

40. M. N. Leshchenko, *Klasova borot'ba v ukrains'komu seli na pochatku xx stolittia* (Kiev, 1968), p. 52.

41. *Agrarnoe dvizhenie v Rossii*, Vol. 2, pp. 111–113.

42. M. N. Leshchenko, *Selianskii rukh na ukraini v roki pershoi rosiis'koi revoliutsii* (Kiev, 1956), pp. 13–14.

43. M. N. Leshchenko, *Selianskii rukh na pravoberezhnoi ukraini v period revoliutsii 1905-1907 rr.*, p. 30.

Table 2.14. **Sugar Beet Output in the Southwest**

1865	1,700,000 *pudy*[a]
1881	9,803,298
1890	13,369,895
1900	27,000,000 (est.)

Source: O. O. Nesterenko, *Rozvitok kapitalistichnoi promislovosti i formuvannia proletariaty na ukraini v kintsi xix i na pochatku xx st.* (Kiev, 1952), p. 41.

[a]One *pud*=36.11 pounds.

over 68,000 workers.[44] Although cereals remained the primary crops in the borderland, the importance of this sort of crop was growing with each passing year, making commercial agriculture the predominant form of estate owning in the borderland.[45]

Thus, agriculture in the borderland, particularly in the southwest gubernias of Kiev, Podol'e, and Volynia, was characterized by a well-developed capitalist basis. Production for profit rather than for subsistence was the rule. Land in the west was bought and sold as if it were a commodity. In other parts of Russia, peasants had acquired huge amounts of land at the expense of the gentry. In the borderland, however, they were being forced off their communal allotments and were becoming proletarianized. To compound the peasants' problems, the profitability of commercial farming was so great in the southwest that landlords were unwilling to rent to peasants. These situations were characteristic of the kind of agrarian capitalism seen in other nations that had experienced what is usually called the "agrarian revolution."[46]

Since the 1890s, there has been extensive debate among scholars and political figures about the extent of capitalism in Russia. There has also been similar disagreement among students of the Russian countryside concerning the proper indicators of agrarian capitalism. Despite these broad differences of opinion, the literature on agriculture in the southwest is virtually unanimous in describing conditions there as predominantly capitalist.[47]

44. Leshchenko, *Selianskii rukh na pravoberezhnoi ukraini*, p. 33.

45. G. P. Pavlovsky, *Agricultural Russia on the Eve of Revolution* (London, 1930), p. 328.

46. See Temma Kaplan, *Anarchists of Andalusia* (Princeton, 1977), p. 39. See also Boguslaw Galeski, *Basic Concepts of Rural Sociology* (Manchester, 1972), p. 29.

47. On this question, early and contemporary Soviet scholars agree with Western historians. See A. M. Anfimov, *Krupnoe pomeshchich'e khoziaistvo evropeiskoi Rossii*, p. 167; A. Shestakov, *Krestianskaia revoliutsiia 1905-1907 gg.* (Moscow, 1926), p. 14; S. M. Dubrovskii, *Krestianskoe dvizhenie v revoliutsii 1905-1907* (Moscow, 1956), p. 29; F. E. Los', *Revoliutsia 1905-1907 rokiv na ukraini* (Kiev, 1955), pp. 180–185; P. Maslov, *Krestian-*

The future Nationalists were well aware of the character of agriculture in the borderland. In a brochure of 1893 on the peasants of Kiev gubernia, Baron I. M. Reva, who would become an assistant Minister of Interior and later a leading party activist on the local level, described the impact of the region's swiftly expanding market economy on the peasantry of the province. In particular, he noted the weakening of the village commune and the emergence of sharp differences of wealth among the peasants. Both of these phenomena were taken by most contemporary observers as indicators of the penetration of capitalism into the countryside.[48]

The production of cash crops forced the west's gentry, both Polish and Russian, into the modern capitalist world of profit, competent bookkeeping, and close control of the daily operation of their estates. These were not their traditional pursuits, and the effect was unsettling. It deprived the landlord of the smug satisfaction and accompanying political passivity that went with the absolute domination of the relatively self-contained setting of the traditional village. Instead, the western landlords moved in an unfamiliar world of moneylenders, shippers, and other middlemen. Moreover, they confronted these new types, many of them Jewish, in the towns of the borderland. The necessity of functioning in an urban economic context was particularly disturbing to Russian landlords, who had only recently left the far more controlled, and therefore less threatening, environment of the bureaucracy. While this situation made them feel less secure than their central Russian counterparts, it also made them more open to modern approaches to economics and politics. Significantly, in Bielorussia, where market relations and commercial agriculture were less extensive, the future Nationalists had less electoral success than in the southwest. This was true despite the fact that relationships among nationalities were similar in both regions.

Self-sufficient communes and dues-collecting landlords were few in the west. The profitability of farming was reflected in the high value of the land, especially in the southwest where land sold for an average of 128.7 rubles per desiatin in 1900, a figure exceeded in value only in the left-bank

skoe dvizhenie v Rossii v epokhu pervoi russkoi revoliutsii (Moscow, 1924), pp. 17–18; N. Mirza-Avakiants, *Selianskii rozrukhi na ukraini 1905–1907 rokiv* (Kharkov, 1925), p. 29; Lancelot Owen, *The Russian Peasant Movement* (New York, 1937), pp. 56–61; Maureen Perrie, *The Agrarian Policy of the Russian Socialist Revolutionary Party* (Cambridge, 1976), pp. 190–195; Pavlovsky, *Agricultural Russia on the Eve of Revolution*, p. 47; Robinson, *Rural Russia under the Old Regime*, p. 85. This section, on the terms of the peasant emancipation, notes that commercial agriculture was being practiced in the western borderland even before the freeing of the serfs.

48. I. M. Reva, *Kievskii krestianin i ego khoziaistvo* (Kiev, 1893), p. 420.

Table 2.15. **Loss of Noble-Owned Land in the Ukraine (1862–1914)**

	Percentage of land lost
Right-bank Ukraine:	
Kiev	28.6
Podol'e	28.0
Volynia	34.0
Left-bank Ukraine:	
Poltava	56.5
Kharkov	61.9
Chernigov	62.8

Source: M. A. Rubach, "Sotsial'naia struktura agrarnykh otnoshenii i rassloenie krestianstva v ukrainskom derevne v 1917 g.," in *Osobennosti agrarnogo stroia Rossii v period imperializma* (Moscow, 1962), pp. 47–48.

Ukraine and the southern steppe.[49] In addition, the borderland exhibited a higher concentration of land in the hands of large holders and a higher level of private landholding than did the rest of Russia.[50]

Noble landlords of the west had lost far less land over the course of the late nineteenth century than had their central Russian counterparts. Since the emanicipation, the dvorianstvo, in general, had been losing its grip on the land, but the pomeshchiki of the southwest still retained 84 percent of what they had owned in 1877. The figure for Bielorussia was 88 percent in comparison with a national average of 70 percent.[51] The research of M. A. Rubach, a Soviet specialist on Ukrainian agriculture, makes the contrast even sharper. Using a variety of statistical sources for the years 1862 through 1914, he indicates that the distinction between the southwest and the other regions of Russia also applied to the rest of the Ukraine. He compared the three southwestern provinces of Kiev, Podol'e, and Volynia (often called the right-bank Ukraine) with the three neighboring "Little Russian" gubernias of Kharkov, Poltava, and Chernigov (often called the left-bank Ukraine) (see Table 2.15). The comparison becomes politically significant when one remembers that Kharkov, Poltava, and Chernigov were all areas of Octobrist electoral strength.

Much of this success in retaining title to land is attributable to the more

49. I. D. Kovalchenko, "Agrarnyi rynok i kharakter agrarnogo stroia evropeiskoi Rossii v kontse XIX–nachale XX veka," *Istoria SSSR*, No. 2 (1973):47.

50. N. A. Proskuriakova, "Razmeshchenie i struktura dvorianskogo zemlevladenia evropeiskoi Rossii v kontse XIX–nachale XX veka," *Istoria SSSR*, No. 1 (1973):61.

51. Ibid., p. 64.

efficient Polish landlords who had never been distracted by the necessity of state service. Many of these men had even studied agronomy formally. Although not always direct participants in this agricultural activity, west Russian nobles, nevertheless, had a notion of landowning that derived from the experience of their more advanced Polish competitors. For this reason, among others, Russian landlords in the west came to perceive agriculture as a modern productive force, which, as much as or more than rank, determined their social position.

The Gaisin district of Podol'e was typical. Roughly two-thirds of the holdings were managed by their owners. One-third had been rented out on long-term leases.[52] Little land was left fallow or given to communes to run on their own in exchange for rent. Crop rotation had become more sophisticated in the west. In Gaisin, 85 percent of the land was under multifield tillage, and the few individual holdings on which we have information were also multifield.[53]

One finds leading Nationalist figures engaged in both renting and farming. Professor V. E. Chernov was vice-president and later president of the Kiev Club of Russian Nationalists. A medical specialist in the city of Kiev, Chernov had no time for agriculture despite his noble ancestry, and so he rented his 1,068 desiatiny in Uman uezd to the Verniachsky sugar factory. The opposite pattern was followed by the Nationalist deputy A. A. Pototskii. A member of one of the Empire's wealthiest landowning families, Pototskii owned land in Podol'e and Kiev.[54] He had fifteen villages in Zvenigorod uezd of Kiev gubernia. Pototskii farmed 14,598 desiatiny and rented out only 891. All his land was planted in a ten-field system.

Information on the estates of several relatives of Nationalist deputies reveals a clearer pattern of agricultural modernity. Of nine such holdings, all but one were multifield, and the one three-field estate provided the grain for a large distilling operation. All the estates had either sugar beet refining or distilling factories, in some cases both.[55] This is concrete proof

52. *Materialy*, p. v.

53. Ibid., p. 3; *Ves'iugo-zapadnogo kraia*, pp. 7, 9, 220; A. I. Yaroshevich, *Ocherki ekonomicheskie zhizni iugo-zapadnogo kraia*, (Kiev, 1908), p. 12; *Materialy*, pp. 4, 122.

54. Anfimov, *Krupnoe pomeshchich'e khoziaistvo*, p. 394.

55. Descriptions of these estates were made by the Ministry of Agriculture. See *Kratkie spravochnye svedenia o nekotorikh russkikh khoziaistvakh*, izdanie vtoroe, vypusk vtoroi (St. Petersburg, 1901). There is no way of specifying the precise relationships of these landlords to the Nationalist deputies, nor can one be certain of the extent and nature of communication that went on between family members. Membership in the same family is no guarantee of shared political opinion, but, as a general indication, this particular connection is meaningful. The estates mentioned in the *Kratkie svedenia* include additional information on the lands of A. A. Pototskii, p. 182, and K. K. Pototskii, p. 242. Others were the heirs of

that the Nationalists' social base was involved in production for the market. In addition, the existence of these establishments meant that their owners had to do business in the city of Kiev, the economy of which was heavily geared to sugar and alcohol. This practical involvement in city life had significant political and institutional consequences for the Nationalists.

While the estates of future Nationalists exhibited a variety of patterns of land use, it is crucial to note that agriculture in the west, regardless of the particular form of tenure, was capitalistically organized, and the importance and profitability of agriculture accordingly reinforced the commitment of Russian landlords to retain their lands. Commercial agriculture existed outside the west, and the mix of nationalities with a less extensive market orientation could be found in Bielorussia. But the coupling of commercial agriculture with the distribution of nationalities, a combination found in the southwest, created a particularly volatile political setting.

The landlords' success in holding onto their property had created an especially acute land shortage for the peasantry of the west. By 1900, the average peasant (individual, not household) in the southwest owned only 1.5 desiatiny.[56] Soviet researchers, using the arbitrary categories of "poor," "middle," and "rich" peasant, have estimated that nearly 65 percent of the peasantry of the southwest could be considered poor.[57] Elsewhere, the vast majority of peasants fell into the so-called middle category.

Lack of land was the historic complaint of the Russian peasant, and the situation in the borderland was especially acute. In central Russia, peasants could always hope that their family's situation might be improved as part of the periodic redistribution of land practiced by the traditional repartitional (*obshchinnoe*) village commune. That possibility did not exist in the west where land tenure in the commune was hereditary (*podvornoe*). New land for the peasants of the borderland could only come from the estates of the gentry.[58] The noble landlords of the west were fully aware of this situation, and it made their fear of the peasants all the more intense.

Many peasants had been forced off their allotments to work as wage laborers on the landlords' huge sugar plantations. Most of those who held onto some land could not make ends meet, and they too had to seek

---

N. A. Bezak, p. 177, P. E. and A. I. Suvchinskii, p. 214, Praskovaia Aleksandrevna Urusova, p. 188, Nikolai Petrovich Balashev, p. 244, Nikolai Matveich Chikhachev, p. 265. Finally, it should be noted that there is no guarantee that this group is in any way typical. It does, however, correspond to most general accounts of the nature of agriculture in the borderland.

56. G. I. Moiseevich, *Sel'skokhoziaistvennye rabochie vo vremia pervoi revoliutsii* (Moscow, 1926), p. 31.

57. P. P. Telichuk, *Ekonomichni osnovi agrarnoi revoliutsii na ukraini*, p. 138.

58. Owen, *The Russian Peasant Movement*, p. 51.

employment, for piteously low wages, on the estates of the pomeshchiki. Thus, the relationship between the landlords of the west and those who worked their lands more closely resembled that of capitalist employers and their employees than traditional feudal landlords and their peasants. In the west, in contrast to much of the rest of Russia, something far more like a class of capitalist farmers confronted a class of agrarian laborers in an intense, bitter, and daily struggle.[59]

The landlords of the west did not have to search their memories to find proof of the seriousness of what could properly be called (at least in the borderland) a class struggle on the land. In the course of the massive peasant revolts of 1905 and 1906, the southwest had had the highest per capita incidence of disturbances of any region; Bielorussia ranked third.[60] Moreover, these events were neither the elemental burnings and lootings nor the sporadic forest offenses typical of the rest of Russia. The peasants of the west engaged in well-planned, highly conscious strikes for higher wages and better working conditions. This movement met with some initial successes, but eventually it was brutally repressed by the autocracy's policemen and soldiers. By the end of 1907, the landlords had been reminded of their ultimate dependence on the state, and the peasants had once again been thwarted in their desires.

Because of their desire and their ability to maintain their estates, the landlords of the west were extremely unsympathetic to the peasants' demands for land. Those west Russian landlords who came to join the Nationalist Party were especially militant in their opposition to peasant demands. One particularly grim case in point is that of A. A. Pototskii, who became a member of the Nationalists' council. On June 14, 1906, he learned of his peasants' intention to approach him with a deputation in the hope of gaining a higher daily wage. Pototskii telephoned the governor of Podol'e, and when a group of fifty unarmed peasants, including women and children, approached his manor house, they found Pototskii protected by a squadron of soldiers. The peasants put forward their request. Pototskii replied, "You want higher wages? Here are your higher wages." Without warning, the soldiers fired, killing one and wounding six before the frightened peasants could find cover in the nearby woods.[61]

Aside from the factors of commercial agriculture, national distribution, lack of zemstvos, and antagonistic peasants, there is one other crucial element that characterized the west. Since the 1860s, when it had been an

59. Kovalchenko and Milov, *Vserossiskoi agrarnyi rynok*, p. 320.

60. Maureen Perrie, "The Russian Peasant Movement of 1905–1907: Its Social Composition and Revolutionary Significance," *Past and Present* (November 1972):128.

61. *Agrarnoe dvizhenie v Rossii*, Vol. 2, p. 194.

Table 2.16. **Population Growth in Kiev (1884 – 1913)**

1884	154,000
1897	247,723 (census)
1907	404,000 (est.)
1908	450,000
1913	594,000

Source: Institut istorii, Akademia Nauk USSR, *Istoria Kieva* (Kiev, 1965) 1:339–341, 464.

administrative and military center of 68,000, Kiev had experienced astronomical population growth (see Table 2.16). By 1910, the city of Kiev had a population of just under half a million, which made it the third largest city in Russia. Of a population of 4,200,354 in Kiev gubernia, 604,135 lived in towns larger than 10,000.[62]

Industrial expansion had been enormous, especially during the 1890s. Much of this expansion was in light industry, organized in relatively small units. Many firms dealt in products closely related to agriculture. As already noted, sugar beet refining and distilling were Kiev's major industries. The city was also a major transport center. Kiev dominated the entire southwest, serving as the central city for landlords from Podol'e and Volynia, many of whom maintained houses or apartments there.

Railroads had played a crucial role in Kiev's growth. However, by 1907, this expansion had cooled somewhat, and unemployment was a serious problem in the city. The political unrest of the previous two years had been suppressed, but the Nationalists' future supporters could not help but feel that they were sitting on a powder keg. During the 1905 Revolution, strike activity had been considerable, and railway workers, who had played such a central role in the events of October 1905, constituted a large portion of Kiev's work force.[63]

City life had a profound effect on the politics of the Nationalists. This aspect of the party's development distinguishes it sharply from the Octobrists. After eliminating from consideration the capitals from which the Octobrists drew most of their industrial and commercial support, one is struck by the absence of large cities in areas that returned Octobrists. Samara, Chernigov, Ekaterninoslav, Poltava, Voronezh, Tambov, Khazan, Kaluga, and Kharkov all elected large numbers of Octobrist deputies, but only Kharkov had a city that could approach Kiev in size. Moreover, in

62. *Ves'iugo-zapadnogo kraia*, p. 7.
63. Institut istorii, akademia nauk USSR, *Istoria Kieva*, Vol. 1, (Kiev, 1965), pp. 339–341, 464.

those areas of Bielorussia that were least urbanized—Mogilev and Vitebsk—the Nationalists did not fare as well. However, in the Bielorussian
province of Minsk, which was roughly similar to the southwest, seven
future Nationalists were chosen.

The precise influence of urban society on west Russian nobles was well
delineated by the future Nationalist leader Vasillii Vitalevich Shulgin in a
1909 pamphlet arguing the case for elective zemstvos in the west. Shulgin,
an intelligent young noble landlord from Volynia and a gifted writer,
provided a highly revealing analysis of the connection between town
politics and the as yet nonexistent zemstvo. Many descendants of the
original *chinovnik* (bureaucrat) landowners had remained on their land to
take up farming. But no institutional framework that could have brought
them into normal contact with one another existed. Rarely seeing their
neighbors, they lived isolated lives. Shulgin called them *dachniki,* those
who lived alone with their families in summer-vacation cottages. Atomized
in this way, they lacked any real community. Public activity represented
both an answer to the political impotence of the west Russian landlords
and a solution to their psychological problems. Yet, with no zemstvo, there
was no arena for these nobles in the countryside. To engage in public
activity, it was necessary to go to the towns. Shulgin continued:

> Often people meet each other, for example in Kiev, and find out to their
> amazement that they are close neighbors or even farm land in the same
> uezd. To such an extent did Russian landowning exist in isolation that men
> were kept in their little cells. It was clear that given such a situation people
> who wished to occupy themselves with public affairs . . . had no place in the
> countryside. They had to run to the city to find both gratification for their
> spiritual [*dukhovnii*] needs and a way to expend their energy. People of an
> exceptional nature remained on the land either scorning society or feeling
> called to the land.[64]

The initial experience in politics for those who later became Nationalist
leaders took place in the cities of the west, particularly Kiev. As a result,
their approach to party work came to be influenced by the urban political
culture and social structure that they found in the city. Only in the towns
could they find the sort of political and personal involvement they sought.

Shulgin's primary complaint was the lack of a satisfactory institutional
infrastructure in the countryside. In keeping with the new political
conditions of the day, he sought a framework that could give the Russian
landowners of the region the possibility of playing an independent political

64. Shulgin, *Vybornoe Zemstvo,* p. 19.

role, apart from the tutelage of the bureaucracy. "The local population must think for itself and be able to help itself."[65] Once granted the kind of infrastructure they sought, the Russian landlords of the west could control local life on their own. Yet, the future Nationalists' approach to the zemstvo institution was entirely different from that which had emerged in central Russia. The Nationalists' exposure to urban politics gave their views on local government a particularly modern tone. The zemstvo was not to be above politics. Rather, it was to be the arena for the struggle for political power in the western borderland. Local elections were to be contested in terms of the party divisions that had emerged in the Duma.

Unlike other conservative parties, the Nationalists saw success in local politics as the necessary basis for gaining power at the national level. Their experience in the cities of the west had led them to the belief that all elections were contestable in terms of the same party divisions that had emerged in the Duma. Speaking on party participation in the Kiev city Duma elections of 1909, A. S. Liubinskii, a member of the Nationalists' local organization, stressed this point.

> Up until now, elections for the most part were conducted on a purely economic [*khoziaistvennyi*] basis or on the basis of personal groupings of electors. . . . The party holding the city and zemstvo bodies in its hands now receives a weapon of immense influence and a powerful tool for the propaganda of its ideas, from which it can direct itself toward participation in the Duma elections, direction of schools, participation in educational bodies, as well as the gubernia assemblies which choose deputies to the State Council.[66]

The Octobrists, on the other hand, denied that there was any direct link between local and Duma politics. They held to the previous zemstvo tradition of electing local men of honor and talent regardless of their views or affiliations. However, the Nationalists felt that the old tradition no longer had meaning in an era of acute social instability, a feeling that was largely derived from their experience in urban politics.

The drive for the western zemstvo was therefore not simply a single-issue campaign to extend a useful institution into an area in which it did not exist. It was seen as an all-embracing answer to the problems of the west Russian gentry, and it was around this demand that the Nationalists coalesced during the first two years of the third Duma's existence.

It is not surprising then that the Nationalist local groups, their Duma

65. Ibid., p. 33.
66. *Sbornik kluba russkikh natsionalistov,* vtoroi vypusk (1910), p. 27.

fraction, their party program, and their relationship with the premier were interrelated in a manner that suggests a structure more commonly associated with modern Western European political parties than with the peculiar proto-parties that had developed in Russia. The social structure of Kiev, with its modern social classes, plus the greater intensity of urban politics were more typical of Western Europe than of rural Russia, and the character of the Nationalist Party was influenced by the exposure of its members, early in their careers, to a relatively modern urban political environment.

As a result of their involvement in capitalist agriculture and their exposure to the increasingly capitalist milieu of Kiev, the people who comprised the Nationalists' social base came to describe their social positions in terms that were more characteristic of capitalist societies. This meant they were coming to define their social positions less in terms of the religious, educational, juridical, and genealogical criteria of precapitalist societies and more in terms of their productive roles, which is a definition of class typical of modern, industrial, capitalist society.[67] Because of strong inducements to economic modernization in the borderland, this tendency to seek a new basis of self-definition was especially advanced in the west. Nevertheless, it would be a mistake to think that those who came to support the Nationalists had entirely abandoned the traditional attitudes associated with state service. Instead, the traditional and modern coexisted among them in a particularly volatile contradiction that was never resolved.

Arising as it did from the capitalist character of much of the region's economy and from the precariousness of the west Russian landlords' political situation, this new awareness of class created a need for independent political activity. Yet, at the same time, this feeling of an acute and immediate threat eventually forced the borderland's Russian gentry back into the arms of the state. Their awareness of danger, so recently seen in 1905 and 1906, drew them back to the one familiar source of support. Moreover, the experiences of state service in either their own lives or in

67. On the differences between class consciousness and estate consciousness, see Georg Lukacs, *History and Class Consciousness* (London, 1971), p. 55; Etienne Balibar, "The Basic Concepts of Historical Materialism," in Louis Althusser, *Reading Capital* (New York, 1970), pp. 220–221; Tom Bottomore, *Classes in Modern Society* (New York, 1966), p. 12; Max Weber, "Class Status and Party," in H. Gerth and C. W. Mills (eds.), *From Max Weber* (New York, 1946), p. 183. See also Karl Marx, *The Poverty of Philosophy*, p. 150, cited in Nicos Poulantzas, *Political Power and Social Classes* (London, 1973), p. 59; Anthony Giddens, *The Class Structure of Modern Societies* (New York, 1975), pp. 111–112; and Ralph Miliband, "Barnave: A Case of Bourgeois Class Consciousness," in Istvan Meszaros (ed.), *Aspects of History and Class Consciousness* (London, 1971), pp. 22–23.

the lives of their fathers made continued reliance on the state a familiar and attractive alternative to charting a new course. In moments of crisis, the rhetoric of independence was forgotten, and the bureaucracy was asked for assistance. Thus, the instability and danger confronted by the west Russian gentry simultaneously drew it away from and toward the state. This ambivalence proved to be a fundamental characteristic of the Nationalists' approach to politics.

III

The Rise of the Nationalist Party

From the outset, the Octobrists assumed a dominant position in the third Duma. They occupied the political center of the lower house, and they had the largest parliamentary group (154 of 442 deputies). But the Octobrists did not constitute a majority, and they were required to form alliances on every vote. In order to support reforms, they could join with the fifty-four Kadets, with whom they shared certain constitutional visions. On the other hand, they could oppose reforms or advance more limited measures with the cooperation of the deputies to their right. To keep these options open, the Octobrists made no formal commitment to any continuous relationship with the other Duma parties. Cooperation with either the left or the right had disadvantages as well as advantages. The Kadets were too closely associated with the "irresponsible" first two Dumas, while the various groups on the right were far too amorphous to offer any prospect for a permanent conservative majority.

Following Lenin's lead, Soviet scholars, adopting the formulation of a number of contemporary observers, have described this situation as a "two-majority system." This view implied that a unified Octobrist group chose its allies on each vote depending on specific circumstances. In practice, however, the Octobrists experienced continual internal division. As often as not, the Duma fraction split its votes on both major and minor matters. This lack of internal cohesion was the direct result of the Octobrists' center position in the Duma. They were pulled in both directions, and, as a result, clear tendencies and factions soon developed inside the party. Only a uniformly accepted program and severe parliamentary discipline could have held the Octobrists together. But their vague constitutionalism never inspired all their members, and they came from a political tradition (the zemstvo) that was suspicious of the notion of party discipline. Their chronic disunity, while evident from the first days of the third Duma, only became obvious after a year of Duma activity. Once these weaknesses were noticed, the Octobrists' dominance of the lower house was soon challenged.

At the beginning of the third Duma's work, however, most public attention focused on the Octobrists. Stolypin's political future rested on his ability to convince an always dubious Nicholas that he enjoyed the support of the social elements represented in the newly restricted Duma. Thus, Stolypin was prepared to work in close harmony with the Octobrists and their leader, Alexander Guchkov. For his part, Guchkov sought to demonstrate his party's responsibility by cooperating with the government. Only real achievements could show educated and propertied society the benefits of the Octobrists' moderation, and without Stolypin, there could be no real achievements. The two men thus established a *modus vivendi*. While there was no personal cordiality in their relationship, they shared certain ideas of Russia's future. Both strongly advocated restoring Russia's military power in order to reestablish the nation's international prestige. In addition, both were committed to a restructuring of local government and administration that would establish private property, rather than soslovie, as a basis for participation in politics at all levels.

The daily press came to describe the Octobrists as the "government party." The Octobrists were prepared to cooperate with the new prime minister on a vaguely understood program of legislation. This relationship was reminiscent of Western European parliamentary structures, and Guchkov and others hoped that it contained the germ of an eventual evolution toward a true parliamentary and constitutional system. However, they were overlooking one crucial element of the Russian political structure: Stolypin remained in office at the tsar's pleasure. If the premier lost the support of the Octobrists, he was not required to step down. But, if Nicholas lost confidence in Stolypin, all the Octobrist support in the world could not save him.

Thus, the Octobrist preeminence of the early third Duma was based on an exceedingly fragile set of political relationships and understandings.

Eventually, as those relationships became unravelled, the Octobrists diminished in numbers and significance. Their decline created a need for a new governmental party, a role the Nationalists sought to fill.

The Moderate Right under Octobrist Preeminence

Most deputies arriving for the Duma's convocation in November 1907 had no formal party ties. As the only organized conservative Duma group, the Octobrists enjoyed considerable success in attracting adherents. However, about 150 other conservative deputies chose not to join Guchkov's camp. Most of them had not yet formulated precise political opinions. They described themselves only in the most general way as right-wing. The pro-government daily, *Rossiia,* was quick to notice this lack of political experience.

> They never were professional politicians. They entered the Duma because they understood that calm, steady people and peaceful, concentrated state [*gosudarstvennyi*] work were now necessary. The vast majority of them knew each other little or not at all. Only in the Duma, in the course of common efforts, will the achievements of each worker become clear.[1]

Within this amorphous group, differences appeared immediately. The fundamental distinction concerned the significance of the Duma itself. A group of seventy of the more extreme rights did not consider the lower house a legislative chamber in any sense of the term. This group's spokesmen, Purishkevich and Markov, used the Duma as a theater for obstructions and dramatic scenes. This behavior alienated those deputies who had come to Petersburg with more serious intentions. On November 8, V. A. Bobrinskii sought to justify the creation of a moderate right group that could engage in real Duma work.

> If the moderates do not split from the extreme rights, I cannot remain in this party. Seventy or eighty persons must either join the Octobrists or form an independent group. Nothing can be done with people who do not even know the technical conditions for [parliamentary] work.[2]

1. *Rossiia,* October 31, 1907.
2. *Novoe Vremia,* November 9, 1907.

A day after Bobrinskii's declaration to the press, the moderate right Duma fraction, numbering some seventy deputies, was formed.[3] Joining Bobrinskii at the head of the new fraction were P. N. Krupenskii and P. N. Balashev. All three were from the wealthiest of the noble landowning families. Most deputies from the west allied with the moderate right fraction, and the program of the new group accordingly stressed the defense of Russian interests in border areas and the extension of institutions of local government to regions where they did not exist.[4] In the early stages of the third Duma, Bobrinskii and Krupenskii, both experienced parliamentarians, were the leading moderate spokesmen. Later, as the fraction's members came to perceive the concrete basis for their cohesion, these two figures were eclipsed by Balashev and others from the west. Unsure of themselves at this stage, the moderate rights kept a low profile and subordinated themselves to the more numerous and active Octobrists.

But following the Octobrists' lead forced the moderate rights into uncomfortable positions. In the Duma's opening address to the throne, the Octobrists had described the Russian state as "renovated by the Manifesto of October 17."[5] The Kadets argued that the new order should have been called "constitutional."[6] The pravye, on the other hand, claimed that Russia was still an autocracy.[7] The moderates agreed with the pravye in substance. P. V. Sinadino, a doctor from Bessarabia and a follower of Krupenskii, argued that because the tsar had created the new institutions, nothing could become law without his signature. Unlike the pravye, the moderates welcomed the creation of representative institutions,[8] but they had no clear position on the character of the new political system. Accordingly, they wished to avoid divisive debate on this question. Balashev called any discussion of the matter "useless and undesirable" and urged his comrades to go along with the Octobrists in order not to provoke sharp differences.[9] But this lack of a clear position on the "constitutional question" was embarrassing. The Nationalists never specified the precise political meaning of their vision of an autocracy with representative institutions, and it proved difficult to arrive at any position because of their strong commitments to both the state and the Duma. So

3. *Rech'*, November 10, 1907; A. I. Guchkov, *Poslednie Novosti* (Paris), September 16, 1936.

4. *Rech'*, November 14, 1907; *Rossiia*, November 14, 1907.

5. Sten. ot. (September 1908), 3.1.1.5.135.

6. Sten. ot., 3.1.1.5.141.

7. Sten. ot., 3.1.1.5.151.

8. Sten. ot., 3.1.1.5.194.

9. Sten. ot., 3.1.1.5.153.

long as the two institutions were not sharply counterposed, the future Nationalists could avoid this contradiction. Therefore, they preferred not to press the issue.

Several months after the opening of the third Duma, opinions in the Duma's right wing had begun to shift toward the moderate position. In January 1908, twenty-three deputies broke with the extreme rights and formed the National Group.[10] The leader of the new fraction was Prince Alexander Petrovich Urusov of Tula. One of the most active of that gubernia's landlords, he was an important member of the provincial zemstvo and a successful and expert farmer. Tula was not the most fertile of regions, but Urusov used an extensive knowledge of agronomy to make his 2,000-desiatin estate profitable. Moreover, he shared this knowledge with others through extensive publication in agricultural journals. The same drive that made him a successful farmer also fired his political ambitions, and his leadership of a parliamentary group was a source of personal pride.

Of the twenty-three deputies in the new fraction, twenty were noblemen. They came from roughly the same areas as did the moderate rights, although none of them was from Kiev or Podol'e. The National Group's leading spokesmen, aside from Urusov, were N. K. von Gubbenet and N. N. Ladomirskii, both from Mogilev. Although these similarities of background and viewpoint promised strong possibilities of cooperation between the moderates and the National Group, little came of the tentative early contacts between Urusov and Krupenskii.[11]

The Duma did not actually begin to deal with the specific concrete concerns of the moderate rights until the spring session. A report of the Finance Committee on the Ministry of Interior's budget estimates for the appointive zemstvos in the borderland touched off a revealing exchange. The committee's reporter, Glebov II, an Octobrist, prefaced his remarks by suggesting that the Duma's ultimate aim should be the "normalization" of the zemstvos in the west.[12] The future Nationalist, S. M. Bogdanov, echoed this view. He demanded elective zemstvos with special national curiae to restrict Polish participation. The already existing appointive zemstvos could not properly plan the construction of roads, schools, and hospitals, because they were fiscally dependent on the Ministry of Interior. Independently elected zemstvos, with their own powers of taxation, Bogdanov argued, could remedy this problem and would give the west Russian

10. *Rech'*, December 8, 1907; PRO, FO 371.513.5462 (February 17, 1908).
11. *Rech'*, January 17, 1908.
12. Sten. ot., 3.1.3.3104.

gentry the possibility of controlling local life on its own without state supervision.[13] At this point, however, the government ignored the demands of the moderate rights. Stolypin's Assistant Minister of Interior, S. E. Kryzhanovskii, stated his superior's belief that any change in the situation in the west had to await a total overhaul of the zemstvo system.[14]

During the spring of 1908, these first halting organizational steps in the lower chamber were matched by the emergence of several nationalist organizations outside the Duma. These new conservative groups differed from those that had arisen in direct opposition to the mass revolutionary violence of 1905. Social stability had been restored, and conservative Russians now had to compete for power and influence in the limited political arena created by the June 3 election law. The future Nationalists were aided in this task by the creation of two groups that shared certain general aims with both the moderate rights and the National Group in the Duma: the Kiev Club of Russian Nationalists and the All-Russian National Union.

The Kiev Club of Russian Nationalists became the strongest and most advanced element of the Nationalist Party. Its initial purpose was simply to unite the various local moderate right-wing elements around nationalist slogans in order to raise national consciousness and combat Polish and Jewish influence in the southwest. The leader of this campaign was a figure possessed of enormous political ambition, Anatoly Ivanovich Savenko. A noble and the owner of a small estate, Savenko spent most of his time as a journalist for the conservative Kiev daily, *Kievlianin.* At the club's first meeting on April 6, 1908, he was chosen vice-president, and A. A. Sidorov, a local landlord, was elected president. Professor V. E. Chernov joined the club's council along with the moderate right deputy, D. N. Chikhachev. D. I. Pikhno, an appointed State Council member and publisher of *Kievlianin,* was a club member, as was almost all the Duma delegation from the southwest. Many nonresidents of Kiev who owned houses or apartments in the city were listed on the club's rolls as homeowners. During its first year, the Kiev Club of Russian Nationalists enrolled 329 men and women, incorporating much of the elite of the southwest.[15]

It was clear from the outset that the club's concern with party politics was far more extensive than that of past conservative organizations, most

13. Sten. ot., 3.1.3.3127–3131.
14. Ibid., 2.2800.
15. *Sbornik kluba russkikh natsionalistov,* pervyi vypusk (1909), p. 5.

of which had sought either to petition the tsar or foster a vague climate of opinion in polite society. The Kiev Club attached great importance to the maintenance of contact between local conservatives and their representatives in the Duma. Accordingly, Shulgin addressed the group's initial gathering, reporting on the Duma debate concerning the budget estimates for the appointive zemstvos.[16] Reports by Duma members continued throughout the spring, summer, and fall. This close relationship between a local organization and the Duma fraction was to serve as the model for the Nationalists' own network of local groups.

The second new conservative formation, which emerged during the spring of 1908, was called the All-Russian National Union. Its founding has commonly been credited to M. O. Menshikov, columnist for the conservative Petersburg daily *Novoe Vremia*.[17] By Menshikov's own account, however, the union did not assume the form he had hoped for, nor was he recognized as its leading spokesman. Prince Urusov was one of the early organizers, along with S. V. Rukhlov, a State Council member who was soon named Minister of Communications. This appointment made him, in Menshikov's words, "the first minister openly belonging to a political party."[18] Urusov's participation made possible a close working relationship between the union and the National Group. This alliance between a public group and a Duma fraction turned out to be even more intimate than that between the moderate right and the Kiev Club.

Rukhlov's relationship to the union and the National Group is particularly significant in this regard: An examination of the bills introduced by the National Group in 1908 and 1909 reveals that nearly two-thirds of these measures were concerned with railroads and ports.[19] This information suggests that the National Group was serving as a funnel for Rukhlov's ministerial proposals. The novelty of this situation was not simply that Rukhlov was a member of a political party but that he and that party actively cooperated on a specific program of legislation.

Throughout the spring of 1908, the organizers of the All-Russian National Union met repeatedly. They were divided over whether the new group should be a political party or a league of parties grouped around a unifying idea. Menshikov preferred the latter concept, but Urusov wanted a genuine party. Urusov's conception was finally accepted.[20] On June 3,

---

16. Ibid., pp. 10–23.
17. A. Ia. Avrekh, "Tret'ia duma i nachalo krizisa tret'eiunskoi sistemy," *Istoricheskie zapiski*, Vol. 53 (1955):76.
18. *Novoe Vremia*, February 3, 1908.
19. TsGAOR 115.1.31.38.
20. *Pis'ma k blyzhnim* (May 1908), p. 314; *Novoe Vremia*, May 20, 1908.

1908, the union's program was officially registered.[21] In close harmony with the views of the moderate right, it stressed the protection of Russian interests in the borderlands of the Empire.[22] This step was soon followed by the union's inaugural meeting, which attracted over 200 people.[23] Urusov and Menshikov were elected to the new group's nineteen-man council, along with six members of the National Group and three State Council members, including Rukhlov.

The emergence of these first shoots of the nationalist movement inside and outside the Duma increased the assertiveness of the moderate right fraction. On the eve of the Duma's second session, in November 1908, the moderates announced that their first legislative priority was the introduction of zemstvos into those regions of the Empire where they did not presently exist. Although slightly muted, the specific demand for Russian domination of local government in the western borderland was unmistakable.[24] This announcement indicated the moderate right deputies' growing awareness of the basis of their unity, and it showed their increasing willingness to make demands in the pursuit of their aims. Once again, the moderate rights discussed the possibility of a merger with the National Group.[25] Bogdanov, writing in *Kievlianin* in early December, was among the first to suggest the possibility of a new party arrangement in the Duma.

> There never was any basis for expecting the realignment of all the Octobrists to the left. Should such a tendency arise, a part of the Octobrists, in fact the majority of them, would leave and move to the right. It would follow that one could expect the formation of either a separate fraction, a right center, or a very strong progressive monarchist party, the result of a union of this group of deputies [the conservative Octobrists] with the moderate rights.[26]

By the end of 1908, the elements of the later general shift to the right had already appeared. Chronic Octobrist disunity, the desire for a new arrangement of Duma fractions, the rise of nationalist groups in both the provinces and the capital, and the concern with the western zemstvo question were already parts of daily political discourse as the Duma met in January 1909 for its spring session.

---

21. *Svet*, June 20, 1908; *Rech'*, June 5, 1908.
22. *Ustav vserossiiskogo natsional'nogo soiuza*, June 3, 1908.
23. *Rossiia*, June 20, 1908; *Novoe Vremia*, June 19, 1908.
24. *Novoe Vremia*, October 31, 1908.
25. *Slovo*, October 27, 1908; PRO, FO 371.513.38892 (November 9, 1908).
26. *Kievlianin*, December 4, 1908.

The Realignment of Forces
in the Duma and the
Ministerial Crisis of 1909

The Octobrist–government entente, which had functioned with surface smoothness throughout 1908, came apart in 1909. The Octobrists began to disintegrate under the strain of right-wing challenges to Guchkov's party leadership, and Stolypin ran into difficulty in the course of the crisis surrounding a bill calling for a naval general staff. Reactionary pressures at court and in the State Council apparently chastened Stolypin and dampened his ardor for the Octobrists, whose concern for military reform, which he shared, had created the debacle. The ministerial crisis of 1909 is commonly seen as a turning point in the premier's career, marking the end of his flirtation with constitutionalism and the beginning of his adoption of more overtly conservative and nationalistic policies. The significance of such a change should not be underestimated, for it marks the abandonment of the government's last attempt before 1914 to cooperate with even the mildest of constitutionalist elements.

In terms of political relationships, this shift toward the right necessitated Stolypin's cutting his ties with Guchkov and the left Octobrists in favor of establishing a permanent right majority centered around the Nationalists. The crisis of 1909 is usually seen as a dramatic switch for Stolypin that, in turn, profoundly affected the realignment of forces in the Duma. Accounts that center around Stolypin give the impression that the Nationalists were the premier's creation rather than a movement of genuine social significance. Yet, the demise of the Octobrists and the rise of the Nationalists were long-term processes that almost certainly would have occurred without the impetus of the crisis. Stolypin's adoption of the Nationalists was not an immediate reaction to his troubles; rather, it was the result of much lengthier processes that developed not only in St. Petersburg but in the provinces as well.[27]

27. In a pro forma manner, the leading Soviet specialist on the regime of the Third of June, A. Ia. Avrekh, has recently accepted the view that the Nationalists were a movement from below. As a Soviet historian, Avrekh had no choice but to give the appearance of Marxist method and make such a statement. See A. Ia. Avrekh, *Stolypin i tret'ia duma*, p. 25. However, the structure of Avrekh's narrative and his attitude toward Stolypin leave the reader with the opposite impression. In an early piece which he has never disowned, Avrekh stressed the crisis as a turning point. See Avrekh, "Tret'ia duma i nachalo krizisa tret'eiunskoi sistemy," p. 76. The Nationalists' rise is viewed from the vantage point of the premier's career; no analysis of social roots is offered, and we are left with the impression that the Nationalists were an artificial creation. This view has been echoed by E. Chmielewski, "Stolypin and the

The drive for a new right majority had begun even before the Christmas recess. By January 1909, Octobrist preeminence was constantly being called into question in the press. The liberal daily *Slovo* described the instability of Guchkov's position with considerable accuracy.

It is well known that the Octobrists can more properly be called Mr. Guchkov's house guard than a party in the strict sense of the word. The leader of the Octobrists is a highly individualistic personality to whom the law of June Third gave the possibility of forming a political organization.[28]

Rumors of an Octobrist split were rife, and with them came anticipation of a new arrangement in the lower house.[29]

The Creation of the Moderate Right Party

Among the future Nationalists, prospects were considerably brighter. Early in February, the moderate rights opened their own Petersburg club for Duma members and public figures.[30] Shortly thereafter, the All-Russian National Union announced plans to hold a national conference to bring its Petersburg center into greater contact with branches recently formed in the provinces.[31]

At the same time, Guchkov came under attack from the right wing of his own party. The Social Democrats introduced a resolution calling for a ministerial explanation of government persecution of trade unions. In parliamentary terminology, such measures were called interpellations. Guchkov and his allies in the Octobrist fraction chose to support this measure despite their usual concern for the interests of private property and big business in particular. However, the Duma committee on interpellations rejected the resolution. The committee's reporter was the conser-

Russian Ministerial Crisis of 1909," *California Slavic Studies* 4 (1967):33. Both writers owe much to the account of the Kadet critic, A. S. Izgoev, *P. A. Stolypin*, p. 81. Recently Hosking has sought to place the crisis in a broader chronological context, seeing the Octobrist decline, the Nationalists' emergence, and the crisis itself as the results of deeper, long-term processes. This has clarified our understanding of these events considerably. See Geoffrey Hosking, *The Russian Constitutional Experiment* (Cambridge, 1973), pp. 74–105.

28. *Slovo*, January 17, 1909.

29. *Rossiia*, January 7, 1909; John Hutchinson, *The Octobrists in Russian Politics*, p. 118; *Russkie Vedemosti*, January 3, 1909.

30. *Novoe Vremia*, February 14, 1909.

31. *Rossiia*, January 17, 1909.

vative Octobrist, Ia. G. Gololobov, who, in direct opposition to the stated desires of his fraction, addressed the Duma in support of the committee's negative decision.[32] Under any circumstances, this breach of discipline would have been a subject of concern for the Octobrists. Given the political climate of the moment, the matter was treated with the utmost seriousness.

Guchkov's decision to support the interpellation on the trade unions, while curious, had a number of understandable sources. He still sought to curry favor with the Kadets, who supported the measure. In addition, investigation had revealed certain bureaucratic abuses that upset Octobrist notions of legality.[33] Guchkov's political balancing act soon became the subject of increasing attacks from the right both within his party and in the Duma. This confrontation, which became known as the "Gololobov incident," dragged on until May when Gololobov and several allies were expelled from the party.

At this early point, it may have been possible to sweep the affair under the rug. However, the growing assertiveness of the moderate right and the attacks on Guchkov within his own party exacerbated the situation. On February 20, P. N. Krupenskii, acting for the moderate rights, invited the Octobrists and the National Group to meet at the moderates' downtown club in order to discuss the formation of a new club of the Duma center.[34] The Octobrists refused to attend, and the National Group, afraid of being subsumed under moderate right leadership, also declined the invitation. Nevertheless, Krupenskii's continued efforts to create a new center threatened Guchkov's position. On February 27, Krupenskii held still another meeting to discuss the creation of a club of the Duma majority to include Octobrists, moderate rights, and the National Group, again without result.[35]

With their attempts to achieve cooperation rebuffed, on March 12, the moderate rights announced their intention to form their own political party with local branches and influence outside the Duma.[36] P. N. Balashev, more a backroom manipulator than a gifted orator, now emerged as the moderate right's leading spokesman and organizer. The owner of a huge estate (10,000 desiatiny) in Podol'e, Balashev supported much of the new party's work with his own funds. In all his statements he stressed the necessity of organizing in the localities. *Slovo* was quick to

32. A. S. Viazigin, *Gololobovskii intsident*, p. 12.
33. Hutchinson, *The Octobrists in Russian Politics*, p. 101.
34. *Rech'*, February 20, 1909,
35. *Rech'*, February 28, 1909.
36. *Rossiia*, March 12, 1909; *Rech'*, March 12, 1909; *Slovo*, March 13, 1909.

pick up the significance of Balashev's emphasis. The moderate rights would be different from the other Duma parties and from the bureaucracy. All these formations, *Slovo* said, "hung in the air" without popular support. By contrast, the new party was to be based on social forces in the countryside through the creation of a network of organizations in the provinces. The moderate rights were, in *Slovo*'s words, "our agrarians."

> Without doubt, they have in the full sense, the physiognomy and politics ascribed to agrarians. In this sense the work in the countryside can be expected to find a spontaneous reaction but only in a limited sector of society [the gentry].[37]

None of the other press accounts even hinted that this step had been inspired by Stolypin, and to this date no evidence has been found to link him to this phase of the moderate rights' efforts.[38]

The moderate rights were also fully aware of the general political implications of such a step. On March 20, 1909, S. M. Bogdanov published an article in *Rossiia* that repeated what he had written in *Kievlianin* in December 1908.[39] As he had earlier, Bogdanov was seeking to pry the Octobrists loose from the Kadets' embrace. He argued that the Duma's work was poorly organized, and only a permanent conservative majority could structure the lower house's labor in an effective and consistent manner. Bogdanov suggested that a loose coalition of Octobrists, moderate rights, and Nationalists, working on the basis of the shared points in their programs, could do a better job. In attacking the two-majority system in favor of a permanent right majority, Bogdanov did not seek to destroy the Octobrists nor did he advertise the moderate rights as the heirs apparent to Duma leadership. Yet, he fully expected that his group's latest step would increase their influence in the Tauride Palace.

37. *Slovo*, March 10 and 11, 1909; Avrekh, "Tret'ia duma," p. 72. Curiously, Avrekh cited these articles, but apparently failed to notice the significance of their meaning.

38. Hutchinson, *The Octobrists in Russian Politics*, p. 120; Hosking, *The Russian Constitutional Experiment*, p. 106; *Rossiia*, March 14, 17, and April 8, 1909. Some efforts have been made to use *Rossiia* as an indicator of the premier's thinking. Stolypin's friend and adviser, I. Ia. Gurliand, was an editor, and the paper usually supported the policies of the Council of Ministers. Throughout January and February, *Rossiia*'s editorials had been minimizing rumors of an Octobrist split. Even after the moderate rights' intentions became public, *Rossiia* was still expressing skepticism about a change in party relations.

39. *Rossiia*, March 20, 1909. This article, an attack on the Octobrists, has been viewed as a turning point for the premier whose newspaper was now supposedly taking Guchkov's party to task. Yet, it is overstating the case to see the piece as introducing something especially new into the plot. *Rossiia* printed articles by a number of commentators, who were far from unanimous in their views. Bogdanov himself had appeared in the paper before this.

Eighty people attended the organizational meeting of the moderate right party on April 19. Balashev was chosen president, A. S. Gizhitskii, of Podol'e, became one of three vice-presidents. A. A. Pototskii was elected secretary, and F. N. Bezak, the new Kiev gubernia marshal of nobility, was given the job of treasurer. Significantly, all but one of these men came from western gubernias. Neither Bobrinskii nor Krupenskii played a major role in this latest step.

Balashev and the others from the west had lacked the experience and confidence at the outset of the third Duma to play an agressive role. But, by 1909, they had learned the ways of the Duma, and they hoped to profit from the Octobrists' mistakes. In particular, they were determined not to repeat the Octobrists' dismal record in the field of local organization. Balashev's acceptance speech stressed the crucial necessity of creating a national network based on strength "in the localities." In addition, Balashev clearly stated that the party's genesis was a provincial phenomenon.

> The idea for the formation of an indisputably progressive and national party arose in the depths of Podol'e. In Petersburg the thought of bringing together all the streams of moderate nationalist tendencies into one mighty river was finally brought to fruition. . . . We must seek support in the country because the Duma cannot work alone. . . . All classes of the population are in need of help, but the landowning class requires it most of all.[40]

Balashev did not view "the country" as one undefined mass. The future Nationalists would champion the demands and grievances of the social elements they claimed to represent.

The creation of the Duma had made the independent defense of noble interests through a political party necessary, and the new electoral law had given the gentry dominant representation in that body. But to be effective, such a party had to have a social base.[41] According to Balashev's conception, a network of groups in the provinces could organize that base. These local organizations would in turn maintain close contact with the Duma deputies. Finally, it was hoped that the new party could establish a close working relationship with the premier by offering him political support in the Duma. This structure was supposed to impress the tsar who would then act in a manner that served the interests of the party's constituency.

Thus, while organized outside the supervision of the autocracy, the

40. *Slovo*, April 20, 1909.
41. *Rech'*, April 20, 1909; *Novoe Vremia*, April 20, 1909.

party was nevertheless structured to direct a forceful appeal to the state. This was certainly an ambiguous approach to building a political party. Modern in its independence and in its representation of clearly defined interests, the new party was traditional in its ultimate reliance on the power of the autocrat. While such an approach achieved certain immediate political gains, it proved ultimately disastrous, for it placed the Nationalists squarely between two institutions that would eventually become polarized.

Writing in *Rossiia* a few days before the moderate rights' inaugural meeting, S. M. Bogdanov sought to characterize the nature of the party's constituency.

> The only correct basis for the creation and existence of parties among us is the recognition of class interest. The Social Democratic party represents the workers. . . . The Trudoviki stand for the interests of the peasants. The Kadet party, in essence, represents no one's class interests. . . . The left Duma fractions are opposed to all the fractions of the center and the right wing which represent the interests of the possessing classes, particularly the landowners. It was only on this basis that the majority of the third Duma was formed, arising in opposition to the left fractions.

Bogdanov's basis for determining social class emphasized property ownership rather than noble status. Bogdanov, a landowner in Kiev where agriculture was geared to the market, owned a moderate-sized estate that was among the most modern and efficient in the borderland. Therefore, it is not surprising that he should define social groups and their political representatives according to terms of reference that were most meaningful in the more commercial economy of the western borderland.

In the same article, Bogdanov emphasized that an essential element of gentry class interest was consistent opposition to forces on the left who sought to change society drastically. Because the Octobrists maintained cordial relations with the Kadets, Bogdanov considered them to be inconsistent defenders of gentry interests.

> The Octobrists readily draw away from their allies [the moderate rights], finding support in the left camp. We, the representatives of the moderates . . . recognize the existence among us of an order brought into being by the will of the autocratic tsar, and we absolutely draw away from the left fractions.[42]

Thus, the future Nationalists distinguished themselves from the Octobrists by claiming to speak for a specific property-owning constituency, defined in terms of shared interests. The new party's approach contrasted sharply

42. *Rossiia*, April 10, 1909.

with that of the Octobrists, who had all but abandoned their network of provincial groups to concentrate on work in the Duma. It was not difficult for the Octobrists to take this step, as they came from a tradition in which the zemstvo and public work were thought to be above politics and therefore separate from them. On the other hand, with no zemstvos in the west, the future Nationalists could quite easily perceive the unity of local and national politics. This consciousness of their interests and their willingness to organize in defense of those interests aided the Nationalists' initial political success. Yet, this sensitivity to the modern, specifically capitalist, world masked the retention of many traditional attitudes, the most lasting of which was continued reliance on the state. At this early stage of their existence, however, the Nationalists were far more concerned with the novel elements of their politics. It would only be later that, in moments of crisis, the older attitudes would reemerge with ultimately catastrophic results for the Nationalists' survival.

Despite the aptness of Bogdanov's analysis, the sense of constituency was less keenly felt among nonborderland Nationalists. While men like Urusov, Bobrinskii, and Krupenskii were all active agrarians, the structure of local politics outside the west did not bind them so closely to those they represented. Duma politics rather than local conditions played a larger role in their eventual adherence to the Nationalist party. Anticonstitutionalism separated them from the Octobrists. Antiliberalism, especially on religious questions, broadened the gap. Yet, most of the nonborderland Nationalists had worked in the zemstvos with their strong consensual traditions. This experience in deliberative bodies marked them off from the more irresponsible pravye. As a result, men like Krupenskii and his coterie from Bessarabia felt most comfortable with the moderate rights and later the Nationalists. But their work with the Nationalists vitiated the new group's character as a modern representative political party with a firm sense of its constituency. It is therefore significant that Krupenskii and many other nonwestern Nationalists would eventually leave the party, making it a far more homogeneous group. However, in 1909, all was harmony and optimism.

The Ministerial Crisis

The plans of the moderate right were made public just as Stolypin's own situation became more serious. On March 19, the State Council narrowly passed a proposal to regularize a permanent general staff for the navy. The plan was a product of Stolypin's early cooperation with Guchkov on questions of military reform. The Duma had passed the plan in 1908 only to have it rejected by the State Council. The Duma had passed it again and sent it once more to the upper house. Foes of the proposal maintained that it violated Article 96 of the Fundamental Laws, which protected the tsar's complete control over the organization of the armed forces. Among the plan's opponents in the State Council were such personal enemies of Stolypin as Count Witte, P. N. Durnovo, V. F. Trepov, and M. G. Akimov, all of whom were members of the State Council's right wing. Stolypin's suporters were led by his brother-in-law, A. B. Neidgart, who headed the Center Group, a collection of deputies with no formal affiliation with the Nationalists. Each side in the debate believed that the passage of such a bill would establish significant precedents for future Duma control of military affairs. Thus, the stakes were larger than the actual issue itself. When the State Council vote came, an ailing Stolypin had to make certain of the presence of the entire Council of Ministers, whose votes were needed in order to pass the bill.

Immediately, speculation spread concerning the tsar's likely stand on a bill that some people had construed as a restriction of his traditional prerogatives. Indeed, Stolypin himself admitted that the proposal as passed by the Duma violated Article 96 of the Fundamental Laws. For this reason, it is not easy to understand his insistence on the bill's passage. However, the specific plan for a naval general staff was consistent with his own program as well as with the demands for military reform made by the Octobrists and the moderate right. Stolypin did not even become aware of the bill until after it had passed through the Council of Ministers, so minor was its nature. Only after the initial rejection in the State Council in 1908 did he become concerned. Stolypin's continued support for the proposal after this rejection is difficult to explain. Details of the staff's organization, which had been attached to the proposal by the Naval Ministry for informational purposes, were specifically included as part of the bill by the Duma. However, it does appear that Stolypin had promised Nicholas that the passage of the bill would not constitute a precedent despite its apparent violation of the Fundamental Laws.[43] Stolypin thought this compromise would fulfill the demands of his Duma supporters while assuaging the tsar's doubts and those of the reactionaries in the State Council. Stolypin had publicly insisted that he had to stand firm on this matter. He argued that fifteen similar bills had become law, and that only the intrigue of his enemies had led them to fasten on the weaknesses of

43. Hosking has noted that Article 14 of the Fundamental Laws contradicts Article 96 on these points. He argues that only a highly literal reading of Article 96 could support the view of the State Council's right wing. This would lend credence to a view that emphasized the personal motive of Witte and his allies. See Hosking, *The Russian Constitutional Experiment*, p. 81; Avrekh, "Tret'ia duma"; and Chmielewski, "Stolypin and the Russian Ministerial Crisis of 1909" for full accounts of the crisis itself.

this relatively minor bill. Throughout April, the press was filled with speculation concerning Stolypin's likely course of action should Nicholas reject the naval general staff bill. If Stolypin left office, he would create the impression that a premier's attachment to his policies came before his loyalty to the autocrat. Remaining in office on the other hand, would reinforce the principle that the president of the Council of Ministers was the tsar's appointee and served at his pleasure. Thus, as a result of this issue, Stolypin's enemies found themselves hoping he would remain in office.

On April 25, Nicholas sent Stolypin a letter stating his refusal to sign the bill and rejecting any thoughts that the premier might have had about resigning. Stolypin chose to remain in office, and the crisis was liquidated along with much of the premier's public image as a reformer. To many, including Guchkov, the premier had compromised the cause of constitutionalism by backing down. Such a view assumed that Stolypin had held such beliefs in the first place. However, he did not emerge from the episode empty-handed. The letter from the tsar contained only part of a bargain that was probably struck during Stolypin's audience with Nicholas on April 22. Stolypin revealed this deal to the French ambassador, who passed the word on to his English colleague, Nicolson.

> M. Stolypin appears to have explained in substance to my colleagues that as the emperor expressed his readiness to state in the Imperial Rescript that he had full confidence in the Cabinet and approved of the manner in which the government was maintaining the Organic Laws, that there was no necessity to insist on resignation. . . . M. Stolypin has also obtained Imperial permission that he, and not the president of the Council of the Empire, should submit to His Majesty the names of candidates to the nominated seats in that chamber. This will be of considerable advantage for M. Stolypin as the president, M. Akimoff, is an extreme right partisan and invariably presented candidates of his own persuasion.[44]

When the new year came, Nicholas lived up to his promise. Akimov's list of four nominees was rejected, and four other men, three of whom joined the pro-Stolypin center group, were named to the State Council.[45] After so severe a challenge, Stolypin must have been receptive to the idea of increasing his base of support in the Council. Thus, the result of the ministerial crisis was less a defeat for Stolypin than a compromise.

Stolypin's relationship with Guchkov and the Octobrists did not change dramatically after the crisis. Stolypin's later political reorientation from the Octobrists to the Nationalists was based on an offensive strategy of

44. PRO, FO 371.729.1934 (May 16, 1909).
45. PRO, FO 371.978.3356 (January 24, 1910).

creating a viable base of support in society and in the Duma rather than on a particular defensive tactic of moving to the right to mollify those reactionaries who had attacked him. When it was absolutely clear that Guchkov could no longer furnish the broad public and political support that Stolypin required, Stolypin abandoned him. This decision, however, came much later.

Stolypin's evolution from quasi constitutionalism and mild reformism to nationalism was the result of his attempt to create a new political base for himself. His adoption of nationalism was not supposed to quiet his critics on the far right. Indeed, these same reactionaries seized on the crown jewel of his nationalist program, the western zemstvo bill, in order to destroy him. If nationalism was supposed to silence those to the premier's right, it certainly did not have the desired effect. It is, then, inescapably clear that, despite the prevailing view in the literature, the ministerial crisis produced few, if any, immediate changes in the political relationships of the regime of the Third of June. Those new elements that did arise came into being later, and they did so largely on their own.

In fact, proof that Stolypin had not entirely abandoned Guchkov and the Octobrists came quickly in the wake of the crisis. Early in May, the Premier was visited by Gololobov, Baron Cherkassov, and several other right-wing Octobrists. They came to discuss three Duma bills that would have eased restrictions on religious freedom. While the measures had been introduced by the government, they had been liberalized by Octobrist and Kadet amendments, and it was known that Stolypin was uneasy with the proposals in their present form. The right-wing Octobrists, who opposed the bills, sought to use the occasion to gain Stolypin's support for a new permanent right-wing majority, but the premier refused to cooperate with their efforts.[46] When word of this maneuver leaked out, the party's left wing was outraged. They imagined that the newly confident moderate rights were behind this latest move, and the earlier cordiality between the two fractions quickly vanished. What had begun as an attempt to draw the Octobrists away from cooperation with the Kadets had backfired. Instead, Guchkov became far more friendly with those to his left in the ensuing months, while Stolypin continued to observe, but not control, events in the Duma.[47]

46. Chmielewski, "Stolypin and the Ministerial Crisis of 1909," p. 28; Michael Brainard, *The Octobrist Party and Russian Society, 1905-1914*, p. 14. Avrekh, *Tsarizm i tret'eiunskaia sistema*, p. 50; Geoffrey Hosking, "Stolypin and the Octobrists," *Slavonic and East European Review*, November 1971, p. 155; *Rech'*, May 12, 1909.

47. *Novoe Vremiia*, May 17, 1909; *Novoe Vremiia*, May 22, 1909, cited in Brainard, *The Octobrist Party and Russian Society*, p. 16; Hutchinson, *The Octobrists in Russian Politics*, p. 124; *Rossiia*, June 4, 1909.

The Pikhno Proposal

Once the ministerial crisis had been settled late in April, Stolypin's next public action was to introduce into the Duma a proposal advanced by D. I. Pikhno, an appointed member of the State Council, publisher of the *Kievlianin*, and a leader of the Kiev Club of Russian Nationalists. This bill sought to revise the system of elections to the State Council from the nine western gubernias. Where they existed, each zemstvo chose a member of the State Council. In the west, special noble assemblies that were dominated by Polish landlords elected State Council members. Thus, all nine gubernias sent Poles despite the numerical preponderance of Russians among the rest of the population. Pikhno sought to introduce national restrictions that would guarantee the election of at least six Russians. Stolypin was probably attracted to this plan, which would place people in the State Council who would probably be loyal to him. Although Pikhno's bill sprang directly from the moderate right's most immediate political needs, Stolypin demonstrated only a partial awareness of the broader concerns of the west Russian gentry whom the moderate rights had come to represent. The Pikhno plan is a textbook example of a legislative proposal that germinated within a specific region, served the interests of its residents, and was advanced by its parliamentary representatives. The process by which it was elaborated and came to Stolypin's attention indicates the manner in which the future Nationalists came to serve their electoral base.

Toward the end of 1908, the attention of local Nationalist figures had shifted from the general question of elective zemstvos to the matter of representation in the State Council. This problem was understood to be an aspect of the broader zemstvo campaign, but it was singled out because of the approaching State Council elections (which were to take place in the summer of 1909). In addition, it was thought that Stolypin, who had expressed doubts about zemstvos in the west in 1908, could be influenced by this more specific proposal. The first public airing of the question of State Council elections occurred on January 9, 1909, at a meeting of the Kiev Club of Russian Nationalists. A plan like that introduced by Pikhno was advanced by the Podol'e marshal of nobility, I. A. Rakovich, who later became the president of the Nationalists' organization in Podol'e. A resolution in favor of the idea was passed and sent to Stolypin. A deputation to F. F. Trepov, governor-general of the southwest region, was organized, and plans were made for deputations to the tsar, Stolypin, and Duma leaders.[48]

48. *Sbornik kluba russkikh natsionalistov*, pervyi vypusk, pp. 11, 56.

In March, Ia. N. Ofrosimov, a deputy from Vitebsk, addressed the moderate right club in Petersburg on the question and, in April, the All-Russian National Union held a meeting on the matter at which the members decided to play host to the planned deputation. Groups from the entire borderland planned to participate, and it was soon apparent that the deputation would represent a broader range of conservative tendencies than that of the moderate right party.[49] Nicholas was scheduled to meet the western Russians on May 3. The night before, the thirty-seven members of the delegation collected at the All-Russian National Union with Duma deputies from the moderate right and the National Group. The evening was a huge emotional success, capped by Menshikov's rousing patriotic appeal.[50]

By contrast, the audience with the monarch was an anticlimax. The visitors were ushered into an anteroom. Nicholas entered; they presented him with a copy of their petition in support of the Pikhno proposal. He thanked them and left.

They did manage to meet with Stolypin. The group briefly described their plan for the State Council elections, and the premier agreed to support it. They had a short discussion of conditions in the west, and very quickly this meeting too was over. The participants' accounts of this encounter demonstrate no particular enthusiasm for Stolypin, nor do they reflect any ardent receptiveness on the part of the premier. In contrast to the warmth of the previous evening, the audience with the Nationalists' future ally was surprisingly tepid.[51]

On May 8, Stolypin introduced Pikhno's bill into both houses. The next day, he sent a letter to the president of the Duma in which he admitted that the introduction of zemstvos in the west was one possible solution to the question of State Council representation. However, he reiterated the government's earlier contention that the solution of the borderland's problems had to await a general zemstvo reform.[52] Stolypin suggested that the forthcoming State Council elections be postponed a year so that they might take place under the new law. Octobrists in the Committee on Local Government objected to this step. They argued that a more proper

49. F. Nikonovich, *Iz dnevnika chlena gosudarstvennoi dumy ot Vitebskoi Gubernii*, pp. 95, 114; *Okrainy Rossii*, No. 19 (May 1909), p. 283; *Sbornik kluba russkikh natsionalistov, vtoroi vypusk*, p. 9.

50. *Okrainy Rossii*, No. 19, p. 284.

51. Nikonovich, *Iz dnevnika chlena*, p. 119; *Sbornik kluba russkikh natsionalistov, vtoroi vypusk*, pp. 1–10.

52. TsGIA 1278.2.885.3, cited in A. Ia. Avrekh, "Vopros o zapadnom zemstve i bankrovstro Stolypina," *Istoricheskie zapiski*, Vol. 70 (1961):67.

constitutional procedure would be to permit the elections to occur and then to hold new elections under the revised law a year later.[53] This distinction eluded the moderate rights, who thought the Octobrists were playing games with a bill that was essential to the west Russian gentry's political survival. The exchange added a further element of mistrust between the two fractions. The moderate rights feared that the Octobrists' apparent belief in rules of procedure made them unreliable allies. Bogdanov accused the Octobrists of insensitivity to the needs of the constituency of the moderate rights.

> We recognize that they [the Octobrists] consider it possible to reject a strictly Russian national policy on the question of relations with non-Russians ... in the western gubernias. Because the moderate rights are absolute nationalists and the greatest number of deputies from the border gubernias are in their fraction, it is clear that an antinational policy will separate the moderate rights from the Octobrist fraction once and for all, making joint work with them impossible.[54]

However, the moderates had no objection to the Octobrists' claim that the only proper solution to the question was the introduction of zemstvos with national curiae.[55] Balashev immediately added his support, and quickly the center and right fractions accepted the creation of zemstvos in the west as an urgent priority. By the time he made his Duma speech in support of the Pikhno plan, Stolypin had also recognized the necessity of the new zemstvos, and he promised to introduce such a bill by the fall session. Thus, by advancing the narrow question of State Council representation for Russians, the moderate rights had succeeded in calling the Duma's attention to their fundamental demand.

Stolypin's willingness to introduce a western zemstvo bill did not signify a complete conversion to the cause of the moderate right. In his Duma speech on the Pikhno plan, he appealed primarily to the Octobrists, whose support was still required for passage of the bill. In advocating a change in the election procedure, he came to separate class and national concerns, arguing that the old "class principle" of election, which had always resulted in the election of Polish nobles, had to be changed in order that the Russian majority of the borderland, peasants included, could make its voice heard in the State Council. By defining the question in this way,

53. Izgoev, *P. A. Stolypin*, p. 91; E. Chmielewski, "Stolypin's Last Crisis," *California Slavic Studies*, Vol. 3 (1964):99; PRO, FO 371.728.23024 (June 19, 1909).
54. *Rossiia*, June 21, 1909.
55. Sten. ot., 3.2.4.2757.

Stolypin implied that the principles of ruling class interest and Russian national interest might be antagonistic.[56] The future Nationalists recognized no such contradiction. For them, Russian nationalism was a form of support for gentry interest. Their aim was to combine class and national interests in a manner that would permit Russian landlords to control local government in the borderland. Because Stolypin did not fully share this conception, some moderate rights considered him, like the Octobrists, an unreliable ally.

The entire exchange over the Pikhno proposal proved enormously revealing to both the moderate rights and the National Group. After May, it was abundantly clear that neither Octobrist notions of justice nor bureaucratic rules of procedure would be sufficient to protect both the land and political influence of the west Russian landlord. Stolypin was to jump on the Nationalist bandwagon only later. At this point, he had committed himself to no special course. The rest of the bureaucracy, particularly the governors-general and the governors, could not be relied on consistently to share the premier's Russian nationalism. There still existed among many chinovniki (bureaucrats) a feeling of loyalty to a multinational empire and a commitment to the even-handed application of rules and procedures. They could not always be relied on to support Russians against Poles. For this reason, the Russian dvorianstvo of the west was forced to go outside the state structure to establish independent political organizations. They did this even though they solicited and accepted the support of the administration whenever they could get it.

The Birth of the Nationalist Party

The Shift to the Right in the Countryside

With politics in the Duma in a state of flux, trends in the countryside were being watched closely. As a result, the zemstvo elections that took place during the summer of 1909 received considerable attention. The last zemstvo elections, held in 1906 and 1907, had produced a stunning victory for the right: Many of the old zemstvo liberals had been driven from the zemstvos in the wake of the nobles' reaction to the events of 1905 and 1906. With them went much of the zemstvos' devotion to selfless service and conciliarity. But these changes did not mean that the party divisions that had appeared on the national level had direct

56. Sten. ot., 3.2.4.2741.

Table 3.1. **Shifts in the Political Tendency of Zemstvo Majorities**

	1906–1907	*1909–1910*
Rightist	5	14
Borderline rightist to moderate	6	9
Moderate	10	5
Borderline moderate to left	2	1
Leftist	3	1

Source: TsGIA 1288 (1907), 2, 2 and 46, cited in Ruth McNaughton, "The Provincial Nobility and Political Trends in the Zemstvo, 1906–1910," p. 114.

counterparts in the zemstvos. Even more acutely than in the case of the Duma elections, political labels presented problems. For example, the broadly descriptive terms of "right," "moderate," and "left" were used by government observers, while the liberal press often used the term "progressive." As a result, the imprecisions of the zemstvo electoral process only permit us to gauge broad trends. Nevertheless, with the political center in the Duma edging toward the right during the spring of 1909, it would be important to determine if a similar pattern was emerging in the provinces that summer. If such a trend were developing, it would be necessary to conclude that much of the pressure from the right on the Duma deputies came not simply from the court camarilla and the State Council but also from the social element that these Duma deputies were supposed to represent, that is, the provincial nobility who dominated the zemstvos.

However, there are certain difficulties in obtaining the specifics of the zemstvo elections.[57] On matters for which government sources provide information on the 1906–1907 and 1909–1910 elections, a certain measure of extrapolation is required. Of the thirty-four gubernia zemstvos, some thirty had noble majorities. If one studies the shift in the political affiliations of the noble majorities of these thirty zemstvos, certain tentative but fairly clear patterns do emerge. (Keep in mind that these zemstvos were not socially homogeneous and that the descriptions of political tendency are those of the government.)

The evidence of a shift to the right in the zemstvos is unmistakable (see Table 3.1). The most dramatic changes are the large increase of right-wing majorities and the obvious decline of moderate majorities. It was commonly accepted that people classified as "moderates" by the government

---

57. Ruth McNaughton and Roberta Manning, "Political Trends in the Zemstvos, 1907–1914," in Leopold Haimson (ed.), *The Politics of Rural Russia, 1905–1914*, p. 187.

were usually sympathetic to the Octobrist program. Thus, it appeared that the sort of zemstvo activists who might have been sympathetic to Guchkov's party were beginning to disappear from local politics.[58]

The shift to the right was far less dramatic than it had been in the previous election, and changes in the character of zemstvo majorities usually involved just a few votes rather than wholesale changes of personnel.[59] Nevertheless, the general trend toward the right among the gentry boded ill for the Octobrists. Since the spring of 1909, it had been obvious that the remaining provincial Octobrists were considerably to the right of the national leadership, and the first results of the summer zemstvo elections of 1909 must have made clear to many that the segment of provincial opinion that had once supported the Octobrists was now beginning to abandon them. The moderate rights must have thought that this turn of events created possibilities for them to expand their influence outside western Russia, but it was still too early in the party's development for them to reap any quick gains from this shift to the right in the countryside.

The trend in the countryside was not duplicated in the towns. City duma elections during the summer demonstrated no similar shift toward the right in urban Russia.[60] Thus, it came as a terrible shock when the Octobrists lost a Duma by-election in the first curia of Moscow, long regarded as their most secure district. Because this seat was regarded as an Octobrist bailiwick, only a perfunctory campaign was undertaken. The result was a defeat at the hands of the Kadets.[61] Octobrist disorganization and division explain much of the disaster. Also, many normally non-Kadet voters supported that party as a protest against the course of the government, which had been linked with the Octobrists repeatedly during the last two years.[62] This association irked Stolypin who had avoided investing his prestige on the side of the Octobrists. It became abundantly clear that open association with the Union of October was no longer a course of political advantage.

A party congress, held in October, was called to put a halt to the erosion of the party's influence. However, the gathering served only to underscore the loss of prestige suffered in the Moscow by-election. Some local groups

58. Ibid., p. 97.

59. Ibid., p. 199.

60. *Rech'*, May 21, and June 5, 13, and 17, 1909; *Russkie Vedemosti*, May 16, 20, 28, June 14, and July 1, 1909.

61. *Novoe Vremia*, September 19, 1909.

62. TsGAOR 102 (1909) 265.395.30. M. A. Shtromberg, Moscow, to E. S. Kariatigin, St. Petersburg (September 28, 1909).

refused to send delegations to the meeting.[63] Worse still, only a limited number of branches were actually sent invitations. Early that summer, the president of the central committee, N. Saposhnikov, wrote thirty members of the Duma fraction, calling on them to ensure the success of the upcoming congress that October. However, the paucity of replies forced him to accept "the fact that in many places, the party organization has collapsed."[64]

In contrast, the future Nationalists were continuing to expand. On August 26, 1909, the Podol'e Union of Russian Nationalists began operations with 200 members. It was led by the Kamanets uezd marshal of nobility, I. A. Rakovich, who also edited the group's newspaper *Podolianin*.[65] The union's leading members, Rakovich and Balashev, also belonged to the Kiev Club of Russian Nationalists. This made the new group essentially a branch of the Kiev Club, which had now expanded from 360 to 567 members. Interestingly, 104 people were listed on the Kiev Club's membership rolls as working for the railroads or for the Ministry of Communications; the list included the highest administrators as well as conductors and ticket sellers.[66] Since Kiev was an important transportation center, it was logical that railroad men would play a role in Kiev politics. The lower ranks of white-collar employees, although probably attracted by the club's nationalism, may have been included to pad the membership rolls. Eventually, these members came to offer strong support for Savenko, who used them against the attacks of rivals to maintain his leadership of the club. The party's special relationship with Rukhlov, now Minister of Communications, may also explain the presence of so many railroad employees on the club's rolls.

Despite the presence of this element, it should be stressed again that the landowning nobility dominated the club's operation. The other elements in the club accepted this situation, choosing to affiliate largely on the basis of a nationalism stimulated by the perceived threat from the Jewish population of Kiev. Nationalistic merchants and professional men played a subordinate role at the outset of the club's operation. The urgency with which they viewed their situation and the manner in which they expressed their sense of struggle had a significant impact on the club's approach to politics. Later on, when splits began to develop within the party, they would begin to play a more independent role.

63. Brainard, *The Octobrist Party and Russian Society*, p. 21.

64. TsGAOR 102 (1909) 265.384.98. N. Saposhnikov, Moscow, to L. G. Liuts, Kherson (June 16, 1909).

65. *Sbornik kluba russkikh natsionalistov*, vtoroi vypusk, p. 61.

66. Ibid., pp. 121-140.

Given the rightward shift in both the capital and the countryside, it was with considerable optimism that the Russian conservative political organizations of the nine western gubernias met that October in Kiev to discuss their mutual interests and plans for the future.[67] Held under the auspices of the Kiev Club of Russian Nationalists, this meeting brought together a variety of right-wing tendencies, and the differences of political approach and interests that were revealed there had an important impact on the eventual shape assumed by the Nationalist Party.

The gathering, called the West Russian Meeting, began on October 4, 1909.[68] Of the 178 participants, 38 were Duma deputies. Since many were pravye, the meeting was not simply a gathering of those forces that would soon make up the Nationalist Party.[69] In fact, a member of the pravye Duma fraction, S. P. Sazonovich, was elected president of the meeting. In an interview with the liberal daily *Kievskaia Mysl'*, Sazonovich sought to counter one of the most serious conservative arguments against the zemstvo plan. Witte and others later argued that the abandonment of a purely property-based requirement for participation would lead to zemstvos that would be "too democratic." But neither Sazonovich nor anyone else present at the meeting wished to support proposals that might permit peasants and small landowners to control local government in the borderland.

> I am a supporter of the large landowners and therefore, as far as the question will pertain to maintaining the advantage for the large landowner in the future zemstvo, I will try with all my strength to influence the resolutions of the West Russian Meeting.[70]

The major point of division at the meeting centered around the attempt of delegates from the Kiev Club to revise the government's proposal that would have extended zemstvos to all nine borderland gubernias. Because of the hopelessly small number of Russian landowners in the northern provinces of Vilna and Kovno, no amount of curial manipulation could guarantee a Russian zemstvo. Under these circumstances, those from the southwest thought it preferable to have no zemstvos at all. They proposed that the northwest region be eliminated from the government's bill.[71] After a bitter debate, Rakovich and Savenko succeeded in convincing the

---

67. *Rech'*, September 17, 1909; *Rizhskaia Mysl'*, September 25, 1909.
68. *Kievlianin*, October 4, 1909.
69. *Sbornik kluba russkikh natsionalistov, vtoroi vypusk*, p. 146.
70. *Kievskaia Mysl'*, October 7, 1909.
71. *Sbornik kluba russkikh natsionalistov, vtoroi vypusk*, p. 164.

meeting to support a resolution that called for zemstvos in just the six southern gubernias.[72] The acceptance of this resolution was a victory for the moderate rights' conception of the western zemstvo bill, but the ten members of the fraction who were present in Kiev hesitated to make political capital of their victory. The absence of unanimity at the meeting and the necessity of avoiding a purely regional image made them reluctant to take major steps at this time. Yet, they must have been impressed by the breadth of concern for the western zemstvo movement.

Stolypin's First Signs of Change

On October 3, the eve of the West Russian Meeting, Stolypin gave an interview to the provincial newspaper *Volga*. Contemporary observers and later scholars have considered the interview to be the public signal of Stolypin's conversion to the cause of the Nationalists—"the replacement of Guchkov by Balashev."[73] The creation of the Nationalist Party shortly thereafter could then hardly be seen as coincidental.

Such a sequence of events leaves one with the impression that the premier had only to give the word for the Nationalist Party to emerge. But a reading of the *Volga* interview hardly substantiates this conclusion. Stolypin's primary concern was with the impact on provincial life of his agrarian and local government reforms. Duma politics were mentioned only obliquely, with references to the need for a "working majority" and "serious legislative efforts." Certainly such terms had been long-standing code words for a new right majority, but it would appear that Stolypin was merely giving Guchkov and the left Octobrists a warning rather than abandoning them entirely.[74] On the other hand, it would be a mistake to deny the *Volga* interview any significance at all. Stolypin may not yet have shifted his loyalties to the Nationalists, but there can be little doubt that he was certainly searching for new sources of support. By itself, the interview may not have been a crucial turning point. Nevertheless, it did contain certain significant signs of change.[75]

At this time, *Kievlianin*, which had become a mouthpiece for the moderate rights, began to take note of new developments. The paper's editorials urged "nonrevolutionary rightists, monarchists, and genuine nationalists" to unite in opposition to the "semiconstitutionalism" of the

72. *Kievskaia Mysl'*, October 6, 1909.
73. Avrekh, *Tsarizm i tret' eiunskaia sistema*, p. 49.
74. *Rossiia*, October 4, 1909.
75. *Kievskaia Mysl'*, October 4, 1909.

Octobrists.[76] A few days later, also in *Kievlianin*, Bogdanov, with his characteristic bluntness, made matters even more explicit. The Octobrists, he argued, never represented a unified ideology, nor could they be called a genuine political party. The loss of the Moscow by-election exposed their weaknesses, and the only proper response of conservatives in the Duma was the creation of a "normal" right majority.

> Recognizing the necessity of a possible union, the right fractions of the Duma, at the present time, are showing an inclination toward a more friendly way of acting, indeed even toward unification. It is possible that they will succeed in uniting the fractions of the Nationalists and the moderate rights under the general banner of the Russian Nationalists.[77]

He added that several Octobrists had already joined the moderate rights, and it was reasonable to expect that in time the National fraction would become the largest in the Duma.

At this point, the various trends finally appeared to be crystallizing. The alignment of Duma forces was clearly changing, and, just as the West Russian Meeting was ending in Kiev, a special ministerial body assembled in Petersburg to discuss the western zemstvo bill. This group, called the *sovet po delam mestnogo khoziaistvo* (Council for Local Economy), had been revived by Stolypin in 1907. It was supposed to serve the function of a "pre-Duma," assisting the Ministry of Interior in working out legislation in the field of local government. The sovet consisted not only of local governors but of marshals of nobility, presidents of city dumas and zemstvo boards, and other representatives named by the zemstvos and approved by Petersburg. The formation of this council was an attempt to marshal local public opinion and give it a voice in an essentially bureau-cratic context.[78] This group was called on to discuss the bill for the introduction of zemstvos into the nine western gubernias. The crucial decision that had to be made was the same as the one that had split the West Russian Meeting. Should the zemstvo be introduced throughout the west or only in the six gubernias where Russian dominance was assured?

Savenko, who had been pushing the six-province plan, was quick to note the coincidence of the closing of the Kiev meeting and the opening of the sovet's activities in the capital. Writing in *Kievlianin*, he contrasted the two groups, calling the West Russian Meeting "much closer to [local] life than the Petersburg council." As was his wont, he conveniently ignored the representatives of the noble assemblies, city dumas, and zemstvos who

76. *Kievlianin*, October 11, 1909.
77. *Kievlianin*, October 17, 1909.
78. A. N. Naumov, *Iz utselevshikh vospominanii*, Vol. 2 (New York, 1954–1955), p. 132.

comprised half the group and claimed that the sovet consisted of bureaucrats who did not know the peculiarities of the western borderland. Their plan to introduce the zemstvo in the north as well as the south reflected their tendency to work by "bureaucratic formulas rather than the living needs of the region." He accused them of applying one and the same electoral law to regions that were by no means the same. For this reason, he applauded Stolypin's speech to the sovet on October 6, in which the premier somewhat half-heartedly opposed the extension of zemstvos to Vilna and Kovno. Savenko was cheered by these remarks, but felt them too weakly put to elicit any sense of comfort that the premier was the true champion of his cause.[79] Strong support had been voiced for the nine-province bill in the sovet, and Savenko was apprehensive.

A month later, only after the Nationalists had organized, Stolypin announced his support for the six-gubernia version.[80] Savenko hailed the decision as a great victory and a major turning point in the development of the renovated state structure. By distorting the intentions of those involved (including Stolypin's), Savenko imbued the limiting of the western zemstvo bill with considerably more drama than it merited. Savenko crowed that all the demands of the West Russian Meeting had been met: Now it was guaranteed (in Savenko's words), "that large landownership should not be dominated by middle and petty landownership." He sought to pit the Kiev meeting against the sovet. Savenko argued that by following the recommendations made by the West Russian Meeting, Stolypin was rejecting the old bureaucratic path and accepting the views of a segment of the local population instead.[81] But this one example hardly constitutes a revolution in the premier's decision making. Again, Stolypin was making a choice between offered alternatives, and, regardless of the institutional implications, it is possible to justify this decision on its own terms, thereby diminishing any feelings that others might have had about important political precedents.

The Formation of the All-Russian National Union

Before the beginning of the third session of the Duma, in the fall of 1909, Cherkassov and Gololobov announced the formation of a right Octobrist group numbering eleven deputies.[82] These Octobrists took pains

79. *Kievlianin*, October 10, 1909; *Kievskaia Mysl'*, October 7, 1909; *Okrainy Rossii*, No. 41 (October 10, 1909): 577.
80. *Kievlianin*, November 14, 1909.
81. *Kievlianin*, November 19, 1909.
82. *Birzhevie Vedemosti*, November 6, 1909.

to separate themselves from the moderate right, thus ending schemes for a grand influx of Octobrists into the National fraction. One right Octobrist sought to pinpoint their position.

> The differences with the Octobrist fraction are on religious and partially on national questions. However, we do not inscribe on our banners "Russia for Russians" and above all we do not want to be cannibals.[83]

The last phrase was a rejection of what some critics called the "zoological" nationalism of the moderate rights. In particular, the right Octobrists, especially Gololobov, did not share the future Nationalists' passionate devotion to anti-Semitism. Rejecting rumors that they would subordinate themselves to any future Nationalist fraction, Gololobov and Cherkassov maintained a verbal loyalty to what were called Octobrist principles. To secede entirely from the union would have implied an admission that their brand of Octobrism was a deviation when, in fact, they sought to prove that Guchkov had erred.[84] By and large, members of the right Octobrist group came from traditionally Octobrist areas. Thus, there did not exist sufficient shared experience with the moderate rights to lead them to surrender themselves entirely to Balashev's leadership.

The right Octobrists, however, were by far the smaller of the two new Duma groups. Months of rumors and abortive attempts finally culminated in the formation, with little fanfare, of the Russian National fraction. Long discussions and arguments preceded the unification of the moderate rights and the National Group. Much of the division had been caused by the inability of the two groups to agree on the distribution of power in the united fraction. At last, it was decided that the fraction would elect an entirely new council.[85] This was a victory for the moderates. Eight moderate rights and three National Group members were elected to the council with Balashev as president. On October 25, the alliance was formally announced, and a program published. Drawing as it did on the platforms of each group, the program offered few surprises.[86]

1. The unity of the Empire, the protection of Russians in all parts of the Empire, and Russia for the Russians
2. Loyalty to both autocracy and representative institutions
3. Development of the Orthodox church, especially in the villages

83. Ibid.
84. *Rossiia*, November 8, 1909.
85. *Golos Pravdy*, October 26, 1909.
86. PRO, FO 371.726.42645 (October 22, 1909); *Rossiia*, October 27, 1909.

4. Improvement of the peasants' economic situation and support for private peasant landowning
5. The inviolability of private property
6. The right to work
7. Development of local government to protect Russians in areas in which they are a minority
8. Opposition to equal rights for Jews
9. National agricultural and industrial planning
10. Development of Russian national self-consciousness in the schools

The new, if limited, concern for the peasants reflected the Nationalists' growing sense of self-importance. They now felt compelled to speak on behalf of other classes. The degree of seriousness with which any particular point in the program was taken varied, but it was clearly necessary for these new claimants to national influence to make some appeal to other classes.

Balashev sought to play down the importance of the fraction's creation and, instead, stressed the necessity of organization in the country.

> The formation of a new fraction is only the first step in an immense task which faces the Nationalists, namely, to organize a Nationalist Party in the localities in order that it may be easier to spread the idea of Russian nationalism.[87]

Because the union of the moderate rights and the National Group had been expected for almost a year, public reaction was predictably low-key. The new fraction simply confirmed a voting pattern that had been apparent for some time in the Duma. The real significance of the latest step was the sense of dynamism that the merger would impart to the nationalist movement elsewhere. Savenko's report to the Kiev Club of Russian Nationalists on the new National fraction was therefore dispassionate and factual. Like Balashev, he cautioned that it was only the first step in a broader campaign and that success in the Duma meant little by itself.[88]

The pravye publicly welcomed the new party.[89] But Guchkov's public pleasure at the National fraction's creation belied the extent to which he felt threatened. Publicly, he applauded the consolidation of any Duma

87. *Russkaia Rech'*, November 1, 1909; *Novoe Vremia*, October 28, 1909.
88. *Sbornik kluba russkikh natsionalistov*, vtoroi vypusk, p. 7; *Kievlianin*, December 29, 1909.
89. *Rossiia*, November 15, 1909.

group and expressed a willingness to work with the Nationalists.[90] But, privately, Guchkov, speaking to foreign journalists, pronounced his readiness to move his fraction into the opposition camp.[91] Guchkov did maintain a steady relationship with the Nationalists, and because of the Octobrists' center position, he was still a force to be reckoned with in the Duma. Nevertheless, the rise of the National fraction spelled the end of his dominance of the third Duma. The Octobrists had diminished in numbers and were no longer *the* party of the government. Balashev's intense expressions of loyalty to Stolypin made it thoroughly clear which group had assumed that role.[92] It remained for the Kiev liberal newspaper *Kievskie Vesti* to sum up the situation.

> The longer the third Duma lived, the more clearly it was revealed that the line of its behavior was not drawn up according to an Octobrist "document" but went past it toward the right. . . . Little by little, hegemony in the Duma slipped from the hands of Guchkov's boys. . . . The moderate rights appeared as the masters of the Duma. In place of Guchkov, stood Balashev.

On the Nationalists themselves, the Kiev daily commented:

> They do not consider it necesary to dress themselves up in constitutional masks. Here have gathered people who do not have in their past any sort of compromising "documents." . . . The Nationalists now become the real government party.[93]

Not only was this recognition of the change in power relationships important, but the paper had singled out a reason for the new situation. As the third Duma and Russian society evolved, appeals to constitutionalism proved increasingly ineffective as a basis for power. The Octobrists' politics of principle and rule were giving way to the Nationalists' politics of interest. This change was occurring not only in the limited context of the Duma but, more significantly, in the country at large.

The next logical step after the unification of the parliamentary fractions was the actual merger of the two public groups. To this end a committee of members of the All-Russian National Union and the moderate right party was established in order to work out whatever changes in the union's charter might be necessary to accommodate the new arrangement. In exchange for acceptance of its name as the title of the new larger group,

90. *Rech'*, October 27, 1909.
91. *Ranee Utro*, October 28, 1909.
92. *Rech'*, October 20, 1909.
93. *Kievskie Vesti*, December 3, 1909.

the All-Russian National Union agreed to the election of a completely new party council. The union's charter was left virtually unchanged. However, later organizational changes increased the strength of the provincially oriented moderate rights at the expense of elements whose primary concern was with events in the capital.[94] By this time, it was clear that Balashev and the men of the southwest would be in control of the new Nationalist Party. Even such well-known members of the moderate right fraction as Bobrinskii and Krupenskii were to play less than central roles.

As a representative of Petersburg elements, Menshikov was predictably less than impressed by these developments. For Menshikov, the creation of political parties was dangerously European and modern. He sensed that the acceptance of a new set of rules in the political game posed a real danger for the still dominant if tattered Russian nobility, and he was not altogether wrong. Menshikov opposed Balashev's emphasis on work in the localities. Obsessed as he was with cosmopolitan bureaucrats and the intelligentsia of the capital that fed on the "Jewish press," Menshikov claimed that nationalism was stronger in the provinces than in Petersburg and that a nationalist party should seek influence at the center in order to make nationalism fashionable once again in Petersburg society.[95] To this end, Menshikov proposed the creation of a satellite organization, the structure of which was much more suited to his notion of politics, namely, a national club designed to foster a spirit of nationalism among the capital's elite.

This idea fit in perfectly with Krupenskii's conception of parliamentary life. He sought to create an informal setting imbued with the nationalist spirit, which would foster compromise on a basis favorable to the new fraction and provide a web of contact and fellowship that would then extend beyond the narrower confines of the Nationalist Party. On November 25, he published an open letter in *Novoe Vremia*, inviting all "patriots" to an organizational meeting on November 29 of the All-Russian National Club.[96] This new club was not entirely synonymous with the Nationalist Party and fraction. Instead, its associations would be broader.[97] The first meeting was well attended, drawing the entire National fraction as well as several pravye, Octobrists, State Council members, generals, professors, publicists, and merchants. Krupenskii, acting as temporary chairman, claimed that 400 men and women had signed the club's membership rolls, paying the considerable yearly dues of fifty rubles.

94. *Rech'*, November 16, 1909; *Rossiia*, November 29, 1909.
95. *Pis'ma k blyzhnym*, November 1909, p. 749.
96. *Novoe Vremia*, November 25, 1909; *Rossiia*, November 27, 1909.
97. *Moskovskie Vedemosti*, December 3, 1909.

Prince Urusov, who had been kept out of the leadership of the new party, predicted to the press that the National Club would serve the same political purpose as the social club in England: "There, in an informal atmosphere, will take place on neutral terrain, if not agreements of a significant political nature, in any event the first steps of such agreements."[98]

Essentially, the club was organized around the idea of nationalism, and those attracted to that particular notion were welcome to affiliate. Although it had a close link with the new All-Russian National Union, which was housed in its headquarters, the club, as an institution, was descended from such amorphous pre-1905 cultural gatherings as the *Russkoe Sobranie*, a collection of polite Petersburg conservatives. The National Club was not to be the center of a national political movement but rather the gathering spot for a collection of like-minded Petersburg personalities. The composition of the council reflected this fact. Most members came from elsewhere than the Duma. Only seven of seventeen on the board were in the National fraction. A retired general, B. A. Vasilchikov, was chosen president, and, as was to be shortly revealed, his world view had little in common with that of the Nationalist Party's leadership.[99] None of the other leaders of the club, all nobles, had been leading lights of the nationalist movement. Rather, they came from an elite segment of Petersburg bureaucrats and generals, the so-called *sanovniki*. Thoroughly secure in their positions, they had no need to join anything so uncouth as a political party. However, a more amorphous club was perfectly suitable. In Petersburg, there were many bureaucrats who were considered cosmopolitan and Western-oriented. Now those bureaucrats and officials who opposed this tendency were seizing on the moment in order to counterattack. In the conservative press and in the salons of the capital, the ideology of nationalism was counterposed to constitutionalism. Menshikov, through his columns in *Novoe Vremia*, was the mouthpiece of this segment of nationalist thought, and for him the so-called national idea always meant loyalty to the autocratic state and the multinational Russian Empire. Along with the sanovniki, Menshikov mistrusted the political parties and the independent activity manifested by the men from the borderland.

Savenko's reaction to the National Club, although restrained, was similar to Menshikov's, at least in one respect. Now it was possible, in

---

98. *Rossiia*, December 1, 1909.

99. *Kievlianin*, December 3, 1909; *Sbornik kluba russkikh natsionalistov*, vtoroi vypusk, p. 41.

cosmopolitan Petersburg, to call oneself a Russian nationalist without embarrassment. In distinction to the sanovniki, Savenko was especially struck by the fact that Russian patriots could now organize such a body independently. Disregarding for the moment the fact that the National Club and the new Nationalist Party had definite structural and social differences, Savenko stressed the importance of independent conservative political units in post-1905 Russia.

> The new conditions of social and political life have created a situation in which not only the government but also patriotic society now stand before revolution. Thus the state has been strengthened among the Russian masses, overtaking the revolutionary tornado.[100]

Nevertheless, much of the National Club and even many Nationalist Party members did not share Savenko's taste for independent activity. At the opening of the National Club's new headquarters in Petersburg, the President, Prince B. A. Vasilchikov, made a speech attacking political parties as divisive of national unity. He clearly reflected the capital elite's mistrust of the kind of movement that had emerged in the west. Vasilchikov argued that nationalism and loyalty to the Empire were the only proper ways of preserving both the state and the nobility's dominant position in the state.[101] In short, the Empire was to be placed above immediate interest. It should come as no surprise that Vasilchikov came to oppose the western zemstvo bill. Savenko was particularly distressed at what he called Vasilchikov's "politics of slogans."[102] Earlier he had noted that such an approach was artificial, based on nothing but words—the very basis of the Octobrists' increasingly apparent weakness. He feared that the Nationalists might fall into the same trap.

> The Octobrists are not a party. They are a collection of people, thoughts and feelings, united by one slogan.... How is this unifying Octobrist slogan the principle of a party's soul? It is not.... This party arose entirely artificially and occupied an influential position due to the powerful support of the government.[103]

Now, of course, the Nationalists were to benefit from the government's support. Yet, if one were to have questioned Savenko on this point, he surely would have replied that the Nationalists, unlike the Octobrists,

---

100. *Kievlianin*, December 5, 1909.
101. *Okrainy Rossii*, No. 9 (February 27, 1910):138.
102. *Rech'*, February 22, 1910.
103. *Kievlianin*, November 29, 1909.

merited that support. Guchkov's increasingly fissured fraction had diminished from 154 to 120 at the start of the third session. The National fraction officially numbered 91 at this time, but, on the crucial national questions that were soon to come up, it could count on the right Octobrists and the less extreme pravye. On issues vital to them, the Nationalists commanded roughly the same number of deputies as the Octobrists. Stolypin took note of this situation, and the legislation introduced by the government in the next few months reflected the changed power relationships.

The demise of the Octobrists and the rise of the Nationalists were only partially attributable to the course of parliamentary affairs. One cannot deny that the institutional tensions among the court, government, and Duma, seen most dramatically in the ministerial crisis, led to the break-up of a galaxy of forces interested in limited reforms. Yet, throughout the country, the Octobrists had experienced an even more dramatic collapse. Their local organizations had ceased to exist, largely by default, and the zemstvo elections of 1909 had been especially damaging. With the Octobrists crumbling and the gentry apparently moving to the right, the opportunity existed for the Nationalists to pick up considerable national support. They were not entirely successful in this task, but they brought to the job an approach and a set of attitudes that contrasted sharply with those of the Octobrists. The modernity of their approach, including the conscious imitation of Western European organizational models, was, in fact, largely attributable to the character of the politics (not to mention the economy) in the area of their greatest strength, the western gubernias. The nobility of the west led the way. Some nobles from elsewhere would follow. Others, however, preferred to work within the context of traditions that had never arisen in the west.[104]

104. The kind of organizational structure that the Nationalists had evolved fits into the scheme advanced by LaPolambara and Weiner to characterize political parties in developing societies. These steps include the creation of a national center, the establishment of local units which maintained contact with the center, and the attempt by both national and provincial organizations to achieve political power by soliciting support at all levels. This definition omits any concern for representation of specific social interests. See Joseph LaPolambara and Myron Weiner, "The Origin and Development of Political Parties," in Joseph LaPolambara and Myron Weiner (eds.), *Political Parties and Political Development* (Princeton, 1966), p. 6.

IV

A Basis for Power

By the beginning of 1910, the Nationalists had good reason for optimism. They had struck a partnership with the most dynamic political figure in the Russian government. Stolypin had just weathered a serious crisis and established a new basis for his political system. The economy had revived after the depression of the revolutionary years, and Stolypin's so-called strong peasants were still leaving their communes in considerable numbers. There was peace on the land, and the strike movement had reached a low ebb.[1] After meeting Stolypin, Savenko saw a bright future for the party and for its powerful new ally.

> Standing firmly along a nationalist path, the ruling circles are now preoccupied with the question of preparing the country for the elections to the fourth Duma, striving to build a permanent, nationalist majority. All elements of society sympathetic to nationalism must give the government their support.[2]

1. Leopold Haimson, "The Problem of Social Stability in Urban Russia: 1905–1917," *Slavic Review* (December 1964):626–628.
2. *Sbornik kluba russkikh natsionalistov*, vtoroi vypusk, p. 81.

The provincial organizations had an immense role to play in such a task. The progress of coming local elections would be closely watched in order to draw implications for 1912.[3] Stolypin hoped that his new relationship with the Nationalists would be the basis of a strong political alliance that would assure him a powerful and loyal majority in the fourth Duma. With the Duma solidly supporting him, Stolypin could enhance his public authority, thwart the intrigues of his more reactionary enemies, and make himself indispensable to the tsar.

Stolypin now publicly adopted the nationalist movement. During the spring of 1910, the progovernment daily *Rossiia*, whose editorials usually mirrored the Premier's views, changed its emphasis from defenses of Octobrism to daily praise for the idea of Russian nationalism. By summer, *Rossiia* was repeatedly linking the growth of nationalism to the coming elections to the fourth Duma.[4]

The National Campaign

In the course of the spring session, Stolypin directed the Duma's attention to several measures that raised questions of nationality. The press dubbed the work of this period the "National Campaign," and it became common to link this reorientation of the premier's concerns with the emergence of the new Nationalist Party. However, the nationalistic legislation of 1910 did not follow directly from the rise of the Nationalists. Most of the ideas raised that year had long histories; some of the bills had been introduced into the Duma as early as the spring of 1909. However, the National Campaign can be seen as the product of the Nationalists' ambitions and Stolypin's search for new political support. Its central elements were the Finnish legislation and the western zemstvo bill, but it has become common practice to include the creation of a new province in Kholm and reform of Polish city government as parts of the same legislative program.

Finland

When Finland became part of the Empire early in the nineteenth century, the Finns were permitted to retain their laws and institutions. Tsarist police did not have free reign, and, by 1905, Finland had become a haven for many revolutionaries. Stolypin wanted to change this situation,

3. Kievlianin, March 1, 1910.
4. *Rossiia*, July 4 and 8, 1910.

but the question of bringing Finland under the same laws as the rest of the Empire was not a matter of central concern to the Nationalists. In a sense, Finland presented clear evidence that the Nationalists were committed to the expediency of nationalism, not its ideology. No vital interest of their constituencies was affected by the Finnish legislation, and the Nationalists paid the Finnish bill only lip service. This indifference dramatically reflected the peculiar character of the party's particular form of nationalism.

A commission of the Ministry of Interior had been instructed in 1908 to draw up a law that would limit many of Finland's historic immunities and protect the rights of those Russians, mainly bureaucrats, who were living there. After an unsuccessful attempt to enlist Finnish cooperation in this endeavor, an all-Russian commission finally worked out a bill that was introduced into the Duma on March 14, 1910. In this bill, laws on subversion were extended to the former Grand Duchy. Its citizens were to become liable to the same taxation and military obligations as the rest of the Empire's citizens. After a short debate, the law passed the Duma on May 10 and the State Council on May 31. The tsar signed it into law on June 17—a stark contrast to the slow pace at which most reform measures had moved.[5]

The Finnish legislation attracted a great deal of attention in both the liberal and conservative press of Petersburg. The question of Finland raised old fears of protected subversive activity so near the capital of the Empire. The provincial Nationalists were, of course, concerned with supporting the fight against revolution, and they were also opposed to Finland's separatist demands. But they were primarily interested in their own local struggles. Thus, the Nationalists were not able to muster the interest in the Finnish bill they had already devoted to the western zemstvo bill. Few business sessions of the Kiev Club, the National Union, or any other constituent group were devoted to discussions of the Finnish problem.[6] Nor did the Nationalists take a very active role in the Duma debates concerning the bill.[7]

Stolypin and his cabinet, on the other hand, devoted considerable attention to Finnish affairs, and their failure to transfer this concern to the Nationalists reflects upon the narrowness of the party's understanding and interests. If the Nationalists had been truly committed to Russian nationalism as a supraclass ideology, it would have been reasonable for

5. A. Ia. Avrekh, *Stolypin i tret'ia duma*, p. 53; Geoffrey Hosking, *The Russian Constitutional Experiment* (Cambridge, 1973), pp. 106–116.

6. *Rossiia*, February 17, 1910.

7. PRO, FO 371.979.9721 (March 2, 1910); *Rech'*, April 8, 1910; *Rech'*, May 4 and 11, 1910.

them to voice an interest in Finnish questions that was at least roughly equal to their concern for the problems of the western borderland. Nationalism, insofar as it had a psychological or ideological meaning for the Nationalist Party, supplied an explanation for the west Russian landlords' economic and political weaknesses in relation to economically successful Polish landlords and highly skilled Jewish merchants who were their neighbors. But the Nationalists' members never expressed this specific kind of resentment against the Finns, with whom, after all, they had little contact in everyday life. This disinterest in the Finnish question revealed that the Nationalist Party's particular version of nationalism was quite unlike that of any other group in Russian society.

The Octobrists, the pravye, State Council conservatives, court hangers-on, and official bureaucrats all claimed to be nationalists. Each group had its particular conception of Russian nationalism, but all of them described the character of nationalism in the broadest of terms. Efforts to find a common basis for the various nationalistic conceptions invariably degenerated into banalities and tautologies. Even certain Nationalist Party ideologues participated in this orgy of the obvious. Professor A. I. Sikorskii, a member of the Kiev Club and professor of psychology at the University of St. Vladimir in Kiev, addressed the club on "the Psychological Basis of Nationalism," which he described as "the moral strength, spiritual power, and psychic energy which represent the most important elements in the national life of humanity.... Nationalities of all countries illuminate the emotional qualities and spiritual power of their peoples."[8] Professor P. I. Kovalevskii of St. Petersburg was similarly vague in describing the task of a nationalist party, which had to "struggle for the welfare, happiness, greatness, power, and consciousness of the entire nation."[9]

In comparison to other conservative and patriotic groups, the Nationalist Party was particularly sensitive to the relatively modern distinction that had emerged between the nation and the state that governed it.[10] Savenko came to talk of an "old nationalism and a new nationalism." He compared the "cosmopolitan bureaucracy" of Petersburg with the true

8. I. A. Sikorskii, *O psykhologicheskikh osnovakh natsionalizma*, p. 1.

9. P. I. Kovalevskii, *Russkii natsionalizm i natsional'noe vospitanie*, p. 89.

10. A broad consensus of historically oriented theorists of nationalism, whose own efforts at defining nationalism are not very useful, do at least agree that the distinction between nation and state became clear only after the French Revolution of 1789. See E. H. Carr, *British Institute Task Force on Nationalism* (London, 1939), p. 3; F. H. Hindsley, *Nationalism and the International System* (London, 1973), p. 19; Elie Kedourie, *Nationalism* (London, 1960), pp. 9–14; Hans Kohn, *The Idea of Nationalism* (New York, 1944), pp. 10–13; and Lewis Snyder, *The Meaning of Nationalism* (New Brunswick, 1954), pp. 74–84.

spirit of the Russian nation, contrasting loyalty to a multinational empire with love of a culturally and linguistically defined nation. The Russian people were the true basis of the Empire; therefore, the state should be a Russian state and not an amalgam.[11] The nationalism of the west Russian gentry was the product of their sense of inferiority and fear of non-Russian national groups. In fact, they were mistrustful of the state, which did not always defend them against Poles and Jews. This mistrust of a "nonnational" impartial bureaucracy distanced the west Russian gentry from the state.

This approach to the problem differed sharply from other recent forms of nationalism. The Nationalist Party did not espouse the sort of conservative integrative or *Étatiste* nationalism that had propelled the unifications of Germany and Italy, nor, for obvious reasons, did it embody the progressive force of an oppressed nationality in a multinational empire. The Nationalists were not a group that fostered the ideology of nationalism. They were a party organized to defend the interests of the dominant nationality in a multinational empire, which was governed by a bureaucracy that did not always support that dominant nationality.

As Professor Kovalevskii later sought to make clear, despite Savenko's distinction between nation and state, any nationalist party was ultimately a party of order.[12] The west Russian gentry could complain about the shortcomings of the state apparatus, but these criticisms arose from a need to make the bureaucracy more responsive to their particular problems, not from a profound desire to change it. Therefore, the Nationalist Party practiced an especially expediential, unromantic, and nonideological version of Russian nationalism. Men like Menshikov, who could become highly emotional and even mystical when talking of the Russian nation, were not comfortable with this more practical approach. Members of the Nationalist Party became aware of themselves as Russians in opposition to the national aspirations of the Germans, Poles, and Jews who shared the west with them. They became disenchanted with the state when it did not create sufficient advantages for the Russian population in the borderland. Their appeals to nationalism were in effect demands that the state that they criticized aid them in their struggle against the Poles and Jews. Just as they sought to maintain loyalty to both the state and the organs of popular representation, the Nationalists sought the advantages of political independence and government support. The passage of the

11. *Kievlianin*, April 1 and September 2, 1912.
12. Kovalevskii, *Osnovy russkago natsionalizma*, p. 14; and *Psikhologia russkoi natsii*, p. 10.

western zemstvo bill would permit them to control local goverment on their own, but they were asking the state to create the rigged conditions that would give them that control. Only Stolypin's support of their cause permitted the Nationalists to maintain this precarious balance.

The Western Zemstvo Bill

One hesitates to characterize the Nationalists as a one-issue party. Nevertheless, it is impossible to minimize the centrality of the western zemstvo bill not only for the Nationalists but, from this point on, for Stolypin as well. The bill was introduced into the Duma on January 21, 1910, just ten days before the formal opening of the National Union. The most controversial element in the western zemstvo bill was its third article, which, by dictating the composition of national curiae, was designed to limit Polish participation.

Acceptance of the extension of the zemstvo principle to the west was never really an issue, and most center and right-wing deputies accepted that principle of national curiae. Left Octobrists, however, sought to reduce the impact of the national curiae.[13] The government wished to allot places in the new zemstvo according to the mean of two demographic percentages: the percentage that each nationality comprised of the total population, and the percentage of all property owned by each nationality. Thus, if the Poles in one gubernia made up 10 percent of the population and owned 20 percent of the property, they would receive 15 percent of the seats in the zemstvo. This formula represented a tortured compromise between the old property principle and the newer national distinction.

Fears had also been voiced, mainly in the State Council, that a zemstvo not based entirely on property qualifications would be overrun by middle and small landowners. Although no more than one-third of any uezd or gubernia zemstvo could be composed of communal peasants, the fear of a peasant zemstvo remained and was used by opponents of the bill. There were other elements in the proposal to protect Russian interests. Three places in each uezd and four in each gubernia zemstvo were accorded to priests; the president of the zemstvo board, which carried out daily operations, and one-half the board were to be Russian; and half the zemstvo employees, always a politically suspect group, had to be Russian. Jews were totally excluded from participation.[14]

Savenko and Rakovich led a deputation of Kiev Club members to

13. *Rossiia*, February 3 and March 26, 1910.
14. E. Chmielewski, *The Polish Question in the Russian State Duma*, p. 100.

Petersburg in order to lobby for the bill. Their special targets were those Octobrists who harbored doubts because of what Savenko called their ignorance of local conditions in the west.[15] However, at a joint meeting of interested Nationalists and Octobrists, held on the eve of committee discussion of the bill, it became clear that differences between the two parties persisted. The Octobrists were also sharply divided among themselves.[16]

The Octobrists in the Committee on Local Government, which began discussing the bill on March 3, quickly opened a campaign aimed at amending the proposed bill. The first of their recommendations involved reducing the full property requirement for participation in the election by one-half. They succeeded in removing all restrictions on employees and zemstvo board members, although the president of each board still had to be Russian.[17] The most bitterly contested Octobrist amendment was made by A. N. Bariatinskii. He suggested that the percentage of zemstvo places be based exclusively on the percentage of property owned by each nationality. The Nationalists did not support this amendment. Because Poles owned so much land, they would have received a few more places; thus, this amendment would have created a solid and vocal Polish minority, instead of a small, weak, and isolated group in each zemstvo.[18] The committee's acceptance of this new scheme outraged the Nationalists.[19]

Pototskii, Shulgin, and Chikhachev led the Nationalists' struggle in defense of the unamended government bill. They were able to win agreement to the notion that those zemstvo employees concerned with education would have to be Russian, but they were unsuccessful in preserving the extensive role for the clergy planned in the government's bill. Only one priest (rather than three) was to be permitted in each district and provincial zemstvo. These defeats soured the Nationalists on the project. They began to talk of voting against the bill and hinted that the government should consider removing it from consideration rather than have it passed by the Duma in an inadequate form.[20]

These developments did not go unnoticed in Kiev. On April 1, Professor Chernov chaired a club meeting on the Octobrists' amendments. He argued that the changes now made the western zemstvo bill "a powerful

15. *Sbornik kluba russkikh natsinalistov*, tretii vypusk (1911), p. 58.
16. *Rossiia*, March 2, 1910.
17. Chmielewski, *The Polish Question*, p. 89.
18. Hosking, *The Russian Constitutional Experiment*, p. 154.
19. *Novoe Vremia*, March 14, 1910.
20. *Rech'*, March 24, 1910; *Novoe Vremia*, March 24, 1910.

weapon for the Polonization of the borderland."[21] Those present agreed that it was better to refuse the law entirely than to accept the version worked out by the Duma committee. Telegrams of protest were sent off to Stolypin and Kryzhanovskii, as well as to the councils of the Nationalists, Octobrists, and pravye. Two weeks later, protest meetings were held in Kiev, Minsk, Vitebsk, and Podol'e.[22] The public outcry of those most affected by the bill must have had some impact, for the entire Committee on Local Government, which had created the amendments, rejected the amended bill. The Nationalists and pravye were joined by those Octobrists who had changed their minds. Thus, in his report to the Duma, D. N. Chikhachev, the committee's reporter, was compelled to oppose the bill as amended by the committee.[23]

The Duma did not turn its attention to the bill until the middle of May. In the interval, the National Club began a series of lectures and meetings, urging passage of the original government version.[24] The National fraction in the Duma was scrambling to assure support for the proposal. Many priests, incensed at the new restrictions on clerical participation, were considering not voting at all. Balashev, fearing that this move would assure the bill's defeat, sent each Duma priest a letter.

> Highly esteemed fathers and pastors:
> It has come to our knowledge that in consequence of the unwillingness of the majority of the committee to allot more than one representative to the clergy in the zemstvos you, spiritual fathers, have decided to abstain from voting for the whole bill. In this manner ... the bill will undoubtedly be rejected.... Undoubtedly when the question of zemstvos for the western and southwestern region again comes before the Duma we shall no longer hear so bold a pronouncement on the part of the government of the principles professed by us....
> Respected Fathers! You are giving our gubernias into the hands of aliens; you are imperiling the significance and local weight of the right parties.[25]

It was in this climate of intense concern that D. N. Chikhachev delivered his committee report to the Duma.[26] Chikhachev was opposed to the bill in the form worked out by the committee and urged its replacement by the

21. *Sbornik kluba russkikh natsionalistov*, vtoroi vypusk, p. 57.

22. Ibid., p. 58.

23. *Rech'*, April 8, 1910; *Novoe Vremia*, April 8, 1910; Hosking, *The Russian Constitutional Experiment*, pp. 121–124.

24. *Okrainy Rossii*, No. 18 (May 1, 1910):276.

25. PRO, FO 371.780.21889 (June 15, 1910).

26. *Rech'*, March 10 and May 18, 1910.

government version. He was especially against making property the sole basis for determining the allocation of zemstvo places for each nationality. He argued against changing the soslovie basis of the 1890 law. Instead, he stressed the loyal services of the Russian nobility and the need to protect them in their struggle against disloyal alien elements. This necessity to protect the Russian gentry required a modification of standard procedures to fit the peculiarities of the region. In no way did he suggest a rejection of the historical dominance of the zemstvo by the nobles, and nowhere in his report did he support the idea of broader representation for the peasantry.[27] Shulgin reiterated the Nationalists' desire to avoid creating "too democratic" a zemstvo in which "cultured" elements would be dominated by the uneducated.[28] Bogdanov was even more explicit in claiming a leading role for the Russian nobility and a subordinate one for the peasantry. He argued that the Russian peasantry could not expect fair treatment from Polish nobles who would control a zemstvo without national curiae. Only the *noblesse oblige* of their brother Russians could assure justice for the peasants.[29] The fact that these brother Russians happened to be noble was purely coincidental.

The Nationalists had no intention of making the western zemstvo into a broadly democratic body. They may have used the term "Russian people" in making their case, but it was clear from their own arguments that what they really meant was the Russian gentry. This is not to say that they denied the peasantry any possible role or that their expressions of concern were hypocritical. Indeed, along with their enemies, the Nationalists envisioned cadres of small landowners, freed by the Stolypin reform, that could function as a source of potential support for conservative nationalism. Nevertheless, they had no desire, as right wingers in the State Council feared, to allow the peasants to gain control of the new zemstvos.

By contrast, Stolypin's presentation of the western zemstvo bill paid considerably more attention to the region's peasantry. He complained that the small percentage of the total population that was Polish should not dominate what was an overwhelmingly Russian region. He opposed most of the Octobrist amendments, although he did come to accept the reduction of the property requirement. This concession, however, was coupled with a warning that the representation of individual small landowners be limited in order to protect "cultured" elements.[30]

The Duma debate did little to clarify the bill's ultimate fate. Much of the

27. Sten. ot., 3.3.4.729.
28. Ibid., 953.
29. Ibid., 791.
30. Ibid., 774 and 1391.

uncertainty centered around the Octobrist fraction, which was evenly divided. The Nationalists prepared their attack on the amendments by calling for an article-by-article reading in order to return the bill to its original state.[31] As things turned out, the Nationalists and their supporters won the most important battles, although they suffered defeats on other amendments.[32] Most significantly, the Duma accepted the government's formula for the organization of the national curiae. However, the property requirement was kept at one-half of that prevailing elsewhere in Russia.[33] The Nationalists were also enormously upset by the Duma's decision to limit the participation of the clergy to the provisions of the 1890 law, which accorded the church one representative per zemstvo.[34] The Nationalists had wanted the clergy to take a major role in the new zemstvos, and their eventual acceptance of the Duma's formula represented a serious compromise of an essential element of their political strategy.

The final version of the bill was accepted by the Duma on May 29, 1910, by a vote of 165 to 139. The majority was made up of Nationalists, many Octobrists, and some pravye. In opposition were the Kadets, the Progressisty, many left Octobrists, and many of the most extreme pravye.[35] The bill now went to the State Council where it encountered fierce opposition.

The Kholm Question

The attempt to create a new Russian gubernia, to be called Kholm, out of the Polish provinces of Lublin and Siedlice is often lumped together with the proposal to extend the law of 1892 on city government to Poland. Although both projects were consistent with the attitudes of Stolypin and his new allies, the specific timing of the two bills makes it impossible to fit them precisely into the framework of the National Campaign. However, the National Campaign did signify a new trend and represented a potentially important institutional precedent of cooperation between a premier and a specific political party. Despite the conservative content of the National Campaign, many old-line reactionaries were highly distressed by its novel form. Neither the Kholm nor the Polish city government bills played central roles in this process. They were originated long before 1910 and were decided after Stolypin's death. Nevertheless,

31. *Rech'*, May 13, 1910.
32. *Rech'*, May 16, 1910.
33. *Novoe Vremia*, May 18, 1910.
34. *Obzor deiatel'nosti gosudarstvennoi dumy, tretii sozyv. 1907–1912 gg.*, ch. 2, p. 86.
35. E. Chmielewski, "Stolypin's Last Crisis," *California Slavic Studies*, Vol. 3 (1964):105.

these bills were an important element of public debate during the period of the National Campaign.

The leading exponent of the Kholm legislation was the head of the Nationalists' clergy group, Archbishop Evlogii. He represented the Russian population of the Polish provinces of Lublin and Siedlice, from which he proposed to create the new gubernia of Kholm. As early as 1906, Evlogii had advanced this proposal before the second Duma. He made the creation of a Kholm gubernia his primary purpose in the third Duma.[36] In 1907, Kryzhanovskii had been entrusted with the task of elaborating such a bill,[37] which was finally introduced into the Duma on May 2, 1909, only to come up for discussion in November 1911.[38]

As early as 1909, Evlogii began actively lobbying for the Kholm bill. Convinced that they disdained serious legislative work and were too isolated to support his efforts in gaining passage of the project, he left the pravye fraction.[39] Since no one in the Duma was exceptionally interested in his plans, Evlogii decided to take his case to what he called the public, but which was in fact educated conservative society. Late in 1909, Evlogii organized a meeting of leading Russian figures in Kholm to demand separation.[40] Throughout the committee sessions on the western zemstvo bill, Evlogii sought to direct attention toward the Kholm question. Concern with the problems of the borderland made the Nationalists more receptive to related matters than the other fractions were, and the National Club devoted a number of meetings to the Kholm problem.[41] V. A. Bobrinskii was particularly active in publicizing the situation there.[42] At the end of the spring session of 1910, Evlogii made use of a device that the Nationalists were to employ later. Riding in a special railway car provided by the Ministry of Communications (still headed by Rukhlov), Evlogii led a group of Nationalist deputies to Kholm in order to demonstrate the seriousness of the local situation and to arouse the interest of the Duma.[43]

The spring of 1910 was the height of the National Campaign, and a special Duma committee on the Kholm question met to discuss the bill at that time. The Nationalists desired to increase the size of the proposed gubernia and the government quickly acceded to their wish. Indeed,

36. Mitropolit Evlogii, *Put' moei zhizni* (Paris, 1947), p. 189.
37. Ibid, p. 212.
38. Chmielewski, *The Polish Question*, p. 117; *Rossiia*, May 2, 1909.
39. Evlogii, *Put' moei zhizni*, p. 213.
40. Avrekh, *Stolypin i tret'ia duma*, p. 110.
41. *Okrainy Rossi*, No. 13 (March 27, 1910):26; *Rossiia*, March 27, 1910.
42. *Novoe Vremia*, March 20, 1910.
43. Avrekh, *Stolypin i tret'ia duma*, p. 109; *Rossiia*, June 6, 1910.

Kryzhanovskii, who appeared before the committee, later claimed that he had received orders from Stolypin "not to oppose the wishes of the Nationalists."[44] But even the Nationalists were not especially concerned with the bill. Disturbed that the committee had not reported the measure as late as 1911, Evlogii went to see Stolypin.

> In the spring of 1911, before the recess, I went to P. A. Stolypin. He was on my side, and because of his clear, nationalist vision, it was easy for me to talk to him. Stolypin promised to take the fate of the bill into his hands that fall.[45]

Soon thereafter, on April 22, 1911, the committee finally passed the bill, preparing it for Duma discussion that fall.[46] When the bill at last came before the lower house that November, it was quickly passed, and, after brief discussion, the State Council also acted favorably on it, permitting Evlogii to retire from the Duma at the end of the last session with his fondest wish granted.[47]

The Polish city government bill represented an attempt to compensate Poland for the loss of Kholm, but the actual structure of the proposal made it apparent that the government was also seeking to preserve the rights of the Russian minority in Poland. The law of 1892 on urban self-government was to be extended to the Polish territories, but with the addition of three national curiae, one for Russians, one for Poles, and one for Jews. Like the Kholm proposal, the issue of urban government in Poland had been raised as early as 1906. However, the Council of Ministers did not begin to work on a bill until October 1909.

The Russian minority was to be protected by a provision entitling it to one representative even if there were only five Russian residents in a city. The tsar retained the right to suspend city dumas, and Russian was to be their official language. Jews were particularly restricted. Even if they composed 50 percent of a city's population, as they did in some Polish towns, they could not receive more than 20 percent of the seats in any city duma. The Poles, opponents of national curiae in the western gubernias, accepted such strictures in Poland in order to ensure a subordinate position for Jews. Anti-Semitism was one of the few issues on which Russians and Poles could agree.[48]

The Nationalists did not devote much public attention to the Polish city government bill until early in 1911. The National Club and various satellite

44. S. E. Kryzhanovskii, *Vospominania*, p. 136.
45. Evlogii, *Put' moei zhizni*, p. 223.
46. *Okrainy Rossii*, No. 19 (May 7, 1910):289.
47. Sten. ot., 3.5.1.2601.
48. Chmielewski, *The Polish Question*, p. 138.

organizations held public lectures on it in the early spring.[49] Not coincidentally, the Polish urban government bill came before the Duma just two days before the Kholm legislation was passed. The Duma finally cleared the proposal in February 1912, but it ran into trouble in the State Council. Numerous changes were made, and attempts to reconcile the Duma and State Council versions dragged on until 1914, when a final version was rejected by the upper chamber in April of that year. As a result, the idea was simply forgotten.

Neither the Polish city government bill nor the Kholm question excited intense passion even during the height of the National Campaign. But they did provide subsidiary issues that permitted the Nationalists to broaden their concerns somewhat and organize on a wider basis than mere support of the western zemstvo bill.

The Early Growth of the Nationalist Party

Although some growth did occur, the creation of the National Union did not result in the immediate influx of large numbers into the ranks of the Nationalist Party. Neither did the reflected glory of being the center of parliamentary events result in the opening of many new branches. The expansion that did occur was the result of intense, specific, and serious organizational work. By the end of 1910, the National Union claimed 1,525 dues-paying members, 711 in the provinces and 814 in Petersburg. In addition to the Petersburg group, the Nationalists now claimed fifteen local branches. However, provincial organizations that had affiliated with the National Union—the most important being the Kiev Club of Russian Nationalists—were not actually listed as branches. Thus, the union's own description of its growth underestimated its strength, because the Kiev Club was the single most powerful element in the nationalist movement.[50] The affiliated units in the west had also grown in 1910.[51] The Kiev Club of Russian Nationalists now numbered over 700, and the Podol'e Union of Russian Nationalists claimed 250 members.

Agitation and organizational activity was concentrated in the localities. The members of the Nationalists' Duma fraction actively toured the provinces to acquaint themselves with local political trends and inform

49. *Okrainy Rossii*, No. 10 (March 3, 1911):156, and No. 11 (March 12, 1911):171.

50. *VNS* (1910), p. 15; A. A. Bobrinskii, "Dnevnik A. A. Bobrinskogo," *Krasnyi Avkhiv*, Vol. 26, p. 143.

51. Ibid.

people of the program of the National Union. The union's council advertised the new party in the provinces through trips, public lectures, and the personal persuasion of important local figures. N. N. Ladomirskii returned to Mogilev for the summer. Soon several branches were formed there. V. A. Bobrinskii and L. V. Polovstov went to Novgorod, and the rest of the fraction agitated in their own constituencies during the summer recess.[52] As Evlogii had done in Kholm, the party organized train trips for deputies to meet local supporters and acquaint themselves with the demands of the local Russian population. In November 1910, the party set up a series of trips whose stated goal was to unify the Nationalists for the election campaign to the fourth Duma.[53]

The Nationalist Party was also faced with the necessity of revising its structure, inherited from the old National Union, in order to accommodate the new provincial forces that had begun to enter the nationalist movement. Because the old union was essentially a Petersburg organization, little provision had been made for the delegation of representatives from provincial groups. The union's official membership lists still numbered more people in the capital than in the localities. But, when the affiliated groups in the localities were included, the direction of the union's evolution toward the provinces was clear. Despite this, no attempt had been made to create a structure that would permit the affiliated organizations to have an influence at the union's center.[54] In fact, there was considerable confusion about the precise roles of the union's *glavnyi sovet* (main council) and its Petersburg branch. Many provincial Nationalists claimed that the *Peterburgtsy* had usurped the role of party center. The capital group remained a stronghold of Menshikov and his supporters. Thus, this struggle was political as well as organizational. Local branches were demanding that the glavnyi sovet, not the Petersburg branch, run the union. They also sought a clarification of procedures that would guarantee them representation in proportion to their numbers.[55]

The Kiev Club, the Podol'e Union, the Viatka Monarchist Party, and several other groups sent representatives to the capital to affirm their solidarity with the Nationalist Party and to request their own representatives on the glavnyi sovet. After much haggling, the glavnyi sovet decided to form a committee to work out the controversy. After a month of deliberation, the committee assigned a lesser role to the branch, granted the meeting of delegates the highest organizational status, constituted the

52. Ibid., p. 13.
53. *Rech'*, November 16, 1910.
54. *VNS* (1910), p. 10.
55. Ibid., pp. 11–15.

glavnyi sovet from among the elected representatives of the local and capital groups, and elected the bureau from among the glavnyi sovet.[56]

These decisions represented a victory for the provincial Nationalists and a significant, politically necessary, redirection of the party's focus. The party had accepted the notion that communication between the national center and local groups was a key element in the modern organization of political power. If the party had not made the change, it probably would have been doomed to lose touch with the provinces; moreover, the local groups would never have been afforded a national forum for their demands. The central body would have passed from the scene, following the path on which the Octobrists appeared to have embarked, and the feelings of the local Russian nobles would have remained just that— sentiments devoid of any concrete political substance. The creation of a structure to marshal those sentiments gave the Nationalists the ability to capitalize on the anticipated western zemstvos in order to strengthen their base in the provinces.

The National Campaign was the first concrete manifestation of the new party's importance. The Nationalists now controlled nearly one hundred votes. Stolypin was quick to solicit their support, primarily by introducing the western zemstvo bill. Since he now began to cooperate with the Nationalists, most contemporary observers began calling them the new government party. For the first time in Russian history, a premier was cooperating with a particular party on a program of legislation, the major part of which was based on the most direct interests of that party's constituents. In return for this cooperation, the party furnished the premier with a base of support not only in the Duma but among the public. The Nationalists, in all but the most formal sense, became Stolypin's party, and he had become their man at the top. At the same time, the Nationalists began the slow, painstaking process of building a power base in the localities on which they could rely in forthcoming electoral tests. Even though it was primarily limited to legislative events, the National Campaign imparted a sense of dynamism and purpose to the Nationalists' cause and enabled them to begin the process of building a national political party. In doing this, they had the support of the most powerful political figure in Russia.

By this point, it was clear that the Nationalists considered the western zemstvo bill to be the necessary basis for the expansion of their political power as well as the control of life in the borderland. If the bill were defeated, the party's efforts throughout the course of the third Duma

56. Ibid., p. 16.

would have been rendered worthless. Such a failure would have exposed them as powerless on both national and local levels. They had placed their hopes on Stolypin, who had advanced this and related projects through the Duma, and they were prepared to render him the support that he expected for his efforts. But, if Stolypin could not deliver the western zemstvo, the entire National Campaign would have been a waste of time. His attempt to enlist and reward the support of the Nationalists would have become meaningless if he had been unable to gain passage of the most important element in the National Campaign. The western zemstvos represented the Nationalists' best hope for an organizational basis for the elections to the fourth Duma, and the Nationalists were in turn the premier's best hope for his own political future. Their combined efforts during the past two years had been leading to the creation of the western zemstvo, which would then permit the creation of a political machine that could assure still further electoral success.

Though the Nationalists had ambitions of power and influence, it was by no means clear what they would do with that power, once it had been won. While Stolypin's agrarian and local government reforms had presented an alternative view of Russia's future to the nation, the Nationalists' commitment to that vision was by no means clear. While the premier had some sense of where he was headed, the Nationalists did not. So long as he advanced their interests and preserved law and order, they were willing to offer support and go along for the ride. As a conservative party, they avoided any explicit delineation of their plans. While they had offered a program at the time of their formation, that document omitted far more than it included. Changing Russia, after all, was not their mission. Concerned more with preservation than renovation, the Nationalist Party did not feel compelled to propose the same kind of broad reforms that Stolypin had advanced. For them, control of the Duma and the support of the president of the Council of Ministers meant only that the tsar would now have to pay greater attention to the needs of the Nationalists and their constituency.

The Western Zemstvo Crisis

The political crisis touched off by the State Council's rejection of the western zemstvo bill proved to be the denouement of Stolypin's career. In the midst of these events, he demonstrated such a fanatical devotion to the project that students of the Duma period have concluded that he was at the end of his rope and therefore incapable of acting rationally. Indeed, if one looks only at the Duma and not at the provinces, it is difficult to find the logic of Stolypin's actions. The few attempts by historians to find a rational core to his behavior stress Stolypin's desire to resurrect his old relationship with the Octobrists in order to go back to the better days of 1908. Neither the so-called irrational nor the rational explanation pays attention to the fundamental structural relationships that gave rise to the western zemstvo bill in the first place. Nowhere in the literature can one find a description of the bill's significance for the Nationalists' constituency, or an explanation of Stolypin's belated acceptance of their demands. Yet, the partnership between Stolypin and the Nationalists provides both of them with a plausible motive for their intense commitment. It is odd that previous explanations of the western zemstvo crisis do not mention this aspect of the situation, when, in fact, the premier's relationship with the Nationalist Party gave rise to the demands that touched off the crisis.

By February 1911, rumors were spreading of intrigues in the State Council against the western zemstvo bill. Count Witte, P. N. Durnovo, V. F. Trepov, and others in the right wing of the State Council had expressed concern about the national curiae and the peasantry's potential role in the new zemstvos. They feared that Stolypin was in the process of creating a novel political system in which his authority might eclipse that of the autocrat. Because the western zemstvo bill had become the central element of Stolypin's political system, his opponents, who were also motivated by personal jealousy of Stolypin's success, realized that they must center their attack on this measure.

Sensing trouble, the Kiev Club sent a deputation to Petersburg to lobby for the bill among members of the State Council. Led by Professor Chernov, the delegation arrived in the capital on January 24 and held a meeting with several right-wing State Council members. The next day, they met at the National Club with the Council's center group, led by Stolypin's brother-in-law, A. B. Neidgart. Many in the center group, who had been the premier's strongest source of support in the upper house, had voiced reservations about the reduction of the property requirement. However, their main concern was the matter of the national curiae, which were defended by Rakovich and a newcomer to Nationalist politics, Vsevolod Iakovlevich Demchenko, a civil engineer who was a member of the Kiev city duma and the Kiev Club. On January 26, they visited the president of the State Council, M. G. Akimov, who also opposed the bill. Later in the day, the Kiev Nationalists were presented to the tsar, who expressed support for their demands, after which they met with Stolypin who assured them that the project would pass.[57]

The reservations of the State Council members quickly became evident

---

57. *Sbornik kluba russkikh natsionalistov,* tretii vypusk, p. 58.

once the bill was discussed article by article. The upper chamber had never been a haven of support for independent public activity. It was to defeat similar proposals for zemstvos in Siberia, the Don region, and Orenburg. Many members of the State Council were distressed by the lowering of the property requirement, which meant that peasants possessing one-tenth of the full property requirement would be allowed to vote and participate independently. It was feared that, with many strong, private, small holders in the west, the new zemstvos would be overrun by a group that might furnish mass support for the premier.[58] Moreover, the possibility of participation by large numbers of peasants was thought to be inherent in the voting schedules the bill established for the national curiae.

It was natural that Stolypin's opponents should attack the national curiae which were the central element of the bill. Thus, Witte's primary argument did not focus on the peasantry. Instead, he stressed the threat posed to a multinational empire by narrow nationalist thinking. National curiae, he argued, constituted an admission that non-Russian nationalities had different interests than Russians did. If this contention were true, it provided a strong justification for their disloyalty. But, according to Witte, the Polish nobility, against whom the bill was aimed, had proven their loyalty to the tsar. The curiae were simply an artificial method of control that greatly inflated the role of the Russian nobility.[59]

It distressed Witte to see conservative Polish and Russian nobles pitted against each other, but in fact, the two groups already had been opposed to each other for years. To the western Nationalists, Witte's homilies on the loyalty of all people to the autocrat in Petersburg were absurd. In the west, these "loyal" Poles were stealing the land of genuinely loyal Russians, while bureaucrats, ignorant of conditions there, were advocating the subjugation of hard-pressed Russians to an outmoded institutional structure. To the Nationalists, Witte's sudden love of all nations marked him at best as a Pollyanna and at worst as a hypocrite.

The right-wing members of the State Council were understandably distressed to learn that Nicholas had expressed support of the project. V. F. Trepov obtained an audience with the tsar just before the crucial vote on the national curiae, and, after much begging, received royal permission for those deputies opposed to the bill to vote "their conscience." Trepov then transmitted this news to his colleagues who had been reluctant to vote against the wishes of the autocrat. Trepov's meeting with the tsar

58. Gosudarstvennyi Sovet, *stenograficheskie otchety* (1910–1911) 6.25.1253.

59. Chmielewski, "Stolypin's Last Crisis," p. 108; Alexandra Shecket Korros, "The Nobility, the State Council and Stolypin," in Leopold Haimson (ed.), *The Politics of Rural Russia, 1905–1914*, p. 137.

remained secret, and neither Stolypin nor his cabinet became aware of it until March 4. On that day, the State Council shockingly defeated the national curiae by a vote of 98 to 62, as Poles, Kadets, and right-wingers joined together in opposition.[60] Sensing that his entire political system was on the brink of disaster, Stolypin, in a tactical move, submitted his resignation to the tsar.

From March 4, speculation about how Nicholas would react to Stolypin's request to resign ran rampant in the capital. After the defeat of the national curiae, the Nationalist Party mobilized its full forces in both the capital and the provinces. In addition to demonstrating public support for the western zemstvo bill, the Nationalists wanted to remind Stolypin of the continued loyalty of his Duma allies. That day, the National Duma fraction held a meeting and issued a protest against the defeat of the national curiae. They cited the Kiev meeting of 1909 as proof that the local population desired such a zemstvo.[61]

Yet, compared to the screams of anguish that emanated from the west, the protests raised in Petersburg were mere whimpers. *Podolianin* defended the importance of Nationalist policies. It traced the history of the national movement, stressing its sense of dynamism, which it likened to "a wave." It was crucial that this feeling of expanding strength and power not be thwarted.[62] The implication was clear enough. Reintroduction of the bill and a second debate in both houses would not repair the damage. Maintaining public interest in a new campaign for the bill would have been too difficult. Obviously, more drastic measures were needed.

With this sense of alarm, the Kiev Club met on the morning of March 10 to voice its protest and plan its course of action. So great had been their anticipation of the bill's passage that "the defeat of the project fell on the Russian population of the borderland like thunder from a cloudless sky."[63] The remarks of the Kiev Nationalists stressed their support for the premier and the thanks they owed him for making their struggle his. As Professor Chernov said:

> P. A. Stolypin firmly believed that the salvation of Russia was both nationalism and the strengthening of popular representation. . . . The hopes and aspirations of west Russian public opinion found in P. A. Stolypin a decisive protector and defender. . . . I cannot . . . I do not want to believe it. . . . P. A. Stolypin must remain in power.

60. *Rech'*, March 9, 1911.
61. *Rossiia*, March 10, 1911.
62. *Podolianin*, March 11, 1911.
63. *Sbornik kluba russkikh natsionalistov*, tretii vypusk, p. 69.

Chernov noted that Durnovo, Trepov, and company picked on the western zemstvo bill because they considered it Stolypin's "creation."

> The bill for the introduction of the zemstvo in west Russia made P. A. Stolypin very popular among the Russian political figures of west Russia, making it [the west] the kernel and the stronghold of the Russian national movement.
> The bill . . . will always be inextricably tied to his name. . . . Now we have a society, a national society in which P. A. Stolypin believes.[64]

The provincial branches of the National Union deluged State Council members with telegrams of protest, stressing the interests of the Russian population and the importance of Stolypin's continued tenure in office. The Kiev Club sent Stolypin a telegram on the morning of March 10.

> We look on you as the hope of the new, reviving Russia. . . . The possibility of your exit frightens us. . . . Your leaving is shrouded in mystery. [We see] an abyss of new adventures into which evil forces push our suffering homeland. Accept from us the most sincere expression of our feeling of deepest sympathy and recognition of all that you have given our homeland.[65]

The next day, Stolypin replied that "I firmly believe that the light of the Russian national idea, having glowed first in the west of Russia, will not go out but shortly will illuminate all of Russia."[66] Clearly, Stolypin attached far more meaning to the western zemstvo bill than the mere satisfaction of regional interests.

It is impossible to be certain what precise role this exchange played in influencing the premier. It seems likely that he had made his dramatic decision prior to the actual exchange of telegrams and that he already assumed that the Nationalists would give him their support. Yet it may have convinced him that part of the nation, if not its leading political figures, was on his side. He may have been dealing a blow to such old allies as the Octobrists in acting as he did, but he had not cut ties to all possible sources of support.

Events in Petersburg did not mirror feelings in the western provinces. At a meeting with the cabinet after the State Council rejected the national curiae, Nicholas, feeling remorse for his concession to Trepov, suggested that the bill be reintroduced. He promised to assure its passage. Stolypin

64. Ibid.
65. *Podolskie Izvestia*, March 13, 1911.
66. *Sbornik kluba russkikh natsionalistov*, tretii vypusk, p. 127; *Volyn'*, March 14, 1911; *Kievskaia Mysl'*, March 12, 1911.

replied that he could not wait for another reading of the bill. The State Council would never admit its mistake, and the current party alignments in the Duma were too unreliable to assure the bill's passage. Stolypin knew that the Nationalists alone could not guarantee the acceptance of the bill by the third Duma. Then, in a private audience, he called on the tsar to prorogue the two chambers for three days. During that time, Nicholas could use the emergency powers of Article 87 of the Fundamental Laws to proclaim the western zemstvos by decree. Trepov and Durnovo were to be banished from the capital until January 1912 for their plotting.[67]

After some deliberation, the tsar sent Stolypin a letter detailing his agreement to the plan. He also agreed to permit Stolypin to name thirty appointed members of the State Council in January 1912. This particular provision demonstrates Stolypin's continued concern with legislative and political support and his desire to build a base in both the Duma and State Council.[68] It suggests that he was looking toward a future in which his political position might be assured. Meeting at Tsarskoe Selo on March 10, the two men agreed on the plan. However, Stolypin was convinced that he had been betrayed in the Trepov incident, and he wanted the tsar's written assurance. This was not an unwise step, but it was an admission of the tsar's unreliability. Nicholas put their understanding in writing, but apparently he was shaken by the incident. His relationship with Stolypin was never the same.

The apparent self-destructiveness of Stolypin's behavior during his meetings with Nicholas—his near-hysterical insistence on getting the western zemstvo bill passed—raises questions about his mental state not only at the time of the crisis but in general. His characteristic bravado made it likely that he would act dramatically. By some accounts, he had grown weary of the reactionaries' attacks against him. One is most often presented with a picture of an exasperated man unaccustomed to and displeased with being thwarted. Stolypin appeared to be committing political suicide by threatening Nicholas and alienating the Octobrists. But his strong commitment to the bill did have a fully rational core. It was based on his alliance with the Nationalists and his hopes for the fourth Duma.[69]

67. TsGIA, Leningrad, 1662.1.325.122; V. N. Kokovtsov, *Iz moego proshlogo*, Vol. 1, p. 453; Chmielewski, "Stolypin's Last Crisis," p. 115.

68. Bobrinskii, *Dnevnik A. A. Brobrinskogo*, p. 149.

69. Kokovtsov, *Iz moego proshlogo*, p. 453; Chmielewski, "Stolypin's Last Crisis," p. 122; John Hutchinson, *The Octobrists in Russian Politics*, p. 163; Hugh Seton-Watson, *The Decline of Imperial Russia, 1855-1914* (New York, 1952) p. 633; Alexandre Stolypine, *L'homme du dernier tsar—Stolypine* (Paris, 1927), p. 133; Alfred Levin, "Peter Arkadevich

News of Nicholas's agreement with Stolypin became known the evening of March 10. On March 11, the Duma and State Council were suspended for the period March 12–15, and, on March 14, the tsar decreed the Western Zemstvo Act. The Octobrists made one last attempt before the actual proclamation of the tsar's ukase to forestall what they considered a disaster. Slight as the chance was, they sought to have Stolypin back down from his plan and pursue a more clearly constitutional course. The Octobrist fraction met the morning of March 12, and, with rare unanimity, they passed a resolution calling the use of Article 87 illegal and promising to vote against the bill when it again came before the Duma as the law said it must. That same day, the conservative Octobrist, M. V. Rodzianko led a deputation of party members to Stolypin, urging him not to go ahead with his plan. Guchkov, Stolypin's one-time ally, wrote him, warning of dire consequences.

> I consider it my conscientious duty to implore you to postpone this step. . . . You know how I was your devoted supporter up to these last minutes. . . . I supported the western zemstvo bill. I must say to you, the step which you are taking is fatal, not only for you but for Russia.[70]

However, Stolypin had already reached his decision by this time. The Octobrists, with their influence in the Duma and the country waning, were incapable of making a convincing case. By having the tsar decree the watered-down Duma version rather than the stronger government draft of the bill, Stolypin thought that he had at least met the Octobrists halfway. In addition, given the Octobrists' chronic disunity, he may have thought that Rodzianko's deputation did not necessarily speak for the entire fraction.

Stolypin: A Political Appraisal," *Journal of Modern History* (September 1965):452; Leonid I. Strakhovskoy, "Peter Stolypin: Progressive Statesman," *University of Toronto Quarterly*, Vol. 20 (1951):252; A. S. Izgoev, *P. A. Stolypin*, p. 93; Ludvik Bazylow, *Ostatnie Lata Rosji Carskiej* (Warsaw, 1972), p. 310; Maria von Bock, *Vospominania o moem otse, P. A. Stolypin* (New York, 1953), pp. 222–223. All these accounts describe Stolypin's actions as political suicide. He is described as acting irrationally at the moment of crisis because of mental stress. Von Bock and Kokovtsov attribute the intensity of his commitment to the bill to love of the western borderland in which he had grown up and served as governor. Only Hosking, *The Russian Constitutional Experiment*, pp. 106–149, and A. Ia. Avrekh, "Vopros o zapadnom zemstve i bankrovstvo Stolypina," *Istoricheskie Zapiski*, Vol. 70 (1961):11, see a rational basis for Stolypin's actions. Both stress his relationship with the Octobrists though he was clearly displeasing them at this moment. Because these authors concentrate on the Duma, they ignore the role of his relationship with the Nationalists which provides a possible explanation. In the absence of any archival evidence from Stolypin himself, any explanation must be seen as possible rather than certain.

70. Cited in E. D. Chermenskii, *Borba partii i klassov. . .*, p. 31.

After all, most Octobrists had supported the bill; in fact, Stolypin argued later that he was only carrying out their will. Still, he must have expected objections from the Duma. The Nationalists were not yet numerous enough to help him weather those attacks without damage, but apparently Stolypin was looking beyond what he saw as a momentary setback to a time when he would have the clear support of those social elements represented in a new, more amenable, fourth Duma. The liberal Podol'e daily, *Podolskie Izvestia*, sensed Stolypin's ultimate purpose.

> What is the reason for such love of a yet unborn zemstvo? Why is it so dear to the government? It is the hope of making the national spirit of Russia into real flesh and blood. Right now its organization is going on. The government is devoting great energy [to the project]. Agitation is going on. National meetings are being organized.
>
> The future "right" zemstvo, which the government wants to create by artificial means, will be of service in the elections to the fourth Duma.[71]

What conservatives and liberals in the capital could not see was obvious to progressives in the provinces.

Despite his willingness to run risks in the Duma and State Council, Stolypin clearly underestimated the intensity of the reaction to his decision. He had won a victory of sorts, but criticism in the capital was nearly universal. Guchkov resigned the presidency of the Duma in protest.[72] Much of the Duma was aghast at having been so easily pushed aside. Because its will had been thwarted, the State Council was even more incensed.[73] The liberal press unanimously condemned Stolypin's action, and many conservatives, notably Menshikov, expressed serious reservations about his methods. But the most dramatic result of Stolypin's move was the near complete evaporation of support for him in the Duma.[74] The attempt to reintroduce the bill into the Duma collapsed immediately, and preparations were made instead for an interpellation demanding an explanation of Stolypin's action.[75]

No doubt Stolypin was shocked by the extent and intensity of the reaction. He must have expected criticism, but he probably did not anticipate anything of this scope. Soon thereafter, he attempted to persuade Guchkov to return to the Duma presidency.[76] But, because the

71. *Podolskie Izvestia*, June 1, 1911.
72. Chermenskii, *Borba partii i klassov...*, p. 32.
73. *Kievlianin*, April 9, 1911.
74. *Rech'*, March 3, 1911.
75. *Minskoe Slovo*, March 12, 1911; *Kievskaia Mysl'*, March 12, 1911.
76. *Podolskie Izvestia*, March 29, 1911.

Octobrists had universally condemned Stolypin, cooperation with them now appeared impossible. On the other hand, Balashev, speaking for the National fraction, announced full support of the premier.[77] With the Octobrists drifting toward the opposition and the Nationalists remaining loyal to Stolypin, the Duma's always fragile right-center majority had collapsed. The Octobrists still outnumbered the Nationalists, and they still occupied the Duma's center. Thus, the breakdown of their relations with the Nationalists meant the collapse of the Duma's efficient operation. The Duma rejected Stolypin's response to the interpellation by a vote of 202 to 82. Only the Nationalists supported him.

Neither party unanimously viewed the Duma split without regret. The Minsk branch of the Octobrists, obviously aware of the desires of the local population, issued a protest against the central committee's opposition to Stolypin and withdrew from the party.[78] The Tsarskoe Selo branch expressed serious misgivings about thwarting the legitimate desires of the west Russians in the name of constitutionalist principles.[79] No sooner had the initial shock worn off when characteristic Octobrist disunity began to reappear. The party was soon unable to decide on a single future course of action vis-à-vis the premier. In fact, the election of the relatively conservative Rodzianko as the new Duma president in place of Guchkov was taken as a sign of compromise with Stolypin.[80] A month later much of the passion had cooled, leading one British diplomat to report that

> M. Stolypin's position would therefore seem to be assured for the moment unless weariness of office and of the constant attacks to which he is exposed should lead him once more to tender his resignation.[81]

While the Octobrists sought to reestablish some semblance of a working right-center majority, the Nationalists were deeply divided on their future course. Several members were reluctant to cut all ties with the Duma center. The majority of the party preferred to let matters rest, awaiting the elections to the fourth Duma, which they hoped would create a more favorable situation. A minority, led by Krupenskii, did not wish to give up the hope of constructive work for the remainder of the third Duma. Krupenskii had appointed himself guardian of the Duma center, and his activities since the beginning of the third Duma had been based on creating the kind of relationships that would assure a functioning center

77. *Rech'*, March 14, 1911.
78. TsGAOR 115.1.76.11.6 and 76.
79. Ibid., 1.3.
80. PRO, FO 371.1214.13149 (April 6, 1911).
81. Ibid., 15140 (April 18, 1911).

majority. He had become something of a social director and a compulsive compromiser. Krupenskii had been eclipsed as a parliamentary figure with the formation of the Nationalist Party. One police agent reported Krupenskii had come to resent the fact that Stolypin paid greater attention to Balashev in his dealings with the Nationalists.[82] In addition, Krupenskii was not part of the inner circle of leaders from the borderland.

As a result, two months after the crisis, Krupenskii formed his own Independent Nationalist Party, which included the entire Bessarabian delegation. Only two men from the west, A. A. Pototskii and K. E. Suvchinskii, were members. Thirteen of the eighteen Independent Nationalists were noble landowners. They planned to occupy the seats to the left of the Nationalists but, curiously, pledged complete solidarity with their former comrades.[83] The most explicit public difference concerned the Independent Nationalists' division of non-Russian nationalities into those who could be assimilated and those who could not. Germans, Tartars, and Armenians could play active political roles, while Finns, Poles, and Jews were beyond redemption. In all other matters, Krupenskii's group pledged to vote with the Nationalists.[84]

The question of different varieties of non-Russian nationalities was directly related to the party's future relationship with the Octobrists. At this time, the Duma Committee on Local Government was discussing a bill that would have prevented non-Russians from acquiring land in Volynia, Podol'e, and Kiev. The proposal was primarily directed against the increasing numbers of German colonists who had been buying land in the west.[85] But several men of German ancestry in the Octobrist fraction swore to oppose the proposal. These men threatened to withdraw from the party unless the Octobrists strenuously opposed this bill.[86] Not wishing to provoke the Octobrists, Krupenskii led his group in opposition to the proposal, though he was mainly concerned with the maintenance of cordiality between the Nationalists and the Octobrists. The substance of the bill was secondary. However, because the regular Nationalists considered the anti-German proposal vital to their interests as threatened landowners in the borderland, they were less concerned with harmony in the Duma.[87] Krupenskii later wrote Savenko that

82. TsGAOR 102.4-oe deloproizvodstvo (1908) 119.310.

83. *Rossiia*, May 5, 1911.

84. *Podolskie Izvestia*, May 4, 1911; *Okrainy Rossi*, No. 19 (May 7, 1911):290; PRO, FO 371.1214.19385 (May 17, 1911).

85. *Kievlianin*, May 11, 1911.

86. TsGAOR 115.1.76.24; *Rech'*, May 12, 1911.

87. *Kievlianin*, May 13, 1911.

all my work is based on one slogan, a moderate, that is Nationalist-Octobrist center in the State Duma. And as for elections to the fourth Duma? In Russia all must unite against the opposition.[88]

Both the regulars and independents sought to minimize their differences. But *Kievlianin* could not hide its concern for the future of the Nationalist Party "about which people have talked most recently as a unifying center, around which a working majority might form in the future fourth Duma upon which the government could base itself."[89] K. E. Suvchinskii, who would later work closely with the other Nationalists during the zemstvo and Duma elections, explained the reason for the creation of the fraction in a letter to *Kievlianin*. The creation of the Nationalist Party had moved the moderates to the right, while the Octobrists had gravitated toward the left. "At the present time," Suvchinskii wrote, "there are only right and left wings in the State Duma.... For the creation of a center, a new party was formed."[90] While *Kievlianin's* response to Suvchinskii was mild,[91] S. M. Bogdanov attacked the new party and accused Krupenskii of acting for personal reasons.[92]

In fact, few differences emerged between the groups. Local organizations continued to function together, especially during elections, and Krupenskii remained a member of the National Club and the National Union. It would be a mistake to view the creation of the Independent Nationalists as a catastrophic blow to the regular Nationalists, but the party's sense of momentum had been blunted. Like the Octobrists, they too now experienced splits and divisions.[93]

As a result of Stolypin's efforts, the Nationalist Party was now ready to elect its people to the zemstvos in the western gubernias. The premier had created many enemies in order to obtain the prize his loyal supporters most coveted. But the Russian nobles of the west had been given control of local government, and their party, the Nationalists, now had the opportunity to develop a broad and effective local organization. The experience gained in the campaign to elect Russians to the new zemstvos would then be put to use during the elections to the fourth Duma. It was not unrealistic to expect that, with Stolypin agitating and manipulating on

88. TsGAOR 102 (1911) 265.510.90; Krupenskii, St. Petersburg, to Savenko, Kiev (October 23, 1911).
  89. *Kievlianin*, May 10, 1911.
  90. *Kievlianin*, May 10, 1911.
  91. *Kievlianin*, May 24, 1911.
  92. *Kievlianin*, May 20, 1911.
  93. *Kievlianin*, April 8, 10, 12, and May 6, 1911.

the Nationalists' behalf, a Nationalist majority could be obtained and that the Octobrists and others with constitutionalist notions would be abandoned by the voters. If so, the unpleasantness associated with the western zemstvo crisis might be forgotten. Given their strong provincial base and steady growth, the Nationalists appeared ready to inherit the Octobrists' position as the majority party. But that goal would have been impossible without the passage of the Western Zemstvo Act. The organizational infrastructure could never have been created. Thus, Stolypin was pursuing what might be called, for want of a better term, a "western strategy." He aimed to build solid support in the borderland that could serve as a basis for a permanent conservative majority in the fourth Duma. Permitting the western zemstvo bill to languish would truly have been an act of political suicide. Despite Stolypin's irascibility, impatience, exhaustion, and ill health, there remains a rational core to his actions that cannot be ignored.

The Nationalist Party therefore represents the missing link in our understanding of the western zemstvo crisis. In the absence of personal testimony from Stolypin, any explanation must involve an element of speculation. But the west Russian gentry's championing of the bill, the rise of the Nationalists, the decay of the Octobrists, and the hope of creating a new power base in both legislative chambers gave Stolypin ample reason for taking drastic action. His entire political system was on the line, and he saw only one way out.

Political Organization in Western Russia

Now that the western zemstvos had been created, the Nationalists faced even more serious challenges. In the elections to these new institutions, they had to demonstrate that fears of peasant domination were groundless. More significantly, the party had to clarify just how much state support and interference it would either seek or allow in the election process itself. Because the Ministry of Interior supervised the election process, it was able to render vital assistance to the Nationalists' cause. Party members welcomed this aid, while continuing to pay homage to the notions of political independence and autonomous action. This ambivalence was directly reflected in their actions during the elections to the new zemstvos.

The election also posed a significant test of state attitudes toward the Nationalists. The bureaucracy was far from unanimous concerning its feelings about the Nationalists. There were supporters of the Nationalists within the government (most notably, Stolypin, Kryzhanovskii, and the governor of Kiev, A. A. Girs), but many other officials were either indifferent or opposed to them. In 1911, the party's supporters in the bureaucracy were able to control the electoral process in a way that was beneficial to the Nationalist cause, but by 1912, during the fourth Duma elections, those supporters had left the government. The new president of the Council of Ministers, V. N. Kokovtsov, was an opponent of the party, and bureaucratic assistance became far less consistent.

The first elections to the western zemstvos were, therefore, of considerable importance. First, they revealed the true character of Nationalists' reliance on the state, and, second, they demonstrated that the government's attitude toward the various parties could have an impact on a particular election. The contrast that the zemstvo campaign presents to the later Duma elections is, therefore, of considerable significance and demands a detailed exposition.

The Nationalists' attitude toward local government was unique. Unlike their counterparts in central Russia or their predecessors in the west, the Nationalists made no attempt to divorce local issues from national politics. This attitude was restated by Professor Chernov in his January 1911 report to the Kiev Club on the city duma elections that had been held during September 1910. In their agitation for the election, the Nationalists had fought the old notion that the city duma was solely concerned with the town's economic interests. Seeking to oppose this viewpoint, Chernov argued for the Nationalists

> that popular representation [the Duma] and local government were inextricably connected with each other. It is impossible to divorce the life of society from the life of the state, and it therefore follows, that it is impossible to divorce the social from the political.[94]

To carry out their task that September, the club members had organized a series of district committees that nominated candidates and electioneered among the Russian population in each section of the city. The intensity and specificity of their efforts contrasted sharply with the leisurely and gentlemanly conduct of many central Russian zemstvo elections. This first organizational effort was successful in reducing the Polish representation on the city duma from thirteen to four, but the lessons learned in the process were of even greater significance.[95] The Nationalists were to apply

94. *Sbornik kluba russkikh natsionalistov*, tretii vypusk, p. 54.
95. Ibid.

the relatively simple organizational techniques that worked in the city to the forthcoming zemstvo elections.

The novelty of this approach disturbed local progressives who sought to preserve the notion of the zemstvo as a purely economic and cultural institution. But economics and culture in the west were so clearly intertwined with nationality and politics that the distinction proved impossible to maintain. The progressive *Podolskie Izvestia* wrote:

> One gets the impression that elections to the Duma and not to zemstvos are going on; that they are electing politicians and not zemstvo workers. . . . Up until the promulgation of the great manifesto of October 17, 1905, there were no officially recognized political parties in Russia. However, this did not prevent people from having different political views and still working together in the zemstvos and considering their work of much benefit to the homeland.
> Why is what was possible earlier now impossible?[96]

The marshal of nobility of the Kamenets uezd (Podol'e gubernia), V. N. Markevich, writing in the conservative newspapers of the west, offered a reply to the liberals' complaints. He argued that the zemstvos had been highly political during the Revolution of 1905 when they had been dominated by Kadets. Now that the Kadets had been swept out, they were trying to deceive the voter into believing something that they themselves did not believe. In the present context, there was no way to divorce politics from the zemstvo. The link between the local and national levels was a central element of the modern party systems of the West, and Markevich was well aware of these models in characterizing the Nationalists' view of politics: "In Western Europe and America, elections to local institutions are considered an indicator of how the elections to parliament will go and what the predominant tendency will be in it."[97] Markevich's approach, which was shared by the rest of the party, is remarkable for its sensitivity to the link between national and local politics. Moreover, this awareness was unprecedented in the development of Russia's political parties.[98] For that reason, it is necessary to do what other students of Russian parties have not done—examine these local elections in great detail to demonstrate conclusively their impact on national politics.

The following discussion of the zemstvo elections focuses on three gubernias in which the Nationalists did well—Kiev, Podol'e, and Minsk—

96. *Podolskie Izvestia*, July 12, 1911.
97. *Minskoe Slovo*, May 28, 1911; *Podolianin*, May 22, 1911.
98. *Volyn'*, March 7, 1911.

and on Volynia, a province where their efforts were unsuccessful. In the first three provinces, electoral committees and organizations sprang up, and full-scale political agitation was carried on. The Nationalists were the most vigorous force in this political activity. Stolypin had staked his career on the success of the western zemstvos and the election of conservative Russian majorities to the new bodies was imperative. Only in this way could he recoup the prestige and influence he had lost in the course of the crisis. (It is precisely this possibility that other students of the period have ignored.) The local Nationalists were fully conscious of Stolypin's hopes. At a meeting of the Kiev Club of Russian Nationalists on May 25, Savenko warned that the failure of the zemstvo legislation would be a severe blow to the cabinet and would have a profound effect on the elections to the fourth Duma. In addition, he applauded the changes in the party charter that had given real control to the provincial branches. These modifications, he argued, would have great meaning for the conduct of the fourth Duma as well as for the zemstvo elections.[99]

Kiev

The most intense organizational effort mounted by the Nationalists was in Kiev, where they had their largest and oldest provincial branch. Moreover, this branch of the party had already been battle-tested in the Kiev city elections. In the zemstvo elections, it was to enjoy the direct and indirect aid of the government. In particular, the governor of Kiev, A. A. Girs, proved extremely cooperative. S. N. Gerbel', the head of the Ministry of Interior's Administration of Local Economy was given the task of administering the elections. Accordingly, it was necessary for him and his assistants to inform local leaders of the procedures to be used. Much of this activity was carried on by governors, governors-general, and ministry officials from Petersburg, acting in concert with district marshals of nobility. Not surprisingly, most of the marshals were Nationalists, and they played a crucial role in organizing support.

This government activity, although extensive, was not especially manipulative. Indeed, there was no need; all the manipulation that was necessary had already been written into the bill. Given this desirable situation, it was only necessary to assure that all eligible Russian landlords voted. The efforts of government officials were limited to technical explanations of rules. However, by organizing local meetings of zemstvo voters in order to

99. *Okrainy Rossii,* No. 23 (June 4, 1911):353.

inform them of procedures, the bureaucracy in effect publicized the elections and brought electors together in a setting in which the discussion of politics was inevitable. Moreover, many leading Nationalist figures participated in these meetings. They established committees in each uezd, plus a gubernia committee, which they patterned after the successful example of the city elections.[100]

The first such gathering took place on April 30 in Kiev. It was organized by the old zemstvo board for the representatives of Russian voters with the full property qualification. The uezd marshals of nobility attended, as did one or two representatives of each district's large landowners. The Nationalist landlord, Baron I. M. Reva, and the newcomer, V. Ia. Demchenko, played leading roles in the discussion, which was chaired by Professor Chernov.[101] Demchenko, a noble, was a civil engineer who also had extensive land holdings. He was also a deputy to the Kiev city duma, and a member of the Kiev Club. He came to play an extensive role in the elections to the zemstvos, and used the notoriety gained in that effort to gain a seat in the fourth Duma. At this meeting of the gubernia electoral committee, he suggested the creation of a series of uezd electoral committees to organize local Russian landlords and acquaint them with technical procedures and political issues. That idea was quickly accepted, and several uezd meetings took place shortly thereafter.[102]

The local meetings had varying degrees of success in bringing Russian landlords into the election process. Little or no effort was made to attract peasants and other small landowners. Thus, in each district, a committee of Russian landowners that acted as a semiofficial source of information in directing the election campaign was created. Important Nationalists, including many in the party's Duma fraction, were leading members of these committees. Members of these groups devoted their energy to tactical and organizational questions, but the general political tendency in the committees was clear to most participants. Most important, a structure had been created for the dissemination of information and the discussion

100. *Kievlianin*, April 4, 1911; *Kievskaia Mysl'*, April 5 and 7, 1911. On April 2, 1911, M. A. Sukovkin, president of the old appointive zemstvo, had attended an unofficial meeting at the home of another member of the old board, A. Vishnevskii. Those present included Professor Chernov; V. Ia. Demchenko; D. L. Davidov, the Kiev uezd marshal of nobility; M. A. Kurakin, the gubernia marshal of nobility; and Baron I. M. Reva.

101. *Kievlianin*, May 1, 1911.

102. *Kievlianin*, May 3, 1911; *Kievskaia Mysl'*, May 1, 1911; *Kievlianin*, May 5, 1911; *Kievskaia Mysl'*, May 6, 1911; *Kievlianin*, May 7, 9, and 12, 1911; *Kievskaia Mysl'*, May 7 and 9, 1911.

of issues throughout Kiev gubernia. Controlled by the Nationalists, this structure represented as effective a political machine as any other party had put together.

The Nationalists had not actually created their own organization in the villages. They used the structures established by the state to administer the election for conveying their own appeals. Thus, a network was set up that was not entirely identified with the Nationalists even though the party exercised control over the decisions of the committees.[103] This network served as an effective organizational structure throughout the province. If the Western Zemstvo Act had not been passed, it would not have been possible or necessary to create such a network. Not only were the Nationalists able to gain control of local government, but they were given the chance of creating an effective political organization encompassing much of Kiev gubernia as well. Without government support in creating the bill and in administering the election their efforts would have been useless. The actions of the government had created the possibility for spreading and solidifying the Nationalists' influence. Nevertheless, if the party had had no true constituency, their efforts would have achieved little, regardless of official support.

Minsk

Prior to the proclamation of the Western Zemstvo Act, a number of political groups existed in Minsk gubernia, but none operated with much effectiveness. With the zemstvo elections approaching and the Russian nobility lacking any active political vehicle of its own, the need for the creation of a branch of the Nationalist Party was clear to many. On April 12, a local landowner, D. V. Skrynchenko, took the initiative and invited a collection of about one hundred friends and colleagues to discuss the possibility of setting up a Nationalist group in the province to carry on the campaign for the new zemstvo and later for the fourth Duma.[104]

In essence, there was little actual organizational work to do beyond declaring that those present on April 12 were members of the new Minsk National Union. A more intense organizational effort was planned for after the formal opening of the branch. That event was set for May 19 with V. A. Bobrinskii and A. S. Gizhitskii slated to deliver speeches.[105] The organizers

---

103. *Kievlianin*, July 4, 1911; *Kievskaia Mysl'*, July 4, 1911.
104. *Minskoe Slovo*, April 14, 1911.
105. *Minskoe Slovo*, May 13, 1911.

had made preparations for a gathering of 300, but the active publicity campaign of the local conservative newspaper, *Minskoe Slovo*, resulted in far more than that showing up for the inaugural meeting.[106] Skrynchenko chaired the proceedings, which had attracted, among many others, the governor and the gubernia's Nationalist Duma members. This close participation of the Nationalist Duma members in the activities of local branches was typical of the western provinces.[107]

By the time the Minsk branch of the Nationalists actually began its activity, preparations for the elections had already begun. Lacking a long-standing organization, the Minsk Nationalists played a lesser role in the technical operation of the election than their more experienced counterparts in Kiev did. Nevertheless, the president of the Minsk branch, O. V. Rodzevich, a local landlord, in his capacity as president of the old gubernia zemstvo board, called a meeting of the old uezd zemstvo boards later in March to establish local committees and begin the process of drawing up electoral lists.[108]

The province was the center of considerable attention from the government. N. N. Antsiferov of the Administration of Local Economy paid several visits to Minsk, as did his superior, Gerbel'.[109] In contrast to similar gatherings in Kiev, the meetings organized by these men appear to have been more clearly official in tone if not in actual content. Less effort was made to enlist uezd marshals of nobility in the process, and the only leading Nationalist who consistently attended official meetings was Rodzevich.

The Nationalists in Minsk had to carry on their efforts outside the electoral machinery because, unlike the situation in Kiev, there was less closeness between government officials and local political figures. This situation posed a more difficult electoral task, but the newness of the Nationalists' organization necessitated this course. However, it was a relatively easy task for the Nationalists to rally their natural constituency. The Minsk organization was less advanced than that in Kiev, but the creation of a unit of the National Union must be seen as progress. This nascent organization was to prove sufficient to assure Nationalist success in the zemstvo elections, and the party structure was to grow as the

106. *Minskoe Slovo*, May 20, 1911.

107. *Minskoe Slovo*, May 20, 22, and 24, 1911; *Rossiia*, May 26, 1911; *Okrainy Rossii*, No. 22 (May 28, 1911).

108. *Minskoe Slovo*, March 29, 1911; *Kievskaia Mysl'*, April 22, 1911; *Minskii Golos*, May 31, 1911.

109. *Minskoe Slovo*, May 11, 1911; Minskoe Slovo, June 3, 1911; *Minskii Golos*, June 3 and 4, 1911.

campaign for the fourth Duma approached. These first steps, taken in the spring of 1911, probably would not have been achieved without the proclamation of the Western Zemstvo Act.

Podol'e

Of all the gubernias in the west, the Nationalists had the least to fear in Podol'e. The province's Duma delegation, led by Balashev, Chikhachev, and Gizhitskii, was solidly Nationalist, and the deputies maintained close contact with the localities. The Podol'e Union of Russian Nationalists had been in existence since 1909 and included among its members nearly all the uezd marshals of nobility. The most notable of them was the Union's president, I. A. Rakovich. With the Russian nobility solidly in line, there was little need for the Nationalists to conduct an especially intense campaign.

Nevertheless, Nationalist figures were prominent in the technical preparation of the election. The cooperative governor, A. A. Eiler, called the uezd marshals together in Zhmerik to begin technical operations.[110] Given the strong Nationalist sympathies of the Russian landlords, few big meetings were required. F. F. Trepov, the governor-general of the southwest, however, attended one large gathering on May 23 along with Gerbel', Eiler, the gubernia and uezd marshals of nobility, D. N. Chikhachev, and A. A. Pototskii. At this meeting, their concern was largely with organizational problems. These were dispatched quickly; they then sent a telegram of thanks to Stolypin.[111] Another notable meeting, conducted by V. N. Markevich, occurred at Liantskorun. Rakovich was present at this assembly, where twenty-five invited Russian landlords took the unusual step of forming a committee of four to select zemstvo candidates.[112] Despite the functional nature of these meetings, the Nationalists did not hesitate to use the electoral committees for explicitly political purposes.

In fact, the Podol'e Nationalists had been well organized for some time. Their province was smaller than Kiev, and, by 1911, the party's organization in the gubernia had developed enough to meet the task. Although the Kiev Club was the largest Nationalist group, its area of concern was larger, necessitating a more intense effort than was required in Podol'e. The Nationalists' success in Podol'e can be attributed to the Duma delegation's prestige and influence throughout the gubernia. At one time or another, Balashev, Gizhitskii, Pototskii, and Chikhachev had all been marshals of

110. *Podolianin*, April 1911; *Podolskie Izvestia*, April 2, 1911.
111. *Podolskie Izvestia*, May 28, 1911.
112. *Podolskie Izvestia*, June 8 and 21, 1911.

nobility, and all had extensive contacts among the province's Russian landlords. They had not lost touch with the localities. All had participated in the creation and growth of the Podol'e Union of Russian Nationalists and had maintained close relations with local figures. The liberal daily *Kievskaia Mysl'* accepted this situation with great reluctance.

> In politics, they are ready to serve their base, and in a sense there are no distinctions between Gizhitskii and Chikhachev in the Duma fraction and the unimportant members of Nationalist committees in provincial towns.[113]

The province had sent Nationalists to the Duma, and the deputies had remained true to their calling. Thus, Rakovich was optimistic at the union's agitational meeting on May 14. He saw the possibility of creating Nationalist groups in all the smaller towns of Podol'e and proclaimed the opening of an era when Russian culture would dominate the schools, courts, and politics of the region.[114] Control of the institutions of local government was to give the party the opportunity to defend the interests of the Russian nobility on all levels of life in Podol'e. Now that they had an actual institutional framework, the Nationalists were able to strengthen their grip on local life, which rendered them an even more powerful force in future elections.

Volynia

Volynia was the least promising of the western gubernias. Commercial agriculture was less developed there than in Kiev or Podol'e. Absenteeism among Russian landlords was extensive. Poles comprised a higher percentage of the population than in the other western provinces, and the Nationalists had no organized groups in the gubernia. In addition, unlike Girs and Eiler, the governor of Volynia, A. P. Kutaisov, did little to aid the party's efforts. Instead, he preferred to restrict himself to purely technical matters. The absence of a branch of the National Union exaggerated the party's weakness in Volynia.

There was little preparation for the elections. Attempts to hold agitational meetings in the provincial capital, Zhitomir, were unsuccessful.[115] Nor did the party do an effective job of informing its supporters of dates

113. *Kievskaia Mysl'*, May 8, 1911.
114. *Podolianin*, May 17, 1911; *Podolskie Izvestia*, May 18, 1911.
115. *Volyn'*, June 8, 1911.

and sites of elections. In addition, there was active opposition to the new zemstvos. Many Russian chinovniki, including Kutaisov, were opposed to zemstvos and preferred that the government operate through bureaucratic structures. In administering the elections, these men sought to minimize the disadvantages against the Poles by giving preference to neither nationality.[116] There was also a bloc of Russian landlords in Volynia with Kadet sympathies. This situation made unanimity among the Russian nobility impossible to achieve. Therefore, the Volynia Nationalists viewed their situation as hopeless and responded to the elections with indifference.[117]

Shulgin and Pikhno sought to influence the election process, but were thwarted by Kutaisov at meetings of the uezd marshals of nobility.[118] Shulgin had just officially shifted from the pravye to the Nationalists, but much of the rest of the province's Duma delegation remained pravye. Unlike him, they were not enthusiastic supporters of the zemstvo principle. Faced with an unfavorable distribution of nationalities, poor organization, extensive absenteeism, and an uncooperative bureaucracy, the Nationalists stood little chance of achieving success in Volynia.[119]

The Zemstvo Elections and Their Aftermath

When the elections to the zemstvos actually took place, the fears of those who expected a democratic, peasant-dominated zemstvo proved groundless.[120] Most Poles boycotted the elections, and the results proved as favorable to the Russian landowners as the framers of the Western Zemstvo Act had hoped.[121] *Kievlianin* offered a breakdown of the elected members by political affiliation, which perhaps painted the situation in an inordinately rosy hue for the Russian nobility (see Table 4.1). In view of their later dissatisfaction with the elections in Volynia, the party's description of loyalties there probably credits the right with too much success. In general, the party did better in the southwest than in the three Bielorussian

116. *Kievlianin*, June 28, 1911.
117. *Kievlianin*, May 19, 1911.
118. *Volyn'*, April 7, 1911; *Volyn'*, April 23, 1911.
119. *Kievskaia Mysl'*, June 26, 1911.
120. *Okrainy Rossii*, Nos. 29-30 (July 23–30, 1911): 432. PRO, FO 371.1218.35056 (September 1, 1911).
121. *Minskii Golos*, June 14, 1911; *Minskoe Slovo*, June 9, 1911.

Table 4.1. **Political Affiliation of Members Elected to the Western Zemstvos**

	Pravye and Nationalists	Moderates and nonparty members	Left	Unknown
Kiev	232	2	10	0
Podol'e	199	14	3	0
Volynia	173	15	3	12
Vitebsk	100	29	9	0
Minsk	93	29	14	10
Mogilev	108	35	17	21

Source: Kievlianin, August 17, 1911.

gubernias. The Nationalists had great success in electing their leaders, including Duma members, to the new zemstvos, and they were by no means inundated by a flood of peasant participation.[122]

Demchenko, Savenko, Bogdanov, Protsenko, Suvchinskii, Chernov, and Bezak were chosen in Kiev.[123] Other club members elected to the uezd zemstvos were K. P. Grigorovich-Barskii, A. A. Kikh, O. L. Davidov, I. N. Diakov, and Baron I. M. Reva.[124]

In Minsk, participation was sizeable only among large landowners. In the two smaller property categories, the turnout was extremely light. Igumen uezd was typical. All forty-four large landowners appeared and chose ten of their number.[125] All were described by the provincial governor as rightists. By contrast, only 10 out of 1,098 peasants in the small land-owners assembly bothered to show up.[126] An analysis of the membership of the Minsk gubernia assembly reveals that the Nationalists fulfilled all their expectations in the election (see Table 4.2).[127]

Podol'e produced a similar pattern of low peasant participation coupled with predictably successful Nationalist showings among the large Russian landowners. Many leading Nationalists were elected to positions in the zemstvos. Balashev, Rakovich, Chikhachev, Gizhitskii, Markevich, Aleksandrov, Pototskii, I. V. Avchinnikov, A. A. Savostianov, I. I. Lozinskii, and I. J. Koval', all party activists, were chosen to places in uezd assemblies, signifying the Nationalists' clear leadership of the province's Russian nobility. In most districts, the Poles boycotted the elections (only one

122. *Kievlianin,* August 17, 1911.
123. *Kievlianin,* July 18 and August 3, 1911.
124. *Kievskaia Mysl',* July 5 and 11, 1911.
125. *Minskoe Slovo,* July 13 and 16, 1911.
126. *Minskii Golos,* July 6 and 15, 1911.
127. *Minskii Golos,* July 9, 13, and 17, 1911.

Table 4.2. **Makeup of the Minsk Gubernia Zemstvo**

By soslovie		By nationality[b]	
Nobles	71	Russian	101
Bureaucrats	28	German	5
Merchants	3	Tartar	1
Honorary citizens	8		
Peasants	11	By occupation[c]	
Priests	1	Agriculture	96
Petty bourgeois	8	State or	
		military	
By education[a]		service	69
Higher	50	Trade	1
Secondary	34	Free professions	1
Primary	16		
Domestic	13		
By land ownership			
Owned land			101[d]
Lived on their land			78
Owned estates larger than 500 desiatiny			65[e]

Source: TsGIA 1288.2.42. 256–338.
[a]Information is available for only 113 out of 130 members.
[b]Information is available for only 107 out of 130 members.
[c]Some members may have practiced more than one occupation.
[d]The average holding was 1,733 desiatiny.
[e]The average holding was 2,547 desiatiny.

Polish landlord was elected to a zemstvo).[128] Russian participation among those with the full property qualification was predictably high, but peasants and small property holders were few in number at electoral assemblies. In Vinits, 73 of over 300 eligible peasants showed up; in Mogilev uezd, 16 of 220. In Gaisin, Olgopolskii, and Letichev districts, no peasants appeared at all.[129]

Thus, the Nationalists had achieved all they could have hoped for in Podol'e. The party's local leaders and Duma members had been elected to the new zemstvos, which were almost entirely Russian and noble. The peasantry had posed no serious threat. The provisions of the Western Zemstvo Act had aided the Nationalist struggle, and their own efforts had assured that the margin for possible defeat left by the bill was not filled. Nonetheless, the Nationalists did not forget whom they had to thank for

128. *Kievlianin,* July 9, 1911.
129. *Podolskie Izvestia,* July 12, 1911.

their victory. *Podolianin* wrote after the elections: "Hail this great man who, with his strong hand, guided the Russian ship of state along the path of national renewal. West Russia will not forget P. A. Stolypin."[130]

Poles were as absent from the election process in Volynia as they were almost everywhere else. The Nationalist deputy Beliaev won a spot in Ostrog uezd of Volynia. Shulgin and Pikhno did not choose to pursue their candidacies, although they probably would have won.[131] Because the new zemstvos would not be bastions of nationalism, there was no point in making an effort. The experience of Volynia proved that the Western Zemstvo Act by itself was not a certain guarantee of electoral success. The intense effort of the local Russian nobility and a cooperative governor were still required for victory.

For the most part, the Western Zemstvo Act had done what its framers and supporters had hoped it would. The Russian nobility had been given control of a fully elaborated system of local government, and this feat had been accomplished without the feared influx of peasants. The Russian gentry had strengthened its position, and, in the process, the Nationalists had developed their organization throughout the borderland. The Western Zemstvo Act created the possibility for the expansion of their influence through the creation of a structure that facilitated the marshalling of their forces. Yet, if the Nationalists had been simply the creation of the government, no amount of manipulation could have assured their success. Only their constituents could do that.

The Nationalists hoped that their victory would strengthen the Premier's position in the capital. Professor Chernov wrote to Savenko after the elections: "I thought that after the brilliant elections of zemstvo members throughout all of west Russia that P. A. Stolypin's situation would be even stronger than it had been up to now."[132] Certainly, Stolypin had every reason to expect that the success of the western zemstvo elections would strengthen his own position and create the possibility for further victories in the elections to the fourth Duma.

The tsar was to visit Kiev that September. Stolypin could be expected to take the occasion to show Nicholas the new zemstvos and to demonstrate the benefits they had brought to the Russian population of the borderland. Despite Nicholas's doubts about the premier, Stolypin could still hope that the new zemstvos would help him to regain the tsar's favor.[133]

---

130. *Podolianin*, July 16, 1911.
131. *Volyn'*, July 3 and 7, 1911.
132. TsGAOR 102(1911) 265.509.29. V. E. Chernov, Kiev, to Savenko, Kiev, (July 24, 1911).
133. Ibid., 504.62. N. Talberg, Kiev, to L. M. Kniazev, Irkutsk (August 12, 1911).

Late in August, before the royal visit to Kiev, the Nationalists of the western gubernias met at the Kiev Club of Russian Nationalists to discuss the party's national congress to be held in Petersburg that January, a conference that would chart the strategy for the fourth Duma elections.[134] When Stolypin arrived on September 1, he spent much time with his allies, going over plans for the fourth Duma campaign.[135] The Nationalists' accounts of their conversations with the premier depict him as healthy, energetic, and extremely optimistic about his political prospects.[136]

That evening, just after his audience with the Kiev Nationalists, Stolypin was assassinated. The murder took place in the Kiev Opera House in the presence of the tsar. Stolypin's assassin, a deranged student named Dmitri Bogrov, had been given a ticket by the police, who were ostensibly using him to keep an eye open for terrorists. This connection with the police and the confusion concerning Bogrov's political loyalty have shrouded the premier's death in mystery. Bogrov had been a member of the Socialist Revolutionary Party and was thought to have been a police spy. However, the Nationalists were less concerned with affixing the blame for the crime than with adjusting to the new political situation created by this sudden turn of events. Their most powerful political ally had been removed from the scene, and the political machine the Nationalists had been developing with his aid now faced a crossroad.

Indeed, without Stolypin, the thrust of the Nationalists' campaign was blunted and the party's sense of dynamism and optimism was sharply diminished. His efforts on their behalf had created the possibility for the party's growth. Working with them, he had been able to balance traditional authority and cooperation with Russia's propertied classes. Through collaboration with Stolypin, the Nationalists had been able to combine support for representative institutions and political parties with continued acceptance of the state structure and its powers. Once Stolypin was gone, this delicate balance collapsed, and with it went the Nationalists' hopes for a strong influence on national politics.

Stolypin was succeeded as president of the Council of Ministers by his Minister of Finance, V. N. Kokovtsov. The new premier was a balancer of budgets and an efficient administrator, but he had no great plans for reform and was indifferent to the Duma. Moreover, his sympathy for Russian nationalism and the Nationalist Party had never been extensive. A

134. Ibid., 505.133. D. Khomiakov, Moscow, to Count D. M. Gonobbe, Mirgorod (August 29, 1911).

135. *Sbornik kluba russkikh natsionalistov*, chetvertyi vypusk, pp. 42–43.

136. Kievskoe gubernskoe zemskoe sobranie, *Stenograficheskie otchety*, August 18–21, 1911; *Sbornik kluba russkikh natsionalistov*, 4-ii vypusk, p. 47.

cosmopolitan used to arranging loans and doing business with the bankers of the West (many of whom were Jewish), Kokovtsov inspired the mistrust of the Nationalists. He had opposed the Finnish legislation and, worse still, had expressed reservations about the western zemstvo bill.[137]

Just after Stolypin's murder, Balashev and a Nationalist delegation met with Kokovtsov. They expressed the party's lack of confidence in him and demanded a pledge that he would continue Stolypin's policies. Kokovtsov was taken aback by Balashev's aggressiveness and developed an instant dislike for the Nationalist leader. Kokovtsov replied that he was willing to accept Nationalist support, but reiterated his opposition to the persecution of Poles and Jews. Then, in an apparent effort to deflate Balashev's sense of self-importance, Kokovtsov sought to insult his visitor by claiming that Stolypin had never considered the Nationalists to be a solid base of support and that he had no need of them either.[138]

The Nationlists now had to deal with a premier who was far less enthusiastic than Stolypin had been about their program.[139] Losing their protector had clearly diminished their faith in their own future. The period of their ascendancy was over. In a sense, the remainder of their history is an epilog to the brief golden era that Stolypin had provided for them.

The most immediate political result of Stolypin's death was a short-lived reconciliation between the Octobrists and Nationalists.[140] While Bobrinskii and Savenko were eager to extend these relations, most Nationalists preferred to hold off until the fourth Duma had been elected. At that time, they expected the balance of power to have changed in their favor. Yet, before that could happen, they had to make significant changes in their political approach.

137. PRO, FO 371.1218.39468 (September 9, 1911).

138. Kokovtsov, *Iz moego proshlogo*, 1: 274.

139. TsGAOR 102 (1911) 265.505.157. A. Suvorin, St. Petersburg, to M. O. Menshikov, St. Petersburg (September 2, 1911).

140. *Okrainy Rossii*, Nos. 37–38, September 10–17, 1911, p. 502. PRO, FO 371.1218.39470 (October 5, 1911).

V

The Elections to the Fourth Duma

The elections to the fourth Duma, the last national elections before the Revolution of 1917, took place in a climate of rapidly decaying social stability in urban Russia. In April 1912, peacefully demonstrating miners at the Lena goldfields were fired on by the police, and more than a hundred men were killed.[1] The massacre revivified the long-dormant workers' movement. A wave of sympathy strikes soon followed, and, in the next months, strike activity reached its highest level since 1906. Unlike 1905, this movement was met with harsh resistance from both industrialists and the government. Accordingly, the strikes became increasingly militant, political, and widespread.[2]

The gentry was somewhat shielded from these disturbing events. Although peasant support for Stolypin's agrarian reform program had declined drastically, the countryside remained calm, and, for the first time in a long time, landlords were feeling fairly secure.[3] This sense of safety led

1. Hugh Seton-Watson, *The Decline of Imperial Russia, 1855-1914* (New York, 1952), p. 291.
2. Leopold Haimson, "The Problem of Social Stability in Urban Russia: 1905-1917," *Slavic Review* (December 1964): 628.
3. Geroid Robinson, *Rural Russia under the Old Regime*, (New York, 1932), pp. 243-263.

many of them to lapse back into the political apathy that had characterized the years before 1905. They did not share the new sense of urgency. This indifference was shared by the peasants, who no longer had any hope that an unrepresentative Duma would give them the land they so desperately desired. Only the clergy demonstrated a strong interest in political activity and, with their newfound energy, had little difficulty in dominating and controlling a passive and disinterested peasantry in the preparatory meetings of small landowners.

Thus, Russia's propertied classes were hardly united during the elections of 1912. Industrialists and professionals in the cities thought that they were sitting on a powder keg, while the rural landlords mistook the peasants' temporary quiescence for acceptance of the status quo.[4] This division between urban and rural property owners does much to explain why the 1912 election campaign failed to excite or energize much of the population. Given this situation, the Nationalists' hopes of achieving a decisive victory were clearly unobtainable.

Preparing for the Elections

The explicit defense of gentry interest had helped the Nationalists develop their base in the west. However, to extend its strength and influence, the party now faced three crucial tasks. First, to expand its base outside the west, it had to broaden and restructure its national and local organizations. Second, it was forced to enrich its impoverished ideological position to attract nongentry support. Third, to prevent political paralysis, it had to clarify its relationship with the government. These problems, which stood in the way of success in the fourth Duma elections, had to be solved before any progress could be made.

Restructuring the Party's Organization

The Nationalist Party's early growth had been asymmetrical. In the wake of the western zemstvo elections, the party had established branches in the smaller towns of the borderland. This expansion was largely the work of Nationalist deputies who traveled the countryside extensively, giving speeches and organizing local chapters.[5] Outside the

4. Geoffrey Hosking, *The Russian Constitutional Experiment* (Cambridge, 1973), p. 215.
5. *VNS* (1911), p. 18. *VNS* (1912–1913), p. 11.

west, success was spotty. The Nationalists claimed to have established branches in several provincial centers, including Tambov, Tver, Kursk, and Chernigov, but few of these branches demonstrated any signs of life. Bobrinskii and Savenko botched a number of attempts at organizing. They found little support in Poltava and Ekaterinoslav, two Octobrist strongholds in the Ukraine. Viatka proved to be even more infertile territory, and, though a branch was formed in Odessa, public response was limited.[6]

In contrast to these failures, the Nationalist deputy from the Russian population of Warsaw, S. N. Alekseev, had some luck organizing among zemstvo members in Kaluga, another area of Octobrist strength. Alekseev sought to characterize the Nationalists as the true party of the dvorianstvo. Archbishop Evlogii and Bobrinskii were brought in for a well-attended agitational meeting. Feeling threatened by the Nationalists' popularity, local Octobrists asked Guchkov to persuade Balashev to call off the drive.[7] The Nationalists also had a good response to their efforts in Kazan, which was far from the western border and had sent four Octobrists to the third Duma. In addition to setting up a branch of the National Club, the Nationalist deputy, N. D. Sazonov, had organized an electoral committee of representatives from so-called monarchist organizations, which began to settle on candidates to run against the Octobrists.[8] Yet, these successes outside the west were relatively few. The Nationalists' uniquely modern approach to the problem of political organization elicited little response in central Russia where institutions, traditions, agricultural practices, and the ethnic mix were different.

V. A. Bobrinskii was also active in Petersburg. Three years earlier, he had organized a group called the Galicia-Russia Society which concerned itself with the protection of Slavs living in Galicia, a region under Austrian control bordering on Volynia. This group was revamped and given a new name. It was now called the West-Russia Society, and its task was marshalling public opinion in the capital in support of the needs of the borderland. If Stolypin had still been alive, such a step would probably not have been necessary, but with Kokovtsov now in power, the Nationalists felt that they needed to create a group that could influence the views of educated society in Petersburg.[9]

6. TsGAOR 102 (1912) 265.506.62. Mirsikov, Odessa, to A. I. Guchkov, St. Petersburg (March 29, 1912). Ibid., 565.974. I. V. Riazanov to A. V. Rudage (March 30, 1912). *Kievlianin*, April 2, 1912.

7. Ibid., 509.125. V. Ilyin, Kaluga, to Guchkov, St. Petersburg (November 16, 1912). Ibid., 565.126. Ilyin to Guchkov (November 17, 1912).

8. Ibid., 509.10. N. Melnikov, Kazan, to Guchkov, St. Petersburg (September 3, 1912).

9. *Rossiia*, November 16, 1912; *Okrainy Rossii*, No. 47 (November 19, 1911): 646.

Thus, there had been real progress in the west, spotty gains in the rest of Russia, and a loss of influence in the capital. These trends were clearly reflected at the Nationalists' party congress, held in Petersburg during February 1912. A year earlier, the party's charter had been changed to afford greater representation to the provincial branches. This shift of power away from Petersburg became clear immediately, as 200 delegates from eighty-three provincial organizations met in the capital. A fierce struggle erupted over the elections to the party council. The provincials demanded an expansion of this body to allow for greater representation of the localities. After lengthy debate, the council was enlarged from fifteen to thirty members. While Balashev retained his presidency, there were seventeen newcomers to party leadership. Savenko was the most notable addition. Several others had played important roles in the western zemstvo election and were now using that experience to gain national positions. Provincial activists from the west were gaining a dominant position in the party.

These elections thus reflected a trend that had been seen elsewhere. At a time when they should have been expanding their influence outside their base in the west, the Nationalists were reducing their national support and becoming more homogeneous.[10] The sanovniki and the Petersburg intellectuals, as well as the nonborderland party members, were diminishing in influence within the Nationalist Party at precisely the moment when their advice and concerns should have been heeded in order to expand the party's appeal.

The Nationalists experienced similar difficulty in working out an electoral platform. The document that finally emerged after fourteen hours of debate superseded the old program of the National Union. Largely because the party had gained the western zemstvos, the new program was different from previous ones. Gone was the overt concern with the defense of Russians in the borderlands. Instead, the party simply presented a few broad demands. Typical of most conservative programs, it omitted more than it included.

1. Support of representative institutions
2. Strengthening the Empire's military power
3. Strengthening the domination of the Orthodox church
4. Improvement of the peasant's lot through cheap credit
5. Strengthening of church schools and patriotic education
6. The "nationalization" of credit, trade, and industry
7. The impossibility of equal rights for Jews

10. *Kievlianin*, February 12, 1912; *Okrainy Rossii*, No. 8 (February 25, 1912): 114.

To call such a program vague would be an understatement. To call it inadequate, given Russia's critical problems and the multiplicity of solutions offered by other parties, would be more accurate. But the trend away from the party's original specificity was unmistakable. The question of assuming control of the Duma and the responsibilities that went with that position forced the Nationalists to go beyond the narrow appeals they had used throughout their earliest organizational drives. It was now necessary to extend their support beyond the borderland. Since the influence of both the Octobrists and the Union of Russian People had declined, the Nationalists had reason to believe that there now existed a mass of uncommitted conservative votes that they could attract. However, securing this potential support necessitated some revision of their views.

Revising the Party's Ideology

The election forced the Nationalists to make a clearer claim for the universality of their views. On the surface, it appeared that they already had a supraclass ideology—nationalism—that could appeal to a broad range of social elements, but the Nationalists were hardly proponents of any familiar form of nationalism. Their early success had been based on the defense of specific interests rather than on the bold proclamation of universal principles. Other parties, most notably the Octobrists and many Kadets, were more comfortable with broadly conceived notions of national pride and with the associated doctrines of neo-Slavism than the Nationalists were. Nevertheless, in response to the challenge of the elections and in the wake of the party congress, several professors and writers associated with the Nationalists attempted to broaden the party's appeal beyond its extremely narrow base of support. The thrust of their arguments was that the Nationalists, who supported both the Russian nation and the state, were a truly democratic party. Moreover, the Nationalists were protectors of the entire nation and were therefore compelled to demonstrate concern for all classes.

This search for new allies was partly a response to the recent concern with nationalism of such right-wing Kadets as Peter Struve. A segment of the capital intelligentsia had lost its earlier antipathy toward nationalism. Accordingly, Professor P. I. Kovalevskii, who had been named to the party council that February, sought to develop the notion of a "national democratic" party that could appeal to intellectuals who were motivated by ideas and repelled by narrow class interest.

In general, the task is to raise nationalism among the masses of the Russian people; to destroy indifference and antinational feeling among the masses of educated people, and to arouse national feeling among the dark masses.[11]

Kovalevskii urged the Nationalists to speak in the name of all classes of the nation. Only if it spoke for the entire nation would the party have the right to call itself a national party. But this openness implied a concerted effort to direct party appeals to a broader audience rather than an actual change of views on important issues. There was nothing in Kovalevskii's remarks to indicate that the actual content of that message had been modified.

Kovalevskii's words produced a response among other party members, notably the writer and poet, Mikhail Baliasnyi, who had been involved in the zemstvo elections in Kiev. He organized the publication of a collection of poetic and political writings entitled *Lado*, which was designed to appeal to the capital intelligentsia as an expression of national-democratic sensitivity. Most contributions to the collection were from conservative Petersburg intellectuals who were seeking a basis of rapprochement with those liberals who had moved to the right during the period of social calm that had followed the coup of June 3. Much of their concern with democracy and the need for a broader social base reflected their own reaction to liberal intellectuals, with whom they came in daily contact, rather than their response to local conditions with which they were not necessarily intimate.[12]

Always sensitive to the latest trends, Savenko, although a representative of local interests, sought to amplify the notion of a nationalism attractive to all of society. In a column in *Kievlianin* entitled "The Nationalist Party and the Class Struggle," he admitted that a new era of class struggle had emerged, but argued that the Nationalist Party was capable of blunting that struggle.

In it [the Nationalist Party] you will not find the old dvorianstvo soslovie tendency ... only those representatives of classes who put state interests much higher than class interests.

By state interests, Savenko meant simply a generalized national welfare as opposed to the interests of a particular class. But still, the state was not to be run by the representatives of all classes.

11. P. I. Kovalevskii, *Osnovy russkago natsionalizma*, p. 16.
12. *Lado*, Sbornik obshchestvennogo postiashchenii narozhdaiushchei russkoi national'-demokratii (St. Petersburg, 1912).

State interests demand that the best people of the land take up the state's affairs. Are the dark peasants really the best people in this sense? The first Duma had 300 and in truth was not a Kadet but a peasant Duma. What good can come of that, and who needs a repetition of it?

   The best people are, above all, the highest, most cultured classes. The first duty of the upper classes is to serve the lower classes, the people.[13]

Thus, in his plea for turning power over to the Nationalists, Savenko offered only *noblesse oblige* as a hope for the future welfare of the lower classes. Given the party's history, it is not surprising that this attempt to develop nationalism into a broadly attractive ideology should have been half-hearted and largely unsuccessful. Men like Kovalevskii and Baliasnyi were hardly at the center of power within the party. On the other hand, Balashev and other west Russian landlords had always been uncomfortable with the broad brand of nationalism now being advanced in their name. Their own nationalism had always been the product of their direct interests. As a result, the efforts of sympathetic intellectuals were given little encouragement by party leaders.

The Party and the State

   The Nationalists' ambiguous relationship with the autocracy had always made them uncertain about the extent of their reliance on traditional authority. Throughout their short history, the Nationalists' attempt to maintain simultaneous support for the new institutions of popular representation and the old autocratic structure had forced them into a delicate political balancing act. So long as the government sought to cooperate with the Duma, the Nationalists had been able to avoid confronting this basic contradiction in their approach to politics. Stolypin had fostered just such a friendly climate between the two branches. He had also been willing to furnish the Nationalists whatever support they might need, especially during the elections to the western zemstvos. Now the government's attitude had changed. Stolypin had been the Nationalists' champion; Kokovtsov was their enemy. In the elections to the fourth Duma, the Nationalists could no longer count on the certain cooperation of the bureaucracy. While they requested assistance wherever they could, they were forced once again to rethink their relationship toward the state.

   The bureaucracy, for its part, was by no means unanimous about taking

13. *Kievlianin*, July 26, 1912.

an active role in influencing the elections. Kokovtsov was suspicious of government interference, and, in any case, he was no friend of the Nationalists. However, the new Minister of Interior, A. A. Makarov, actively sought to furnish assistance to assure the election of deputies favorable to the government.[14] Makarov's attitude naturally encouraged the Nationalists. Publicly, they might praise the new political system with its possibilities for independent action, but, as was clear during the western zemstvo elections, they privately welcomed the support of the bureaucracy when it was offered.

More significantly, when help was not offered, it was often solicited or even demanded. When governors or other administrators refused to cooperate with them, the Nationalists sought their removal. Party members, who had historically been protected by the state, did not hesitate to return to the government for help in moments of crisis. Even in the west, where they were able to organize effectively, assistance was not spurned, and, in central Russia, reliance on the bureaucracy was even more necessary. Open electioneering in the west was contrasted to the closed-door naming of deputies found in many central provinces. Yet, even in the west, the Nationalists had no qualms about seeking the support of local chinovniki.

The elections of 1912 afford numerous examples of the Nationalists' desire for government assistance. In most cases, the demand for such help took the form of petitioning Makarov to appoint sympathetic local administrators. For example, the Nationalists had been trying to organize a branch of the National Union in V. A. Bobrinskii's home province, Tula. Their efforts had met with little support from the governor, who had even refused permission for Nationalist speakers to appear at agitational meetings. After much effort, the Nationalists finally succeeded in organizing a group, but the governor had restrained their efforts to recruit state officials. One local leader wrote Bobrinskii asking for help.

At the governor's office there is a "secret circular" of 1908 or 1909 which forbids bureaucrats from joining any kind of union. Please seek to inform Makarov that this circular does not apply to the All-Russian National Union and that entering it is not forbidden. This will help to increase the number of members, many of whom fear to join because of the circular.[15]

14. TsGAOR 102 (1911) 265.508.90. F. F. Trepov, Kiev, to E. F. Demidova, Zhitomir (October 14, 1911).

15. Ibid., 556.39. Mikhailovskii to Bobrinskii, January 5, 1912.

A similar situation arose in Vitebsk, the least politically active of the western gubernias. There a local Nationalist, distressed at the absence of much electoral activity, implored the Duma deputy, Ofrosimov, to persuade Makarov to name a more active governor, one who was well acquainted with the region.[16] Likewise, in Mogilev, local landowners had petitioned the governor to permit a particular state councillor to remain in the province because of the "good effect" he would have on the Duma elections.[17]

The Nationalists even went so far as to suggest candidates for appointive positions. The Nationalist deputy from Kiev, F. N. Bezak, wrote to the governor of Kiev, Girs, suggesting the nomination of a local Nationalist named Shvindt as mayor *(gorodskoi golov)* of the town of Berdichev. Bezak explained that he had written to Girs because he realized that Makarov would be unwilling to appoint someone over the governor's objections.

> Will it be possible to count on the nomination of Shvindt as chief of Berdichev in the near future? This could have meaning for the elections to the Duma, for Shvindt can become an elector from Berdichev and he would be a right-wing candidate.[18]

While the Nationalists correctly considered Girs an ally, they were extremely mistrustful of the governor-general of the southwest, F. F. Trepov. Typically, Savenko promised that the Nationalists would oppose Trepov and read him out of the "national camp."[19] Rakovich had sensed Trepov's indifference toward the Nationalists even earlier, and he had written to S. N. Gerbel' (who had organized the zemstvo elections for the government) demanding Trepov's ouster before the elections.[20]

The Nationalists' most flagrant attempt to assure themselves of sympathetic bureaucratic support came in Volynia where they campaigned against the governor, A. P. Kutaisov. Kutaisov had not been well disposed toward the Nationalists during the zemstvo elections. Some even accused him of supporting Kadet and Polish blocs. Blaming their defeat on Kutaisov's interference rather than their own failures, Shulgin, Savenko,

16. Ibid., 265.512.27. A. von Rosen, Vitebsk, to Ia. N. Ofrosimov, St. Petersburg (November 7, 1911).

17. TsGIA Leningrad 1327.2.210.19.

18. TsGAOR 102 (1912) 256.561.510. F. Bezak, St. Petersburg, to Girs, Kiev (February 12, 1912).

19. Ibid., 265.513.86. Savenko, Kiev, to Ilia Nikolaevich (November 20, 1911).

20. Ibid., 508.37. Rakovich, Podol'e, to S. N. Gerbel', St. Petersburg (October 19, 1911).

and several other western Nationalists began a campaign against the governor, even though they had not received permission or support from the party center. As early as October 1911, local criticism of Kutaisov began mounting. He was well aware of the intrigues against him.[21] He sensed that dissatisfaction within the Ministry of Interior was the result of Shulgin's attempts to influence Makarov. Feeling threatened, Kutaisov began talking privately about tendering his resignation.[22] He wrote Trepov, discussing a meeting with Pikhno held January 17, 1912.

> He [Pikhno] and the leaders of his party considered it possible to name candidates for the elections.... They talked with the Ministry of Interior which was completely persuaded by these arguments, and, on that basis, not only did they not agree with me on the state of affairs, but quite transparently led me to understand that I was not fully informed of the situation.[23]

Kutaisov stated that the Nationalists were advancing Rakovich's candidacy for the governorship. However, Rakovich did not wish to become governor of Volynia.[24] Savenko and Shulgin had been acting on their own initiative and had not received Balashev's support. The party leader, sensing the bad impression that the campaign would make in the capital, sought to call off Savenko and Shulgin. He argued that the ouster of Kutaisov was "untimely and impossible." In Balashev's opinion, Kutaisov was someone who could be persuaded.[25] Balashev mentioned that he had known Kutaisov for many years, and, on the basis of this friendship, he felt that he could reason with the governor.

Balashev's position reveals the persistent reliance on old family ties and traditional attitudes among the Nationalists. These relationships made it impossible to oppose forthrightly and consistently all bureaucratic figures. This loyalty to tradition would operate more for Balashev, who was from one of Russia's wealthiest and most prestigious families, than it would for Savenko, who owned little land and was something of a parvenu. It also provides a possible explanation for the eventual split in party ranks. Savenko, the journalist, was free to spout off publicly about independent action and post-1905 political conditions. Men like Balashev, on the other hand, were still too comfortable and familiar with traditional Russia ever

21. Ibid., 53. P. Demidov, Volynia, to F. F. Trepov, Kiev (October 10, 1911).

22. Ibid., 256.557.141. Kutaisov, Volynia, to M. A. Melnikov (January 14, 1912).

23. Ibid., 162. Kutaisov, St. Petersburg, to M. A. Melnikov (January 14, 1912). In this letter, Kutaisov describes his letter to Trepov.

24. Ibid., 147. Savenko, Kiev, to Shulgin, St. Petersburg (January 15, 1912).

25. Ibid., 193. Bezak, St. Petersburg, to Demchenko, Kiev (January 18, 1912).

to forsake it entirely. In any case, Balashev's intervention came too late to forestall Kutaisov's resignation.[26]

The Kutaisov affair, if one may call it that, demonstrates that the Nationalists were unsure about the extent to which they were willing to welcome government involvement. This uncertainty reflected a deeper ambivalence about the government. The party clearly wished to develop electoral strength independently. The escape from bureaucratic tutelage was a standard element of party rhetoric. Savenko, despite his actions concerning Kutaisov, was among the most insistent on this point. However, the incidents mentioned above, and they appear to be only a few among many, reveal the Nationalists' desire to create optimal conditions for their own electoral activity. Despite their rhetoric about independence, where the Nationalists were weak and incapable of mounting any real effort among the electorate, they came to rely on the bureaucracy.

As for the attitudes of the bureaucrats, some chinovniki were well disposed to the Nationalists; others were not. Even among sympathetic bureaucrats, the structure of rules and procedures made it impossible to accede to all Nationalist requests. In reality, it was simply impossible for the Nationalists either to run the election campaign on their own or to leave it in the hands of the state's officials. Thus, neither the zemstvo nor the Duma elections provided a solution to the problem of the party's proper relationship with the state and its agents.

Of the three preelection tasks facing the Nationalists, only the internal restructuring of the party was completed. The development of broad ideological appeals was stillborn, and the relationship with the state remained murky. As a result, while they had hopes for success in the fourth Duma elections, they were uncertain and apprehensive about the results.

The Elections of 1912

Since few scholars have studied the elections of 1912, the entire process must be approached in close detail. Only by examining the last national elections before the 1917 Revolution, can one establish the links between national and local politics that are such a central element of the party's practice. Only by studying the roles of such national figures as Savenko and Balashev in their home territories, can we learn what made the Nationalist Party unique in Russian history.

26. Ibid., 559.304. F. F. Trepov, Kiev, to E. Demidova, Nice (January 27, 1912).

The West

Kiev. The selection of deputies from Kiev involved not one but two different elections: the direct elections of one deputy from each of the two city curiae of Kiev, plus the regular, indirect selection of deputies from the rest of the gubernia. Thus, it is interesting and important that the Nationalists, who were primarily agrarians, were able to meet the challenge posed by the Kiev city elections. Unlike the gubernia elections, which ended up in the gentlemanly confines of an electoral assembly of 150, running candidates in the city required a more direct approach to voters.

The electorate was no longer an amorphous mass that somehow magically brought forth a group of vyborshchiki who then chose the Duma deputies behind closed doors. The Nationalists were always acutely aware of the complexity and, more important, the actuality of the electorate. The result of this closer contact was a greater feeling of urgency and a more detailed organizational approach than had been evolved by conservatives elsewhere. The Nationalists agitated extensively in the city of Kiev on a district-to-district level, working meticulously to ensure the unity of potential allies. Many of the same men who helped the Nationalists in the city were also involved in the zemstvo and gubernia Duma elections. They brought the notions and feelings acquired in the city to the rural setting of the gubernia electoral process. In no sense did these political practices involve any special devotion to particularly abstruse organizational techniques. But the Nationalists' urban experience did give them a sense of struggle, an attention to detail, and an awareness of the need for organization that were far greater than those of conservative parties in other regions.

During the summer, the Nationalists had organized a "patriotic" bloc of right-wing groups and had settled on candidates for both curiae. V. Ia. Demchenko, who had played so large a role in the zemstvo elections, was named in the first curia, and Savenko had become the choice in the second curia after the original candidate dropped out.[27] A series of district meetings followed, to which the groups in the bloc invited large numbers of potential supporters. These gatherings took place in six districts of the city throughout September. According to the possibly exaggerated accounts of *Kievlianin*, the meetings were well attended for conservative gatherings, and drew between 300 and 600 people.[28] At some meetings, the candidates appeared, while at others leading members of the Kiev

27. *Kievlianin*, September 17, 1912.
28. *Kievlianin*, September 24, 1912.

Club spoke in favor of the nominees of the "patriotic bloc." There is no clear indication of the social composition of those who came to the meetings, nor is it clear that all of them attended voluntarily. It is reasonable to assume that not all those in attendance were nobles. *Kievlianin* gave no specific indication concerning the content of the speeches and appeals that were made, although Savenko's column for this period, which was much the same as it had been all along, must have reflected, in some manner, what he was saying to the voters.[29] Similar meetings, organized on behalf of Professor S. I. Ivanov, the Kadet candidate in the second curia, were harassed and broken up by the police.[30]

The culmination of the local conservative gatherings was a citywide meeting of the right-wing bloc at the end of September to work out a plan for election day that would assure the participation of those voters who were thought to be sympathetic. As a result, lectures and agitational meetings, although on a smaller scale than those of September, continued up to election day, October 18.[31] Sensing that their best chance was in the first curia, the Nationalists began to concentrate more attention on Demchenko's candidacy.[32] The Nationalists' premonition proved correct: Demchenko defeated the progressive candidate D. N. Grigorovich-Barskii by 816 votes to 756. However, Savenko lost to Ivanov by a vote of 6,527 to 6,244. Since the city's lower and middle classes participated in the second curia, Savenko admitted that he had not seriously expected to win, but he took his defeat less than graciously, attributing it to the "lying Jewish press."[33] Nationalist appeals to the city's other classes did have some effect: Savenko's margin of defeat was surprisingly small for a conservative in the second curia of a major city.

The extent, seriousness, and effectiveness of the party's organizational effort are striking. To the observer of Western European political campaigns, the idea of establishing district electoral committees, striking alliances, and holding agitational meetings may not sound particularly advanced. However, in the context of Russian conservative politics, in which political parties had only just begun to coalesce, these sorts of practices were new. Moreover, the entire effort was guided by members of a social class—the gentry—that had not previously deigned to engage in politics.

29. *Kievlianin*, September 19, 21, and 25, 1912.
30. TsGIA, Leningrad 1327.2.203.131–132, 141.
31. *Kievlianin*, September 27, 1912.
32. *Kievlianin*, September 27, 1912.
33. *Kievlianin*, October 20, 1912; TsGIA Leningrad 1327.2.203.118.

Because many of the Kiev Club's members were active both in the city and the gubernia elections, the character of the campaign in the countryside was inevitably influenced by events in the city. Full-scale mobilization of the Nationalists' forces in the countryside did not really begin until the middle of September. Prior to the campaign, the Nationalists of the southwest met in Kiev early in September to assess what had been achieved so far. Leaders from Kiev, Podol'e, and Volynia attended, and Balashev presided. He announced the creation of an Octobrist-Nationalist bloc throughout the southwest[34] and made public the party's nominees in Kiev and Podol'e.[35]

The official prepatory meetings that chose electors from the small landowners were thoroughly dominated by the clergy.[36] Nevertheless, great care was taken in selecting appropriately reliable peasants. However, the Nationalists were not especially subtle in their methods of assuring the proper kind of peasant deputy. When a peasant named Kozenko, from the village of Kagarliuk, publicly announced his intention to run for the Duma and made no secret of his left-wing sympathies, a local landowner explained to him "the heavy consequences of becoming a member of the opposition."[37] Earlier, the Nationalist deputy, Garkavenko, wrote to Savenko, discussing a peasant named Matrosov who might have become a candidate if the previous Kiev Duma peasant, Kovalenko, had decided not to run.

> He decided that at the present moment it was not wise to be left-wing because with the help of the right he could go to the Duma and with the help of these same people [he could] attain a better position than village clerk.[38]

Clearly, the Nationalists were not above rewarding loyalty, whether it was genuine or the result of threats.

34. TsGAOR 102 (1912) 265.580.2485. N. Talberg, Kiev, to B. V. Nikolskii, St. Petersburg (October 31, 1912). Ibid., 577.2150. Talberg to A. A. Shirinskii-Shikhmatov (October 2, 1912).

35. *Novoe Vremia,* September 8, 1912; *Okrainy Rossii,* Nos. 35–36 (September 1–8, 1912):500.

36. TsGIA Leningrad 1327.2.203.85. Of 513 representatives chosen by *volost's* to actually choose electors from the small landowners curia, 477 were priests and only 35 were peasants.

37. TsGAOR, 102 (1912) 265.579.2386. S. Vykhristenko, Kagarliuk, to Savenko, Kiev (October 23, 1912).

38. Ibid., 577.2155. Garkavenko, Fastov, to Savenko, Kiev (October 2, 1912).

Table 5.1. **Comparison of the 1907 and 1912 Gubernia Electoral Assemblies (Landowners' Curiae) in Kiev**

	1907	1912
Nobles	26	34
Priests	41	35
Honorary citizens	6	2
Merchants	1	1
Petty bourgeois	3	2
Others	1	1

Source: TsGIA 1327.2.203, 233.

However, the Nationalists' concern about the peasantry was unnecessary. The vast majority of peasants stayed away from the initial meetings. In Kiev uezd, 370 owners of small property were eligible to participate, but only 157 appeared, and 124 of them were priests.[39] In Berdichev, no peasants at all took part.[40] Reports from other districts were similar.

The Nationalists approached the district meetings, which chose the electors, with a clear idea of whom they wished to see elected. In the past, many parties had nominated particular individuals in certain districts, but it was unusual for a party to name full slates of candidates in several gubernias as a matter of policy. Particularly in Kiev, this phenomenon reflected a position of strength. Participation of large landowners was extensive. At least three-fourths of those eligible voted, along with a high number of clergy.[41] As a result of their preparation, the uezd meetings went very well for the Nationalists.

A comparison of the 1912 gubernia electoral assembly with that of 1907 reveals that the position of the Russian gentry had been strengthened somewhat, although there were no fundamental changes in the relationships among social groups (see Table 5.1). The landed nobility was still threatened and still relied, perhaps to a lesser extent, on the clergy.[42]

With their supporters in force among the vyborshchiki, the Nationalists had good reason to look ahead to the gubernia assembly with optimism. A last preelectoral meeting held two days before the final election added to the list of nominees. Among the new Nationalist candidates were Savenko (fresh from his defeat in the second Kiev curia), Baron Shteiger, K. P. Grigorovich-Barskii, G. A. Vishnevskii, and N. A. Zhilin. This preliminary

39. *Rech'*, September 19, 1912.
40. *Kievlianin*, September 19, 1912.
41. *Kievlianin*, September 28, 1912.
42. *Vybory*, p. 154.

gathering was attended by fifty-two of the seventy-eight vyborshchiki of the landowners' curia.[43] Savenko was quick to note the novelty and significance of this sort of discipline. He claimed that it was a clear sign of the Nationalist party's development since 1907.[44] The organizational effort paid off: The Nationalists swept the gubernia assembly. Savenko and F. N. Bezak led the field of vote getters. Of the 150 electors, 149 took part in the election. In most cases, the deputies were elected by a vote of about 110 in favor and 40 opposed (the assembly voted for or against the candidacy of nominated individuals). Seventy-eight landowners gave the Nationalists their working majority.[45]

Podol'e. Like their comrades in Kiev, the Podol'e Nationalists had begun organizing themselves around a slate of candidates. Agitational meetings were set up for specially invited audiences of Russian landowners, local officials, and teachers. A successful meeting was held in Balt uezd where right-wing voters agreed to unite behind the Nationalists' nominees.[46] In many cases, the clergy, who had pledged to cooperate with the Nationalists, played a role in organizing these district gatherings. At Novyi Ushits, D. N. Chikhachev addressed a meeting of local landlords on behalf of his own candidacy. He talked to a similar meeting of 140 in Nemirov shortly thereafter.[47] Balashev and Gizhitskii organized a series of meetings, designed to acquaint voters with the men the Nationalists wished to see named as electors by the uezd assemblies. In most cases, these candidates were already well known in local affairs.

Until now, the bureaucracy had played little role in aiding the Nationalists' early agitation for the Duma. However, as the election approached, Balashev sought official assistance. As had been the case earlier, the Ministry of Interior did not blindly submit to all of the party's requests. Balashev's attempts to have several electors added to the landowners' curia were reluctantly denied by Makarov.[48] Although the Nationalist Party had no qualms about enlisting the bureaucracy's aid, its reliance on the

43. *Kievianin*, October 24, 1912; *Sbornik kluba russkikh natsionalistov*, 4yi i 5yi vypusky, p. 114.
44. *Kievlianin*, November 1, 1912.
45. TsGIA, Leningrad 1327.2.33a. 111–156.
46. *Podolskie Izvestia*, September 2, 1912.
47. *Podolskie Izvestia*, September 18 and 25, 1912.
48. TsGIA Leningrad, 1327.2.220. 34, 36, 40, 41, 42, 43. For reasons he did not spell out, Rakovich telegraphed the Assistant Minister of Interior, Kharuzin, on the eve of the uezd assemblies, and requested the addition of one more elector for the Russian landlords in Kamenets uezd. Kharuzin quickly wrote back that this sort of change was impossible under the electoral law.

Table 5.2. **Political Tendencies of Members of the Uezd Assemblies (1912) in Podol'e**

Right wing	274
Nationalists	85
Monarchists	46
Moderate rights	3
Left wing	7
Unknown	7

Source: TsGIA 1327.2.220.47.

state was not consistent and simple. The constantly shifting relationship between the party and the bureaucracy during the fourth Duma elections simultaneously reflected and explained the Nationalists' ambiguous relationship with traditional authority.

The Nationalists faced the district meetings with considerable confidence. The assemblies of small landowners had been overwhelmingly dominated by the clergy, and the Poles boycotted the elections.[49] Thus, the political complexion of the uezd assemblies appeared to guarantee a favorable result. The governor, Ignatiev, using his personal system of political nomenclature, broke down the political tendencies of those at the district meetings (see Table 5.2). The term "monarchist" was usually interpreted as referring to a person who was specifically loyal to the Duma pravye. If one accepts Ignatiev's figures, and they seem reliable only in a very general sense, there still remained a broad category of voters who characterized themselves as merely right-wing in the manner so common during the third Duma elections. However, the presence of a sizeable number of people now actually calling themselves Nationalists demonstrated that the specificity of party labels had increased since 1907. In the actual choosing of electors, those described as "right-wing" supported the Nationalists. As a result, the party succeeded in having all its nominees named to the final electoral assembly.

Forty-one priests, forty peasants, and forty-six landowners were chosen to the gubernia assembly.[50] *Podolskie Izvestia*, the liberal daily, divided them according to political tendency (see Table 5.3). Without much difficulty, this gathering, faced with the well-prepared strength of the Nationalists, elected the full slate of the party's candidates to the Duma: Balashev, Gizhitskii, V. A. Anchinnikov, N. N. Mozhaiskii, Pototskii, and

49. Ibid., 11, 39, and 45.
50. TsGAOR 102.4-oe deloproizvodstvo (1912) 274.109.

Table 5.3. **The Political Tendencies of Delegates to the Podol'e Gubernia Assembly**

Right wing	54
Nationalists	42
Nonparty	24
Progressives	21
Octobrists	1
Monarchists	1
Left wing	1

Source: Podolskie Izvestia, October 9, 1912.

D. N. Chikhachev. The average vote was 95 to 45, indicating that progressive candidates had some support even in Podol'e.[51]

Volynia. With the failure of the Nationalists' campaign to replace Kutaisov, they were left with a new governor, M. A. Melnikov, who was scarcely any more sympathetic to their cause. Absenteeism and confusion among the local Russian nobility persisted, and the Nationalists were never able to gain the loyalty of the large mass of those landowners actually residing in the province, most of whom, as elsewhere, simply considered themselves right-wing.[52] The situation was so unpromising that Shulgin considered not running.[53] A listless campaign, if one could even call it that, produced a generally right-wing gubernia assembly that, with the exception of Shulgin, elected a Duma delegation composed entirely of pravye.

As in the zemstvo elections, Volynia did not follow the examples of Kiev and Podol'e. Russian absenteeism was higher in Volynia and the Polish population was larger. Of the three southwest gubernias, its agriculture was the least commercial. Thus, the social conditions that supported Nationalist success in Kiev and Podol'e simply did not exist in Volynia.

Minsk. The Minsk Nationalists had reached a preelectoral accord only with certain members of the now defunct Octobrist branch. Despite smaller numbers than the Nationalists, the pravye maintained a separate identity. As a result, efforts to nominate a slate of rightist candidates were unsuccessful. Despite a number of agitational meetings, which attracted between eighty and one hundred people who usually heard exhortations

51. TsGIA Leningrad 1327.2.252.138–150.
52. TsGAOR 102. (1912) 265.577.2103. F. F. Trepov, Kiev, t V. F. Gindin-Levkovich, Lipovets (September 28, 1912). Ibid., 578.2297. P. Demidov, Zhitomir, to F. F. Trepov, Kiev (October 15, 1912).
53. Ibid. 576.2044. Shulgin, Volynia, to Rein, St. Petersburg (September 29, 1912).

to support broad Nationalist principles, few candidates were nominated. Much of the party's inability to specify candidates was due to the absence of any outstanding local leaders in the Nationalist camp. Only twenty Russian landlords were in the final electoral assembly. However, assistance came from the usual sizeable delegation of priests. The forces of the right combined against a fairly sizeable national opposition of sixteen Poles and seventeen Jews to elect a slate of largely unknown men to the Duma. Seven of these men called themselves Nationalists, while two more became pravye.[54]

Vitebsk. The Nationalists had been represented in Vitebsk by the Vitebsk Electoral Committee for some time, but this group had not been especially active in anticipation of the election. Only the clergy, working among the peasantry, had devoted much time to preparatory work. Party life in Vitebsk was poorly developed, and it was more by default than through any serious organizational effort that the Nationalists were able to emerge victorious in the election.[55]

The Vitebsk gubernia was the least populous, least urbanized, and least commercial of the six western provinces. There existed little focus for agitational activity in the province. The few newspaper accounts of events in Vitebsk generally describe apathy and indifference to the elections. Certainly the presence of larger cities in the gubernia might have created more active political traditions. In a sense, Vitebsk stands in direct contrast to the intense activity in Kiev. However, despite this situation, five of the gubernia's six places in the Duma went to men who later came to call themselves Nationalists.

Mogilev. Like Vitebsk, Mogilev did not have clearly developed party distinctions. The gubernia's towns were among the smallest in the west. Lacking an urban focus, few trends of political thought ever became crystallized in any organizational form. As a result, much of the work of assuring a result favorable to the government fell on the shoulders of the governor, Pilts. However, unlike Vitebsk, there were voters in Mogilev who were loyal to the Octobrists and pravye as well as to the Nationalists. As elsewhere, an agreement between the clergy and the governor had been worked out, and, as a result, the assemblies of small landowners were dominated by priests.[56] However, the harmonious relationship broke down when Bishop Mitrofan, with whom Pilts had been cooperating,

54. *Minskii Golos*, October 4, 1912.
55. *Novoe Vremia*, September 9 and 10, 1912.
56. TsGIA Leningrad 1327, 2.210.62.

began to campaign against the candidacy of V. S. Dribintsev, a right Octobrist who was an Old Believer. However, Dribintsev had Pilts's support as well as that of much of the rest of the gubernia's gentry.[57] The accord with the clergy evaporated, and Mitrofan began to agitate for his own slate of candidates even though he and his allies were clearly outnumbered in the gubernia electoral assembly. The bishop's supporters, among whom was the secretary of the third Duma, P. V. Sazonovich, were largely pravye sympathizers.[58]

Mitrofan's new assertiveness led to the breakdown of the orderly election process. Pilts sought to have the Holy Synod call Mitrofan to Petersburg at the time of the city elections in which the Bishop was a candidate in the second curia.[59] The results of the elections of vyborshchiki were a reaction against Mitrofan's "crude and open" agitation against Dribintsev, leading to the defeat of the bishop's supporters, including Sazonovich.[60] This unforeseen tumult led to uncertainty among the members of the gubernia assembly. N. K. von Gubbenet, the Nationalist who had represented Mogilev, was advised by friends to appear on the scene quickly if he wished to be reelected. He did not follow this advice, and, as a result, was not chosen to the fourth Duma.[61] The confusion led to the election of a rather mixed Duma delegation that included Dribintsev and the Nationalist, Ladomirskii, but no priests at all. In all, four Nationalists, two Octobrists, and one pravyi were elected.

The Nationalists did well, as indeed they had to, in the six western gubernias included in the Western Zemstvo Act. Only in Volynia did they fail to win a majority of the Duma delegation. Elsewhere, their electoral success corresponded directly to the strength of their local organizations and the extent of government assistance. Kiev and Podol'e had the oldest and largest Nationalist groups. In Minsk, the potential for a successful effort existed, and the party drew most of the gubernia's seats, even though its branch there was young and its leaders relatively inexperienced and unknown. The two northernmost gubernias, Mogilev and Vitebsk, lacked the sizeable cities in which the Nationalists had come to base much, though by no means all, of their operations. Party organizations in these two provinces were weakly developed, and the Nationalists exercised no special influence. The final count for the western gubernias gave fifteen

57. Ibid., 76.
58. Ibid., 80.
59. Ibid., 89.
60. Ibid., 95.
61. TsGAOR 102 (1912), 265.577.2181. No signature, Roslavl, to von Gubbenet, St. Petersburg (October 4, 1912).

pravye, forty-four Nationalists, one Center Group member, two Octobrists, and one Kadet. The key agitational roles played by Duma deputies, plus their active participation in electioneering and organization demonstrate that, at least in the west, the Nationalists could create a solid organizational base that could be politically effective.

The Rest of Russia

Outside the west, concern with the Duma elections took even longer to manifest itself. In most gubernias in which the Nationalists were a force at all, they were not sufficiently strong to manage an electoral campaign and thus were forced to seek the creation of blocs. With the majority of Octobrist local branches all but gone from the scene and the Nationalist groups still in their infancy, no single party was capable of carrying on its own campaign. Therefore, the burden of assuring results favorable to the government most often fell on the provincial governor.

The need for independent party organizations had never arisen in central Russia. Either the zemstvos or the bureaucracy had provided an outlet for the gentry's political energy. Thus, the rise of relatively self-sufficient political parties had made little headway throughout the rest of the Russian countryside, where the special conditions of the west (commercial agriculture, hostile nationalities, large cities, and different local institutions) were not found. Membership in the Nationalist Party outside the west had a different and less precise meaning than it did in the borderland.

Like much of the gentry, the Nationalists were neither constitutionalist nor demagogic, and they hoped that this large and indistinct mass of landowners would come to support them. However, much of the gentry's desire or need to affiliate had diminished by 1912. Their political involvement during 1905 and in the early phases of the regime based on the revised election law had been extensive, but with peasant revolution seemingly contained and the government apparently aimless without Stolypin, their direct concern with politics had waned. Most landowners clung to the general categories of right-wing or progressive. Increasingly, fewer local landowners were bothering to call themselves Octobrists, and most were too moderate to ally with the last remains of the Union of Russian People. Landlords felt no special compulsion to affiliate with any party, although a few chose the Nationalists.

The Nationalists were unable to score any sweeping victories of the kind they achieved in the borderland. Only in Grodno, just west of Minsk, and in Pskov, which bordered on Vitebsk, did they succeed in electing large numbers of deputies. Elsewhere, one, two, sometimes three Nationalists went to the Duma from gubernias where the Duma delegation was dominated by some other party.

But Octobrist dominance of the central provinces and the left-bank Ukraine had also diminished. No single event demonstrated the Octobrists' general decline as dramatically as Guchkov's defeat in Moscow. The party's traditional commercial and industrial support in the city had moved to the left, embracing the Progressisty and Kadets. Guchkov and his supporters had permitted the party's local organizations to erode in the hope that the success of their cooperation with the government in the Duma would so impress Russian voters that they would support the Octobrists in 1912. Yet, as early as 1909, that attempt had collapsed and with it went the Octobrists' hope of gaining control of the fourth Duma. While the Progressisty were making gains among the middle classes, Octobrist support among the gentry was waning as that group returned to its former lethargy. Despite their hopes, Nationalists did not directly displace the Octobrists as the party of the nobility in central Russia. As might be expected for a centrist party seeking to occupy a swiftly eroding vital political center, the Octobrists lost seats in all directions, not only to the Nationalists and Progressisty, but to Krupenskii's new Center Party and the Kadets as well.

In Kazan, the Nationalists had sought to establish a union with the Octobrists in order to guarantee themselves some minimal measure of representation. However, the Nationalists' attempt to negotiate an electoral bloc was hampered by demands from local pravye for some representation in any such combination.[62] This move apparantly succeeded in frightening the Octobrists away from any cooperation. For reasons that were not clear, the Nationalists refused to disown the pravye, and so the Octobrists concluded a secret agreement with the Kadets, while publicly announcing that they had decided to go it alone.[63] Very shortly thereafter, the Nationalists split with the pravye, as the two parties found themselves competing for the support of peasant electors.

As a result of all this confusion, no party was able to achieve a clear advantage in the gubernia electoral assembly. By the governor's account, twelve of the vyborshchiki called themselves monarchists, seventeen were committed pravye, forty-seven were nonparty rights, and only three

62. Ibid., 576.2011. M. Kapustin, Kazan, to K. E. Lindeman, Moscow (September 17, 1912). Bariatinskii, Kazan, to A. I. Guchkov, St. Petersburg (September 11, 1912).

63. Ibid., 509.84. N. A. Melnikov, Kazan, to Guchkov (September 26, 1912). TsGAOR 102.4-oe deloproizvodtsvo (1912) 274.80.

actually claimed to be Nationalists. There were thirteen Octobrists (eight of them left-wing), four Kadets, eight nonparty lefts, one Social Democrat, and one Social Revolutionary.[64] This body ultimately produced seven Octobrists, one Nationalist, one pravyi, and one member of the Center Group. One hesitates to say that Kazan was typical of central Russian gubernias, but it does furnish a good example, which was repeated elsewhere, of a relatively young Nationalist organization failing in its attempt to expand the party's influence in an area where it had not done well previously.

Pskov, on the other hand, provides a case of a province in which the future Nationalists had experienced good success in 1907 and in which they had established a fairly strong local branch. A relatively small province, Pskov had been well organized by the Nationalists, who maintained a good relationship with the governor. The result of this smallness and good organization was an exceptionally high rate of electoral participation, particularly among small landowners. According to the provincial governor, over 72 percent of those eligible actually took part. Fifty-one percent of the large landowners voted.[65] The clergy did not outnumber the peasantry in the assemblies of small landowners to the extent they did elsewhere. In any case, both groups were dominated by men with reportedly right-wing sympathies.[66]

Ultimately, the province elected a final gubernia assembly whose character in terms of soslovie and political complexion was reasonably typical of most of the other provinces. Of the electors, there were thirty-seven nobles, four priests, nine honorary citizens, three merchants, two from the meshchanstvo (petty bourgeoisie), and fifteen peasants. Fifty of these men called themselves right-wing, six said that they were moderates, and fourteen sympathized with the left.[67] A complete slate of five Nationalists was sent to the Duma, confirming once again that the only reliable prescription for Nationalist electoral success was long-standing, well-entrenched organization.

In the wake of the elections, the Nationalists' hope of dominating the fourth Duma was unrealized. The Octobrists had lost many seats, but they had by no means been wiped out. In fact, no party was in a position to control events in the Duma. The Nationalists' plans for broadening their base had failed. Their success in the west had made the party even more homogeneous than before. Many of the party members from outside the

64. TsGIA Leningrad 1327.2.201.146.
65. Ibid., 222.44.
66. Ibid., 13.
67. Ibid., 56.

borderland had now drifted away, leaving the Nationalists a narrow interest party of the west Russian gentry with little claim to national leadership.

The indecisiveness of the election was ominous. It indicated the deep divisions among Russia's propertied classes at a time when their dominance of society was being increasingly challenged. Participation in Stolypin's attempt to allow peasants to leave their communes had diminished considerably. Moreover, the overriding cause of peasant discontent—lack of land—still had not been addressed. In the cities, workers were striking in ever greater numbers, and the character of the movement was becoming increasingly oppositional. A united front of large property holders might have contained the discontent, but the elections of 1912 revealed the absence of such unity.

VI

The Fourth Duma and the New Crisis

The third Duma had begun its work in 1907 after the suppression of a massive revolution, while the fourth Duma started operations at the beginning of a new revolutionary upsurge. The streets of Russia's cities, quiet since 1906, were once again filled with striking and demonstrating workers. Between November 1912 and the outbreak of the world war in 1914, the relationships and understandings on which the revised electoral system had been based collapsed. Stolypin had demanded the achievement of social stability before the institution of any serious reform, but the revival of the labor movement quickly eroded that necessary stability. At the same time, the propertied elements represented in the Tauride Palace lost their limited capacity for united action. All the parties began to disintegrate, and their internal disarray made the achievement of a steady, functioning Duma majority virtually impossible. This weakness paralyzed the Duma at the most inopportune time, because the tsar, under pressure from various bureaucratic elements, was now contemplating making further inroads on the concessions he had granted the Russian people in 1905.

On the eve of World War I, the autocracy, the gentry, and the various segments of Russia's bourgeoisie were thoroughly disunited. It proved impossible for these forces of order to present a united front to the increasingly revolutionary urban proletariat. At the same time, the attempt to restructure relations on the land (the Stolypin reform) had lost its momentum. Peasants remained quiet, but their essential, long-standing demands for more land were still unsatisfied.

Confusion and Ambiguity
(The First Session)

Despite their mixed showing, the Nationalists retained some hope of expanding their influence and power in the lower house.[1] The vast majority of deputies had not formally declared their party affiliation, and no one expected the large number of deputies described by official sources as rightist actually to join the far right group. On the Nationalists' left, the Octobrists had suffered severe losses at the polls, and Guchkov's defeat had deprived them of their most dynamic leader. As a result, the Nationalists believed that they might replace the Octobrists as the largest and most powerful fraction in the fourth Duma. However, when the Duma convened and the deputies formally declared their choices of party, the Nationalists were shocked to find that the size of their group was virtually unchanged. They still numbered around ninety deputies. The Octobrists, with ninety-five members, remained the largest fraction; and they continued to occupy the Duma's political center.[2] Thus, although severely diminished, Octobrist strength was still substantial. The Nationalists had hoped to become masters of the situation. Instead, in the months ahead, they were forced to scramble to preserve any influence at all.

Although the new Nationalist fraction retained roughly the same social composition, it was by no means a carbon copy of its predecessor (see Table 6.1). The turnover of deputies was extensive. Only twenty-one party members were veterans of the third Duma (overall, 140 of 440 deputies had served previously). But, most of the party's leaders—Balashev, Bogdanov, Bezak, Gizhitskii, D. N. Chikhachev, and Shulgin—did return. There were also important additions—namely, N. N. Chikhachev, Demchenko, and Savenko—who had all played important roles in the Kiev Club of Russian Nationalists. Many of the new Nationalists had been active in local politics, most notably in the new zemstvos of the western gubernias. Thus, the number of Nationalists reporting zemstvo experience

1. *Kievlianin*, November 2 and 17, 1912; *Novoe Vremia*, October 28, 1912.
2. *Rossiia*, November 27, 1912.

Table 6.1 **The Nationalist Delegation in the Third and Fourth Dumas**

Soslovie	Third Duma	Fourth Duma
Nobles	52	54
Priests	14	20
Peasants	16	17
Others	5	0

Source: Potrety (third and fourth Dumas).

rose dramatically from twenty-five in the third Duma to forty-four in the fourth.

The Western Zemstvo Act had its intended effect of increasing the Nationalists' strength in the borderland, but this led to a sharp increase in the regional character of the Nationalists' Duma group. Thirty-three of eighty-eight third Duma Nationalists had been from the nine western provinces. Now fifty of the party's deputies were from the west. This greater geographical homogeneity reflected their inability, in Stolypin's absence, to attract the kind of uncommitted deputies from the rest of Russia who had previously affiliated with the Octobrists for want of anything better to do. With Octobrist strength declining, the Nationalists had an opportunity to acquire twenty or thirty nonwestern deputies at the start of the Duma's first session, but their hopes were quickly thwarted.

In the beginning of November, P. N. Krupenskii announced plans for a new Duma fraction that would sit between the Octobrists and National-ists.[3] Krupenskii's devotion to the idea of a smoothly functioning centrist Duma majority had always been greater than his commitment to the Nationalists' programs and aims.

> I had hoped that the ... Nationalist fraction would advance the unity of the Duma's center groups and work hand-in-hand with the Octobrists. More and more the Nationalists moved to the right. Less and less was their nationalism "independent."[4]

Krupenskii opposed what he called the "combative" nationalism of Balashev and Bobrinskii.[5] He was also distressed that the party had taken over the operation of the National Club, driving out "moderates" and members of other parties.[6] In response to these trends, he announced the

3. *Russkie Vedemosti*, November 3, 1912.

4. *Rech'*, November 4, 1912.

5. TsGAOR 102 (1912) 265.2742. Krupenskii, St. Petersburg, to Prince I. V. Bariatinskii, Yalta (November 19, 1912).

6. *Novoe Vremia*, November 4, 1912; *Rech'*, November 4, 1912.

Table 6.2. **Political Composition of the Fourth Duma**

Pravye	63
Nationalists	91
Center Group	31
Octobrists	95
Progressisty	41
Kadets	53
Trudoviki (labor group)	10
Social Democrats	15
Polish kolo	9
Bielorussians	6
Muslim group	7
Nonparty	11

Source: Kievlianin, November 2, 1912.

formation of his new Center Group, issued a program and began recruiting members.[7] By the beginning of the first session, thirty-one deputies had allied with Krupenskii. Twenty-two of the Centrists were nobles, and only one was from the west. Many of these might otherwise have drifted into the Nationalist fraction. If they had done so, the Nationalists would have been the largest Duma group. As a result, the Nationalists were furious with Krupenskii for spoiling their chances.[8]

The creation of the Center Group undermined the kind of permanent conservative majority the Nationalists desired.[9] As each new Duma fraction emerged, the task of setting up any interparty agreement became more difficult. The Octobrist–Nationalist cooperation that had characterized the early work of the third Duma proved an insufficient basis for a permanent majority in the fourth Duma. In view of the strength of the various party groups, any new arrangement would now have to involve three or four fractions (see Table 6.2). Nonetheless, the Nationalists still hoped that they might become the center of a permanent right majority that would include the pravye, the Center Group, and most of the Octobrists. But finding a common program on which these groups could agree proved impossible.[10] The fourth Duma then drifted through a series of shifting alliances until the formation of the Progressive Bloc in the dark days of 1915.

7. *Rech'*, November 6, 1912; *Russkie Vedemosti*, November 4, 1912.
8. *Kievlianin*, November 15, 17, and 22, 1912.
9. TsGAOR 102 (1912) 265.583.2760. Savenko, St. Petersburg, to A. S. Liubinskii, Kiev (November 20, 1912). *Rech'*, November 8, 1912.
10. *Novoe Vremia*, October 28, 1912.

The impermanence and uncertainty of party relations in the fourth Duma became apparent immediately. The presidium elections, normally a formality, produced a chaotic scramble for power. Every party entertained hopes of gaining some control and influence; the winning of presidium offices was a secondary matter. Far more important was the character of whatever coalition would form in support of the various candidates. Would these combinations simply be temporary alliances or would they have the potential for developing a joint program that could serve as a basis for a permanent Duma majority? The Nationalists now thought that their time had come to assume command of the Duma.[11] At the party's first meeting on November 13, Balashev was reelected party leader. Immediately, he began advancing himself as a candidate for the Duma presidency.[12]

The fourth Duma opened on November 15. Its first meeting was a disaster for the Nationalists. With the support of the left, Rodzianko defeated Balashev for the presidency by a vote of 234 to 147.[13] The party's hopes for control of the new Duma had been smashed in the very first vote. The Octobrists had refused to cooperate with them, although the Nationalists had cooperated with them throughout the third Duma. To demonstrate their outrage, the Nationalists and the pravye walked out of the chamber as Rodzianko began his acceptance speech.[14] Realizing that this step had been a mistake, the Nationalists hastened to apologize to Rodzianko and the Octobrists. Talks on the other presidium positions were opened and broadened to include the chairmanships of the various Duma committees.[15] These negotiations, however, soon destroyed whatever goodwill had been established. The Nationalists sought to drive a

11. TsGAOR, 102 (1912) 265.584.2812. G. Lerkhe, St. Petersburg, to Mme. Guchkov, Russian Embassy, Sofia (November 24, 1912). Lerkhe, an Octobrist deputy, said he was told by a Nationalist deputy, "In the Third Duma, the Octobrists commanded us. Now we will command the Octobrists."

12. *Novoe Vremia*, November 13, 1912.

13. M. I. Simonov, *Pervye dni gosudarstvennoi dumy-IV-ego sozyva-vybory presidiuma* (St. Petersburg, 1913), pp. 15–18; *Rech'*, November 15, 1912; *Novoe Vremia*, November 15, 1912.

14. TsGAOR 102.00.307a (1912) 47; *Rech'*, November 16, 1912.

15. *Rech'*, November 25 and 27, 1912; TsGAOR 102 (1912) 0.265.584.2827. Savenko, St. Petersburg, to N. K. Savenko, Kiev (November 25, 1912); TsGAOR, 115.2.4.39. Shidlovskii, Savich, and Shubinskii, on behalf of the Octobrists, suggested to Balashev, Bobrinskii, and Vetchinin that the Nationalists could be compensated for their losses in the presidium with the leadership of key committees. The Nationalists responded favorably and reciprocated by dropping objections to the election of the Progressist, D. D. Uvarov, as one of the Duma's vice-presidents. V. M. Volkonskii, the Nationalist vice-president of the third Duma, then announced willingness, after several refusals, to assume the other vice-presidency now that he could be assured of Octobrist and Nationalist support.

hard bargain, and, for some time, the Octobrists refused to go along.[16] The Nationalists were willing to work with the Octobrists, if the Octobrists disowned the Kadets, while the Octobrists wanted the Nationalists to cut their ties with the pravye. Neither party would take such a step.[17] Thus, the entire episode of the presidium election was thoroughly indecisive.

The third Duma had been marked by Stolypin's attempt to forge a link between *tsenzovye elementy* (propertied classes) and the state. His proposals had provoked the parties into politically meaningful alliances, and those ideas had given the deputies a sense that their work was important and potentially fruitful. No party had benefitted more from this situation than the Nationalists. Now, with Kokovtsov's accession, they found themselves in the impossible position of being a "governmental" party that despised the head of the government.[18] Thus, the Nationalists were cut off from the access to ministerial power that they had enjoyed under Stolypin. This new circumstance made their position particularly difficult. Unlike the Octobrists, the Nationalists did not have the political option of extending their opposition to Kokovtsov into broader and more profound opposition to the government. Loyalty to the state was never in question. Instead, they concentrated on criticism of Kokovtsov's program or, as the Nationalists saw it, his lack of a program. More than any other party, they missed Stolypin's leadership. "We are a ship without a rudder," moaned Savenko. "The government has no course. We live from day to day."[19]

A working conservative Duma majority might have forced Kokovtsov into advancing more concrete proposals. But the Nationalists stood in no position to gain from any such arrangement. The leader of a right-wing majority would have had to work harmoniously with the president of the Council of Ministers. Therefore, neither Balashev nor any other Nationalist could have chaired the permanent right-wing majority they had publicly advocated. In response to this situation, the Nationalists became suspicious of any long-term Duma arrangements.[20]

16. TsGAOR, 102. (1912) 9.265.585.2912. Savenko, St. Petersburg, to N. K. Savenko, Kiev (December 1, 1912); TsGAOR 115.2.4.43, 54, and 57; *Rech'*, November 29 and December 7, 1912; *Novoe Vremia*, November 28 and 30, and December 1, 1912.

17. TsGAOR 102 (1912) 269.585.2935. N. Khomiakov, St. Petersburg, to A. N. Bariatinskii, Kazan (December 3, 1912); *Kievlianin*, December 6, 1912.

18. V. N. Kokovstov, *Iz moego proshlogo*, Vol. 2. p. 133.

19. *Kievlianin*, November 25, 1912, and *Novoe Vremia*, March 14, 1913.

20. Geoffrey Hosking, *The Russian Constitutional Experiment* (Cambridge, 1973), pp. 197–214; Leopold Haimson, "The Problem of Social Stability in Urban Russia: 1905–1917," *Slavic Review* (December 1964):619–642; E. D. Chermenskii, *IV-aia Gosudarstvennaia duma i sverzhenie tsarizma v Rossii*, pp. 53–57.

The inability of the Duma parties to establish a permanent majority made it clear that, by the spring of 1913, the vital center of the lower house was eroding. That political fact reflected the more fundamental disintegration of the political and economic consensus among the nation's propertied classes. In both these processes, the Nationalists played a centrifugal role. The party's activity during this period undermined the stability of the Third of June system in two ways.

First, in the case of the Nationalists, the intraparty divisions that emerged over tactics and alliances corresponded almost exactly to the fundamental institutional and political problem that the party had sought to avoid solving since its inception—how to reconcile their support of the state with their participation in an independent representative assembly. With no answer to this crucial question, the Nationalists were in no position to bridge the quickly expanding gap between the autocracy and the parties in the Duma.

Second, on the relatively rare occasions when the issue arose in the Duma, the Nationalists staunchly defended the immediate interests of the agrarian sector of the economy when those interests came into conflict with the needs and demands of the expanding industrial sector. This led them into conflict with all the parties that gave expression to the needs of the bourgeoisie (the Kadets, Progressisty, and even the Octobrists).

Although both problems were thoroughly interrelated, the first of them—the institutional question—initially emerged as a source of tension within the Nationalist fraction. From the outset of the fourth Duma, the party had begun dividing into camps. Differences over tactics reflected broader political disagreements, and these tensions were exacerbated by personality clashes. Savenko, on the party's left wing, and Bogdanov, on its right, were immediately at each other's throats.[21] Although new to the Duma, Savenko wasted no time in assuming as visible a posture as possible. Enormously ambitious, he spoke often and long in the Duma, made numerous appearances at the capital's political clubs, and began to write for the Petersburg press, most notably for *Novoe Vremia.*[22]

Savenko's closest ally and friend was V. Ia. Demchenko. Also a newcomer, Demchencko, like Savenko, had risen to prominence as a result of his role in developing the party's organization in Kiev. Bogdanov had also participated in the growth of the Kiev Club, but he had been less prominent locally than either Demchenko or Savenko, and he was less

21. TsGAOR 102 (1912) 265.584.2870. Tvoi "M", St. Petersburg, to Father G. N. Sobolev, Kiev (November 19, 1912). "M" in this case appears to be the right-wing Nationalist deputy from Kiev, Father Mitrotskii.

22. Ibid., 585.2924. Savenko, St. Petersburg, to N. K. Savenko, Kiev (December 2, 1912).

than thrilled to see these two upstarts come into the Duma and immediately assume the positions of leading Nationalist spokesmen[23]. However, the election of a new party bureau in the fall of 1912 did not bring these divisions into public view. Balashev, who at this point sought to remain neutral, was reelected president, and all the tendencies within the fraction were represented in the new council. The public finally learned of this problem in December 1912, when Bogdanov expressed his fears of a Nationalist split in the pages of *Kievlianin*.[24]

The question of cooperation with the Octobrists (who had cooperated with Kadets on the presidium and other questions) raised fundamental problems for the Nationalist party. The Nationalists had always attacked the Kadets as revolutionaries and "Jew lovers." Ever since the beginning of the third Duma, they had urged the Octobrists to reject the Kadets. It was now clear that the Octobrists had no intention of doing so. Therefore, a Nationalist agreement with the Octobrists, as some left-wing Nationalists urged, required a muting of the party's attacks on the opposition at a time when the opposition was drawing still further away from the state.

The Nationalists' political position had been based on the cooperation of the state with those social groups represented in the third Duma. Simultaneous loyalty to the institution of the autocracy and to the organs of popular representation had characterized Nationalist politics from the outset. Now the Nationalists were being pushed into making the very choice that their entire program and political approach had been designed to avoid. It is therefore not surprising that this problem produced bitter divisions within the party on the local as well as the national level. In fact, the Nationalists eventually split over this apparently institutional issue in 1915.

The party's situation was further complicated by its severe dissatisfaction with Kokovtsov's handling of the affairs of the state. As the Octobrists and the Center Group moved toward the left, the Nationalists could logically have been expected to drift into further support for the government. But their profound hatred of Kokovtsov made this course impossible. Some momentary advantage could be gained through appealing to other factions within the Council of Ministers, and the Nationalists could, of course, agitate for a new premier. But by this time, most ministers were

23. Ibid., 2964. Savenko to N. K. Savenko, December 5, 1912. Ibid., 2988. "M," St. Petersburg, to A. Ia. Mitrotskii, Kiev (December 7, 1912). The right-wing priest, Mitrotskii lumped Balashev with the left. Mitrotskii also noted privately that the left tendency, which favored cooperation with the Octobrists and was centered around Savenko, represented the majority sentiment of fraction members.

24. *Kievlianin*, December 24, 1912.

indifferent to appeals from Duma members, even those who were conservatives.

Thus, by the spring of 1913, the Nationalists were too weak to control affairs on their own and were cut off from any other possible politically meaningful alliance. As a result, party members became demoralized and apathetic. Absenteeism of party leaders had resulted in a series of embarrassing parliamentary defeats that then spread disaffection among the rank and file.[25] Even so loyal a figure as F. N. Bezak deserted the Duma in June 1913 to devote all his energies to the post of Kiev gubernia marshal of nobility.[26] By the end of the first session, the Nationalists found that none of their hopes for power had been realized, and their options for regaining even a diminished measure of influence were quickly disappearing.

The second centrifugal tendency, the defense of agrarian interests, did not often surface in the Duma. The kinds of agreements the left-wing Nationalists proposed to make with the Octobrists, or even with the Kadets and Progressisty, were to be strictly parliamentary. They were to pertain only to interparty relations in the Duma and were in no way supposed to signify a broader cooperation between those social classes the Nationalists thought the various parties represented. In the fourth Duma, the Nationalists opposed those few measures designed to aid the industrial sector of the economy. They specifically opposed the interests of the industrial bourgeoisie. They criticized government policies that supported industry.[27] More significantly, the Nationalists perceived the industrial bourgeoisie to be a profound and menacing threat to their political and economic interests. During debate on the budget estimates of the Ministry of Trade and Industry, Savenko attacked the power of the large industrial syndicates.[28] Despite protective tariffs and large state orders, Savenko claimed, the representatives of the industrial classes were still not satisfied. He quoted the Progressist leader A. I. Konovalov's criticism of the Ministry of Trade and Industry.

Here are Konovalov's words. "These kinds of policies cannot be continued because they contradict our economic interests." If you think about what this means, you can see that he wants all state and popular matters decided

---

25. TsGAOR 102 (1912) 265.918.287. Savenko, St. Petersburg, to N. K. Savenko, Kiev (February 17, 1913).

26. *Novoe Vremia*, June 21, 1913.

27. *Rech'*, June 9, 1913. *Novoe Vremia*, June 9, 1913.

28. Sten. ot., 4.1.3.1185–1212.

exclusively from the point of view of the big industrialists and merchants. It is necessary to struggle decisively and seriously against this calamity.[29]

But Savenko's mistrust of the bourgeoisie ran deeper than mere accusations of selfishness. Earlier, writing in *Kievlianin*, he had warned that the growth of the industrial sector would spell doom for both the landed nobility and the state that had created it.

> Everywhere, the development of trade and industry has been a sign and a cause of revolution. The bourgeoisie, as it grows in strength and influence, begins to aspire to the seizure of power and enters into a struggle with the aristocracy in order to take its place. We already see the beginning of this. Our bourgeoisie, especially the Moscow bourgeoisie, is extremely oppositional.[30]

Coming from a member of the Nationalists' left wing, these views were especially striking. Unlike their German counterparts, Russian Nationalists feared industrialists and refused to cooperate with them.

On such matters of direct and concrete economic interest as taxation, the Nationalists were especially opposed to urban industrial interests. In the fall of 1913, with political relationships even more scrambled, they voted with the pravye and the far left to defeat a Kadet-Octobrist-Progressist proposal to lower taxes on immovable property in the cities.[31] Although these sorts of direct clashes of economic interest occurred infrequently in the Duma, they do reveal a firm unwillingness to find a basis of cooperation with large urban property owners.

By this time, the hope of achieving a permanent rightist majority had vanished. The Nationalists found that the Duma, whose existence had necessitated the party's creation, was now dominated by hostile forces. Those forces opposed the state to which the Nationalists were still loyal, and, moreover, they sought to enact laws that would directly harm the interests of those agrarian elements represented by the Nationalist Party. The Nationalists could not help but feel that their position in 1913 was as precarious as it had been in 1907, but now conditions had changed. There was no longer a Stolypin to propose laws that benefitted them directly.

29. Ibid., 1344.

30. *Kievlianin*, February 14, 1913.

31. *Rossiia*, November 23, 1913; *Novoe Vremia*, November 19, 20, and 21, 1913; *Rech'*, November 21. 1913. In opposition to the rest of the Nationalists, Demchenko spoke for the lowering of the tax from 6 percent to 4 percent. He was not censured for violating party discipline. See Sten. ot., 4.2.1.1166.

There was no longer a strong, united, moderate Octobrist party to aid the passage of those proposals through the legislature. And, most frighteningly, the forces of movement were no longer quiescent. The Nationalists found themselves confronted by forces they understood but were in no position to control. The party had come into being at a time of social peace when either-or decisions were not necessary. As a result, the party found itself poorly equipped to deal with the multiple processes of polarization that were leading to the disintegration of Russian society.

Drift and Division
(The Second Session)

With the government offering the Duma little new legislation, and the Duma too disorganized to develop its own program, legislative activity ground to a virtual halt. With rare unanimity, the press began to complain of the boredom of life in the Tauride Palace. Indifference and absenteeism were rampant among the deputies. The other parties soon succumbed to the apathy already felt by the Nationalists.

The Duma's slumber came at a particularly dangerous moment. Since early spring, the reactionary wing of the Council of Ministers, headed by N. A. Maklakov (Interior) and I. G. Shcheglovitov (Justice), had been pressing for a restriction of the Duma's rights and powers.[32] Maklakov, a firm opponent of popular representation, had replaced Makarov in the powerful Ministry of Interior. His appointment was seen as a sign of Nicholas's growing disenchantment with the Duma. During the next year, the deputies' parliamentary immunity and freedom of expression came under attack. Attempts were made to restrict the Duma's budgetary rights, and it was feared the lower house would be reduced to consultative status. Only fear of popular response and international pressure restrained the reactionary ministers.[33]

In May 1913, Maklakov and his allies found a pretext for increasing the pressure on the Duma. Speaking on the budget, the pravye deputy, Markov II, had accused Kokovtsov of bribery and theft. Such language was usually ruled out of order, and more often than not, an apology to the

32. Chermenskii, *IV-aia Duma*, pp. 51–52; TsGAOR, 102. (1913) 307a.35. This police report noted that N. A. Maklakov had been conducting a campaign of petty harassment against opposition deputies for some time.

33. Hosking, *The Russian Constitutional Experiment*, pp. 199–200.

accused followed. However, the Nationalist deputy, Prince V. M. Volkon-skii, who was presiding at the time, merely slapped Markov II on the wrist. Kokovtsov demanded satisfaction, but the Duma's Council of Elders, sensing the larger issues involved in the dispute, declined to take any action.[34] Kokovtsov and the other ministers then refused to appear in the Duma either to explain bills or to answer interpellations until Markov II apologized.

At first, the Nationalists joined in the widespread protest against what was called the "ministerial boycott." Savenko argued that Markov's remarks were only a pretext for a long-planned attack. The government, he claimed, was now splitting even with the parties of the right.[35] However, the rest of the Nationalists were far more hesitant. The boycott represented just the sort of direct confrontation between government and Duma that they had always hoped to avoid. They withdrew their initial support for an Octobrist-Center Group resolution condemning the ministers and instead adopted what they called a neutral position.[36] When the Nationalists were attacked for not joining the criticism against the government, Balashev gave the cryptic reply that his fraction's position toward the government was "clearer" than that of any other group.[37]

The crisis dragged on through the summer. Rodzianko met repeatedly with Kokovtsov during these months to find a way out of the impasse.[38] Ultimately, Maklakov's group proved unable or unwilling to push their aims to the logical conclusion, and when, on the eve of the second session, Markov, under considerable pressure, offered a formal apology, the boycott was lifted.[39]

While this episode further poisoned the already tense relations between the government and the Duma, it proved particularly damaging to the Nationalists. Those outside the party now viewed it as the weakest of bulwarks against archreactionary attacks on the Duma.[40] Those inside the party were once again forced to face the divisive issue of the tensions between representative and state institutions. The more often the Nationalists were forced to choose sides in this conflict, the more intense became their internal argument. For this reason, the ministerial boycott was an important step in the eventual disintegration of the Nationalist Party.

34. Ibid.
35. *Kievlianin,* June 9, 1913.
36. *Rech',* June 1 and 5, 1913; *Novoe Vremia,* June 5, 1913.
37. *Novoe Vremia,* October 15, 1913.
38. *Rech',* September 7, 1913.
39. *Novoe Vremia,* November 2, 1913.
40. PRO, FO 371.2090.3312 (January 23, 1914).

The erosion of political relationships that had characterized the Third of June system accelerated during the fall of 1913. The internal unity of the Octobrists, the Nationalists, and even the Kadets disappeared. For the Octobrists the result was a formal split of the Duma fraction. For the Nationalists, the events of the fall were merely a dress rehearsal for the final schism of 1915.

Even at the height of their power, the Octobrists had never demonstrated exceptional solidarity or party discipline. Now, with their strength diminished, their ties to the government cut, and their leader ejected from the Duma by the Moscow voters, the Octobrists had lost their excuses for sticking together. Signs of division had become especially evident in the spring of 1913.[41] For some time, Guchkov had been arguing that Octobrism's original approach of cooperation with the government had failed, and he sought to extend partial and occasional cooperation with the Kadets and Progressisty into a complete shift into the camp of the opposition.[42] At a special conference of the Duma fraction, he drew a harsh picture of the present situation.

> This is the last chance for a peaceful outcome to the crisis. Let no one mistake the mood of the nation, let no one be lulled by external signs of tranquility. . . . Never have Russian society and the Russian people been so profoundly revolutionized as by the present policies.[43]

Guchkov gained the support of the Octobrist central committee for a shift of tactics, but the Duma fraction was divided on acceptance of his views. At a fraction meeting on November 29, 1913, only a small left-wing minority voted to follow the new policy. By the Christmas recess the split became formalized. The majority of the fraction (sixty-five members), now calling itself the Zemstvo Octobrists, centered around Rodzianko; twenty-two deputies allied with S. I. Shidlovskii and N. N. Opochinin in a left Octobrist group; and some fifteen others drifted into the nether world of the nonparty deputies.[44]

The Octobrist split completely reopened and reordered the question of

41. *Rossiia,* February 14, 1913; *Rech',* May 4 and June 6, 1913; *Rossiia,* May 3, 1913.

42. Chermenskii, *IV-aia Duma,* p. 213; Hosking, *The Russian Constitutional Experiment,* pp. 185–187; *Rech',* October 18, 1913.

43. *Golos Moskvy,* November 9, 1913, cited by Hosking, *The Russian Constitutional Experiment,* p. 186; Michael Brainard, "The Octobrists and the Gentry in the Russian Social Crisis of 1913–1914," *Russian Review* (April 1979):160–179.

44. Chermenskii, *IV-aia Duma,* p. 228; John Hutchinson, *The Octobrists in Russian Politics,* p. 228; *Rossiia,* December 3, 1913; Hosking, *The Russian Constitutional Experiment,* p. 188.

interparty relationships in the Duma. A new working majority could perhaps have come out of the latest development, but the debate over the new political options opened up serious fissures within the Nationalist camp.

Savenko and Demchenko had always held the leading left Octobrist, S. I. Shidlovskii, in high personal regard. Accordingly, they must have been struck by his comment on the Octobrist split given to *Rech's* parliamentary reporter.

> The [present] parties came together during years of crisis [1905–1907]. This is abnormal. They must be formed in peaceful times. I think that a process by which the nature of our parties will change has begun.[45]

What were the Nationalists to make of this statement? The Octobrists had been born in the revolutionary years. The Nationalists had been formed in the years of social peace. Was Shidlovskii thinking of them as a party that could best succeed at the current political moment? Savenko thought that this was the case, and he immediately began to raise the possibility of cooperation with the left Octobrists in a broad new majority.[46] Because this suggestion touched on all the issues that had been dividing the party since the beginning of the fourth Duma, Savenko succeeded in setting off a furious debate within Nationalist ranks. Ultimately, the party was unable to paper over the splits that emerged at this point.

Conflicting tendencies within the Nationalist fraction had been evident from the very first days of the fourth Duma. However, these tensions did not become broad public knowledge until the beginning of the second session in November 1913. At the first fraction meetings that fall, Savenko and Demchenko led an attack on Balashev's leadership and tactics. Their two major points of criticism were the failure of the fraction to discuss bills in advance of floor debate and the increasing tendency of the leadership to work closely with the pravye.[47] An anonymous right-wing Nationalist responded to the charges in an interview with *Rossiia.* He admitted the inadequacy of preparatory work, but defended cooperation with the pravye. He claimed that the ambitions of Savenko and Demchenko, and not matters of principle, were the actual basis of the left's campaign.[48] Both men, Savenko in particular, had become very visible in a short period of time. Their energy, combined with exceptional oratorical and

45. *Rech'*, December 8, 1913.
46. *Kievlianin*, December 11, 1913.
47. *Rech'*, November 1, 1913.
48. *Rossiia*, November 3, 1913.

writing skills, had assisted their personal advancement. Yet, both were seen as parvenus by the party's more titled old guard. Savenko, while a noble, was first and foremost a journalist. Demchenko, despite great personal wealth, a large estate, and noble status, was primarily engaged in civil engineering. Their attempt to take over control of the Duma fraction aroused not only political differences but also deep personal resentment.

The divisions over tactical alliances revealed far more profound political disagreements. When these tensions were exacerbated by personal animosities, the results were, predictably, a series of stormy and acrimonious fraction meetings throughout the fall. Speakers attacked the party's failure to introduce bills or dominate floor debate. These complaints received broad support, and only Bogdanov and D. N. Chikhachev rose to defend the present leadership.[49] Despite the attacks, Balashev was reelected president of the fraction, but this time his election, previously always unanimous, was opposed by twenty-one of the sixty-eight deputies present and voting. The divisions within the Duma group were further revealed in the election of the fraction's council. The members had planned to choose a twelve-man council, but only seven could get a majority; only one of them, Demchenko, was clearly on the left. Count Bobrinskii, who would later side with the left, was the leading vote getter. The others were holdovers from the previous council.[50] Thus, the left-wing Nationalists had succeeded in convincing the fraction of the justice of their complaints, but had failed to translate this agreement into personal political power. As a result, the party split dramatically and embarrassingly on the vote for Duma president at the beginning of the second session. Despite Balashev's renewed efforts against Rodzianko, only twenty-five Nationalists opposed the Duma president.[51]

Almost two weeks after the presidium election, Savenko and Demchenko published a conciliatory appeal in *Kievlianin*. They admitted the existence of two wings in the fraction. They argued that the differences were tactical and, in any case, should be kept within the party. Contact with the pravye should be maintained. They stated that the Nationalists had come to the Duma for serious legislative work. For that, they needed a working majority, and, to form a working majority, they needed all the Octobrists.[52] In response to this appeal, the fraction passed a compromise

49. *Novoe Vremia*, November 3 and 6, 1913.

50. *Novoe Vremia*, November 8, 1913; *Rech'*, November 8, 1913. The vote was Bobrinskii (64), Father Drozdovskii (54), Vetchinin (53), Shmiakov (50), D. N. Chikhachev (49), Demchenko (38), Prince D. Shakhovskoi (36).

51. *Rech'*, November 9, 12, and 16, 1913.

52. *Kievlianin*, November 28, 1913.

resolution. According to the agreement, the fraction would maintain its independence, but would enter into "business-like" agreements on important bills with no one to the left of the Octobrists.[53]

The Split in Kiev

The close connection between the situation in the Duma and local politics had been characteristic of the Nationalist Party during the period of its growth. The best example of this relationship had been the constant contact the deputies of Kiev gubernia had maintained with the Kiev Club of Russian Nationalists. Accordingly, the debate that had undermined the unity of the Duma fraction actually split the Nationalists in Kiev. The struggle on the local level was far more bitter than the conflicts in Petersburg. Since previous scholars have not studied these kinds of provincial disputes, it is worth examining the Kiev party schism in some detail. The issues that were confronted and the manner in which they were discussed revealed all the fundamental weaknesses of the Nationalist Party's approach to politics. On the national level, those tensions and difficulties had not been exposed in a full and direct manner. But in Kiev, no issue was side-stepped; no personal antagonism was avoided. For these reasons, it is worth taking a closer look at the split of the Kiev Nationalists.

During 1913, two grand old men of the Nationalist movement—D. I. Pikhno and Professor V. E. Chernov—had died. Both men had possessed the kind of personal prestige that had been able to smooth over petty squabbles. With their passing, the Kiev Club soon fell victim to internal bickering.[54] Much of the earlier tension had been due to personal jealousies and rivalries. Now, however, the debate within the Duma fraction created poles around which various groups and individuals in Kiev came to coalesce. The Kiev deputies took advantage of the Christmas recess to participate in the meetings of the Club of Russian Nationalists, where they struggled over the issues and fought for control of the party's largest and most important local organization.

With the deaths of Pikhno and Chernov, Savenko had expected to assume a position of preeminence in the Kiev Club. Bogdanov's opposition threatened that goal. At the end of November, Savenko wrote to two supporters in Kiev, urging them to begin preparing his candidacy for the

53. *Rech'*, December 2, 1913; *Novoe Vremia*, December 12, 1913.

54. TsGAOR 102 (1914) 265.986.522. "Your son Pierre," Kiev, to M. N. Maksimovich, St. Petersburg (April 9, 1914).

club's presidency. He estimated that his prestige had been enhanced by his work in the Duma, but he thought that it alone would be an insufficient basis for his election.[55] In his opinion, detailed and serious organizational work had to precede the annual meeting at which the president and council would be chosen. On November 30, 1913, Savenko wrote to his ally, E. A. Dvorozhitskii.

> You must prepare well for the meeting on the 13th of December, and get us the kind of huge majority we need. We will make a strong appearance and convince many people, but we require serious preparatory work and agitation.

He urged Dvorozhitskii to organize a caucus of "reliable people, especially from among your railroad men."[56] Clearly, Savenko was taking no chances. It is extremely interesting that he was eager to gain the support of the railroad employees. This group made up the largest nonnoble contingent in the club (about 120 of 800 members), but they had nearly always been invisible in club affairs. Savenko's insistence on obtaining their votes suggests that they had performed a similar function at other moments in the club's development, but this is the only documented instance of the railroad men playing such a role. Savenko's campaign for their support quite clearly reveals his opportunism and his willingness to solicit support from whatever group might offer it. That tendency alienated more traditional and titled elements in the party and the club. A month after the Kiev Club's annual meeting in January, Professor Kulakovskii, one of the club's founders, wrote about Savenko to a friend:

> He is a complete cad who lacks any nobility whatsoever; a modern-day know-nothing who never reads anything. He never was anything but a reporter who spends his time spreading sensational rumors.[57]

During December 1913, these divisions were fully exposed at the club's meetings and in the local press. On December 7, Bogdanov opened an exchange of views in *Kievlianin* by scoffing at rumors of a split. Savenko and his allies, he claimed, had raised the possibility of a new majority in which even the Progressisty might be included. However, he reminded Savenko that the fraction had rejected such a course, and he was pleased

55. TsGAOR, 102 (1912) 265.585.2927. Savenko, St. Petersburg, to G. Ia. Prozorov, Kiev (December 2, 1913).

56. TsGAOR 102 (1914) 15.307a.1.

57. TsGAOR 102 (1914) 265.983.225. Prof. Yu. Kulakovskii, Kiev, to A. I. Sibolevskii, St. Petersburg (February 19, 1914).

to see that they had accepted the views of the "majority" of the fraction.[58]

Savenko quickly accused Bogdanov of distorting the balance of power in the fraction. He reminded Bogdanov that a majority of the Nationalist deputies had teamed up with the left and center to vote for Rodzianko. More significantly, Savenko took pains to point out that he and his allies had, in fact, agreed to the resolution, drafted at the last fraction meeting and mentioned by Bogdanov. That agreement forbade alliances with anyone to the left of the Octobrists. The issues between the two wings of the fraction now concerned the extent of cooperation with the Octobrists, particularly the left Octobrists.[59] Two days later, Bogdanov admitted that the left-wing Nationalists had made no official proposal to break with the pravye, but he claimed that their support for Rodzianko demonstrated their intention to join an opposition bloc in order to provoke dissolution of the Duma.[60]

This disagreement over tactics reveals a profound personal mistrust not only between Savenko and Bogdanov, but one may assume between the two wings as well. However, the personality conflicts also had a firm political basis. For the left, cooperation with the pravye meant playing into the hands of the archreactionaries of Maklakov's ilk who wished the destruction of the Duma. For the right, any work with the Octobrists, especially the left Octobrists, signified cooperation with the "revolutionaries and Jews" who controlled the Kadets and Progressisty.

Despite the antagonisms, no element of personal hostility surfaced at the Kiev Club's meeting of December 14 when the issue was debated publicly for the first time. Demchenko and Savenko had prepared their case well in advance and so were able to dominate the gathering. Bogdanov soon realized that Savenko's assistants had done an effective job of marshalling extensive support within the Kiev Club.[61] Bogdanov quickly found himself outnumbered, but continued to press his case.

In the aftermath of the meeting, Shulgin, who had become the publisher of *Kievlianin* after Pikhno's death, ran an editorial in which he urged a compromise, but Bogdanov, in a letter to the editor, ignored this advice and instead stepped up the attack. The left-wing Nationalists, he claimed, had "fallen under the Octobrists' influence." These were the very same Octobrists who had united with the Kadets and Progressisty in the presidium elections. By contrast, "a part of the Nationalist fraction thought an agreement with other parties could only be worked out by

58. *Kievlianin*, December 7, 1913.
59. *Kievlianin*, December 11, 1913.
60. *Kievlianin*, December 13, 1913.
61. *Kievlianin*, December 15, 1913.

maintaining a strong position, based on what the party had already achieved."[62] This statement meant no compromise of program, no betrayal of party principles. On the next day, Savenko replied bitterly that the left had not opposed a single point of the party's program. The argument was supposed to be about tactics, but now, he warned, broader issues as well as personal antagonisms had entered the debate, making resolution of the conflict all the more difficult.[63]

As the press debate became more bitter, so did the meetings of the Kiev Club. At a tumultuous gathering on December 18, speakers were repeatedly interrupted by the audience, and K. P. Grigorovich-Barskii, an ally of Bogdanov, was actually shouted down while delivering an address. The meeting was then adjourned.[64] This kind of disorder was shocking. The Nationalists had been used to achieving easy consensus in orderly, even uneventful, gatherings. Shulgin, in an unsigned editorial, was saddened that "people who are friends should fight," but he made it clear that his loyalties were with the left. He accused the rights of attacking the left and turning a political debate into a personal campaign against Savenko and Demchenko. Didn't the right wing of the party realize that without the Octobrists no majority could be formed in the Duma, and did they not know that without a permanent majority, the Duma was politically meaningless?

Then, Shulgin put his finger on the crux of the issue that had been tearing apart the Nationalists. The fundamental disagreement between the Octobrists and the pravye, he continued, was "whether or not there exists in Russia a constitutional structure." Shulgin sought to downplay the differences as "purely theoretical," but, in fact, the issue was fraught with the most serious consequences.[65] By choosing to ally with either the Octobrists or with the pravye, the Nationalists would, in essence, be answering this crucial and divisive question one way or the other. However, their entire approach to the institutional relationships of the regime of the Third of June had been based on avoiding this very issue. But this problem could no longer be side-stepped, and the divisions within the party persisted.

On January 4, 1914, the Kiev Club held its annual meeting. Because of the challenge to Savenko, the elections for president and council had attracted national attention. Yet, Savenko need not have worried. He had prepared well and was reelected, in a secret ballot, by a vote of 111 to 6.

62. *Kievlianin*, December 17, 1913.
63. *Kievlianin*, December 18, 1913.
64. *Kievlianin*, December 19, 1913.
65. *Kievlianin*, December 20, 1913.

The eighteen-man council was dominated by Demchenko, N. N. Chik-hachev, and his other allies.[66] Bogdanov and his supporters were ridden out of the club. In response, they announced their intention to establish a Kiev branch of the National Union.[67] Since the Kiev Club of Russian Nationalists presented itself as an independent organization that was merely affiliated with the National Union, the creation of such a group was formally possible.

Significantly, Balashev, who had been attacked by Savenko, made no attempt to discourage the formation of the Kiev branch. F. N. Bezak was chosen president of the new group. Bogdanov, K. P. Grigorovich-Barskii, and Baron S. E. Shteiger were elected to the council. About ninety members were enrolled when the group opened operations in February 1914 at a ceremony presided over by the governor-general, F. F. Trepov, numerous bishops, and most of the gubernia's marshals of nobility.[68] The new group was far more dominated by figures of traditional authority, most notably present and former marshals of nobility, than the Kiev Club was. Its members were thoroughly familiar and comfortable with state functionaries. Despite their participation in the emergence of the National-ist Party, they retained much of their loyalty to the autocracy and its bureaucracy. Bezak, the gubernia marshal of nobility, best typified the more wealthy and traditional Nationalist who now left the Kiev Club. With the loss of a segment of its dominant gentry element, the club became somewhat less a gathering of the borderland's elite. Many Kiev Nationalists had never considered Savenko a paragon of good breeding in the first place, and he had been forced to rely on nonnoble elements to secure his position.

The collapse of Nationalist unity in Kiev may be attributed to the exit of one particular group of noble landowners from the club. By virtue of longer-standing cooperation with state institutions, these men still had not completely abandoned traditional attitudes derived from state service. Men like Bogdanov, Grigorovich-Barskii, Bezak, and Shteiger had never entirely forsaken the psychological set of their service backgrounds, even though they had supported the party's attempt to organize the border-land's gentry during the third Duma. The experience of these men made them less antagonistic to traditional bureaucratic authority than such newcomers as Savenko and Demchenko, who owed their positions to the far more spontaneous political processes that characterized the period of

66. *Kievlianin*, January 6, 1914.
67. *Kievlianin*, January 9, 1914.
68. *Kievlianin*, February 10, 1914; *Kievskaia Mysl'*, March 11, 1914. TsGAOR 102 (1914) 265.982.184. Unclear signature, Kiev, to Savenko, St. Petersburg (February 9, 1914).

the Nationalists' emergence. The new branch's involvement with the governor-general, F. F. Trepov, long mistrusted by Savenko, revealed the greater comfort of its members with representatives of the state apparatus. However, not all the club's wealthy and titled gentry left. Rakovich, N. N. Chikhachev, A. A. Pototskii, and K. E. Suvchinskii—all from honored families—remained in the Kiev Club of Russian Nationalists.

These kinds of experiences and attitudes obviously cannot explain the behavior of all participants in this controversy. But there is a social basis, albeit imprecise, to the split of the Kiev Nationalists. Bogdanov's branch of the National Union, which became the base for the party's right wing, did not attract all the leading gentry activists of the gubernia. However, it was dominated by people who had close personal ties to bureaucratic figures and who had had far more extensive experience, especially before 1905, in serving the interests of the state as chinovniki or army officers. By contrast, the Kiev Club, with part of its gentry element removed, now took on a more "democratic" and urban cast. It was now the center for the party's left wing. Russian merchants and others were no longer so thoroughly dominated by landlords from the countryside. The local power struggle, sparked by the debate over Duma tactics, had, in fact, revealed far more profound social, political, and personal divisions within the broad Nationalist movement. The Duma fraction did not break up at this time; instead, it stumbled on with neither wing able to assume complete control.

The break-up of the Kiev Nationalists proved to be a dress rehearsal for the final schism of the party that came during the summer of 1915. We know far less about the intraparty struggle of 1915 than we do about the local schism of 1913. However, the immediate political issues were substantially the same during the war as they were in 1913, and the social characteristics of the members of each of the two Duma groups that came out of the split roughly corresponded to the social divisions that had emerged locally in Kiev during the winter of 1913–1914. Thus, extrapolating from our extensive knowledge of events during 1913 may help to clarify the final break-up of the Nationalist Party.

Because of the seriousness of these problems, Savenko was troubled by the collapse of Nationalist unity in Kiev. He had minimized the significance of the new group's formation in his public statements, but privately he told E. K. Roshko, an ally in the Kiev Club, that he underestimated "the significance of the split. True, it began as a personal thing, ... but that doesn't diminish its force."[69]

69. TsGAOR 102 (1914) 265.983.276. Savenko, St. Petersburg, to E. K. Roshko, Kiev (February 9, 1914).

The squabbling in Kiev had barely subsided when the party's unity was still further undermined by Shulgin's involvement in one of the most intensely emotional issues of the day—the Beilis case. A Jewish bricklayer, Mendel Beilis, had been accused of the 1911 ritual murder of a Russian boy. The scheme to saddle Beilis with the blame for a crime that was sure to enflame popular anti-Semitic emotions originated among Kiev's extreme right-wing groups. These groups, eclipsed by moderate conservative groups like the Kiev Club of Russian Nationalists, had been moribund for some time. The local prosecutor collaborated in the plan, which soon attracted the support of the Minister of Justice, Shcheglovitov; even Nicholas himself apparently approved it.

The matter quickly became a cause célèbre among liberals who rushed to defend Beilis. Reactionaries and some conservatives led the counter-campaign, which sought not simply to convict Beilis but to prove that the ritual murder of Christians was a common Jewish practice. The Vilna pravye deputy, A. A. Zamyslovskii, headed a team of prosecution lawyers. Beilis's defense was organized and led by V. A. Maklakov, the Kadet deputy and brother of the Minister of Interior.[70]

The patent falsity of the charge had proved embarrassing to more moderate conservatives, nationalists, and even anti-Semites. Shulgin, who had loudly and often proclaimed his anti-Semitism, urged the prosecution to drop the case. On September 27, 1913, he published an editorial in *Kievlianin*, reminding conservatives that they had bigger problems and more serious worries than this particular case. "What," he asked, "is Beilis to us?"[71]

Shulgin quickly found out that Beilis meant a great deal to some of his closest allies. In October, the Kiev Club announced its intention to hold a testimonial dinner for Zamyslovskii and the other prosecutors in the case. Shulgin had not even been invited to the meeting at which the dinner was discussed. In shock, he resigned from the club and began to involve himself actively in Beilis's defense.[72] In retaliation, the club cut its ties with *Kievlianin*, refusing to invite correspondents to meetings and, at times, not even announcing meetings in the paper. But the club very quickly found

70. Hans Rogger, "The Beilis Case," *Slavic Review* (December, 1966):629. See also A. S. Tager, *The Decay of Czarism: The Beilis Trial* (Philadelphia, 1935); and M. Samuel, *Blood Accusation* (New York, 1966).

71. *Kievlianin*, September 27, 1913. The liberal press gave Shulgin a great deal of attention, and during this period he and some liberals developed a mutual personal respect that carried over to the formation of the Progressive Bloc.

72. *Rech'*, October 16 and 24, November 5 and 24, 1913.

that they needed the paper more than the paper needed them. Apologies were offered, and soon everyone was friends again.[73]

The matter rested briefly until the verdict in the case was handed down. Beilis was acquitted, but the jury affirmed that the act had been a ritual murder. In the aftermath of the case, in January 1914, Shulgin was sentenced to three months in prison for printing "untrue statements" about the prosecution (he never served the time).[74] In response, the Nationalists' right wing launched a campaign to expel Shulgin.[75] The attacks lasted for over a month. Some friends even advised Shulgin to quit the party.[76] Finally, in March 1914, the party, meeting at Balashev's apartment, voted not to expel him. However, they did decide that a ritual murder had occurred and that the state had acted properly in prosecuting it. Shulgin had simply been "mistaken."[77]

Despite the resolution, the solidarity of the Nationalist party, both in the Duma and in Kiev, had been shattered. Shulgin had been forced to side even more decisively with the left-wing Nationalists, and *Kievlianin* now became the voice of the party's left wing. Bogdanov ceased to appear on its pages. Deprived of control of any major newspaper, the right wing of the party became less visible to the public. Therefore, it appeared at this point that most fraction members leaned to the left, especially in Kiev. However, there is no way to gauge local sentiment elsewhere, although it is doubtful that party members outside of Petersburg and Kiev had moved in any direction with much decisiveness. In fact, only the leaders of the various tendencies within the party had made definite commitments to particular positions. The rest of the Nationalists stumbled around in confusion and indecision.

By the spring of 1914, nearly all the relationships on which the Nationalists had based their strength in the third Duma had evaporated. The Duma was at sword's point with the government, and the government either ignored the lower house or contemplated destroying it. The Nationalists had lost the tangible support of the President of the Council

73. TsGAOR 102 (1914) 265.981.40. E. Roshko, Kiev, to A. N. Karger, St. Petersburg (January 25, 1914); ibid. 982.103. No clear signature, Kiev, to G. G. Zamyslovskii, St. Petersburg (January 25, 1914).

74. *Rech'*, January 21, 1914; *Kievlianin*, February 2, 1914. When the war broke out, the tsar relieved Shulgin of the sentence.

75. *Rech'*, January 23 and 25, 1914.

76. TsGAOR 102 (1914) 265.985.426. "Your K," Kiev, to Shulgin, St. Petersburg (March 23, 1914).

77. *Novoe Vremia*, March 22 and 23, 1914; *Kievlianin*, March 24, 1914.

of Ministers, which they had enjoyed under Stolypin. The Octobrists, with whom they had formed the working majority of the third Duma, had withered in strength and drifted into the opposition camp. The pravye had now lost whatever limited capcity they had had for common action. Finally, the solidarity and sense of purpose that had been the Nationalists' greatest strength had now disintegrated almost completely.

Nationalist Activity
outside the Duma

The New Zemstvos

Although events had not gone well in the fourth Duma, the Nationalists had every reason to believe that they could dominate and make use of the new zemstvos that they had helped bring to the western gubernias. This attempt to politicize the zemstvos was most overt in Podol'e. However, Nationalist attempts to use the Podol'e zemstvos for their own ends met with resistance.

When it began operation in 1911, the new Podol'e gubernia zemstvo voted an annual subsidy of 2,800 rubles to the Nationalists' local newspaper, *Podolianin*, which was edited by Rakovich, who was president of the Podol'e Union of Russian Nationalists and had now become president of the new zemstvo. In return for this money, *Podolianin* was to publish a supplement devoted to zemstvo news. Liberals had opposed this use of funds, and during the year they had become thoroughly dissatisfied with *Podolianin's* coverage. At the annual meeting of 1912, they became incensed when the National Union requested an additional 16,000 rubles for free subscriptions for zemstvo teachers.[78] P. P. Dmitriev, a local liberal landowner, attacked *Podolianin* for "setting one soslovie against another and one nationality against another."[79] He repeated the liberal zemstvo bugaboo that politics had entered the organs of local government. The Nationalist deputy A. S. Gizhitskii replied that politics had entered all of Russia's zemstvos long ago.[80] The debate on the matter was intense and

78. *Stenograficheskie otchety Podolskogo gubernskogo zemskogo sobrania,* December 19, 1912, p. 729.
79. Ibid., p. 730.
80. Ibid., p. 749.

disorderly. The vote, on a secret ballot, was 25 to 19 in favor of the subsidies and subscriptions.[81] Each year thereafter, the otherwise placid annual meetings of the gubernia zemstvo were rocked by intensely emotional debates on the question of subsidies to *Podolianin*. The Nationalists always won the crucial votes but never by overwhelming majorities. They had always considered Podol'e their stronghold. But, even in an institution specifically designed to assure their dominance, they could not be confident of gaining support for a measure they considered crucial to their political survival.

The Nationalists also soon found that the weak financial position of the new zemstvos made it difficult for them to support typical zemstvo programs at an adequate level. During their first two years of operation, the zemstvos in the six western gubernias spent one ruble, sixty kopecks per citizen on social services. During the same period, the thirty-four old zemstvos had spent two rubles, fifty-two kopecks per citizen on the same services.[82] Insufficient financial resources meant diminished political leverage. Having demanded control of local government for so long, the Nationalists were disappointed to find that the power conferred by attainment of their goal was far less than they had imagined.

Local activists had little hope that the situation could be improved. Early in 1913, Baron I. M. Reva presented the Kiev gubernia assembly with a pessimistic picture of the zemstvo's financial future. He saw no possibility of squeezing additional revenue from taxes on land, which left factories and urban property as the only other sources of tax money. But the left-wing Nationalist Demchenko had coauthored a Duma bill that would make the city of Kiev a separate zemstvo unit, and Kokovtsov had suggested limiting taxation of factories. If these proposals became law, Reva argued, the new western zemstvos might just as well close down.[83] He proposed that the zemstvos be given the proceeds of direct taxes and the right to tax church and railroad property.[84]

The Nationalists had found that the zemstvo, for which they had fought so hard, had failed to live up to their expectations. They were unable to control resources on the local level to their advantage, nor were they able to convert their political strength in the borderland into power on the national level. The result, predictably, was apathy and zemstvo absentee-

81. *Zhurnaly Podol'skogo gubernskogo zemstva*, December 19, 1912, p. 108.

82. *Mogilevskii Vestnik*, August 17, 1913.

83. *Stenograficheskie otchety Podol'skogo gubernskogo zemskogo sobrania*, January 15, 1913, pp. 10–12.

84. *Kievlianin*, January 18, 1913.

ism, especially among those who also served in the Duma.[85] Accordingly, the zemstvo elections, which took place just on the eve of the war, produced far less interest than those of 1911 had. Although leading Nationalists did maintain control of the zemstvos, the turnover of members (40 to 45 percent, depending on the gubernia) was considerable, reflecting the apparent willingness of many west Russian landlords to abandon zemstvo work.[86]

The Party's Groups Outside the Duma

The Nationalists' difficulties in the Duma affected the operations of the clubs and societies associated with the party. The pace of activity outside the Duma slowed considerably. Groups met less often, meetings attracted fewer people, and the party seemed to be searching unsuccessfully for a galvanizing issue to replace the now-completed western zemstvo campaign.

The National Club had grown in membership and prestige during the third Duma, but it immediately ran into problems with the opening of the fourth Duma. Upon his arrival in Petersburg, Savenko began demanding that the club assume a more specifically political character. This insistence meant expelling the many non-Nationalist members and coordinating the club's work more closely with that of the party. Krupenskii took sharp exception to Savenko's demands. He had organized and run the club on a nonpartisan basis. Now, having formed the Center Group, he found himself outside the Nationalist Party. Krupenskii and several supporters then quit the National Club, claiming it had become "too narrowly political."[87] Krupenskii's exit did not have the effect of redirecting the club's activities, but it did lead to a considerable loss of prestige for the club

85. Because annual gubernia assemblies usually took place during the Christmas Duma recess, deputies did not have the excuse of the press of Duma affairs. Balashev was especially guilty on that count. Demchenko was especially active. However, there is no correlation between zemstvo participation and membership in one of the party's wings. See Sten. ot., *Kievskogo gubernskogo zemskogo sobraniia*, January 15, 1913, p. 3; *Zhurnal Podol'skogo gubernskogo zemstva*, December 10, 1912; *Mogilevskii Vestnik*, June 13, 1914. TsGAOR, 102 (1913) 265.916.82.

86. *Novoe Vremia*, May 1, 1914; *Kievskaia Mysl'*, April 1 and 15, and May 18, 1914; *Mogilevskii Vestnik*, June 20, 1914; *Kievlianin*, March 30, June 14 and 20, 1914.

87. *Kievlianin*, November 11 and December 2, 1912. From unnamed Duma member, St. Petersburg, to Doctor L. A. Kuznetsov, Atbusar (November 8, 1912).

among public figures in the capital. Meetings and cultural evenings took place less often. No consistent themes emerged during this period. Membership declined, and the treasury was soon bare.[88] The National Club did not close its doors, but its significance as a force in Petersburg politics had been seriously diminished.[89]

The decline of the National Club was offset by the continued work of two groups closely associated with the party—Bobrinskii's revived Galicia-Russia Society and the West-Russia Society, headed by D. N. Chikhachev. Once again, these were separate entities. Although both organizations had provincial branches, their activities were centered in Petersburg, where they were able to keep issues of concern to the party before the attention of the public in the capital.

The West-Russia Society now numbered almost 300 members and devoted its attention to organizing public support for Duma bills that affected the borderland. It conducted campaigns for the construction of a Russian university in Vilna, the establishment of elective zemstvos in Grodno, and the restriction of German colonization in the southwest.[90] Deputies from both wings of the party often spoke at meetings, which were frequent and well attended. It is revealing that the officially nonpartisan, broadly focused National Club should be eclipsed by a group that concerned itself exclusively with the interests of the party's so-called base area. In essence, this phenomenon duplicates the party's experience in the fourth Duma, where ties to other groups deteriorated and greater attention was paid to what were seen as more specifically Nationalist concerns.

While it held its meetings at the National Club, the Galicia-Russia Society embraced a broader circle of Petersburg public figures. Bobrinskii had been the only leading Nationalist to express extensive and consistent interest in questions of international politics. Although the society's concern for the fate of Slavs outside Russia was, in part, an extension of the party's broader internal nationalism, Bobrinskii's particular form of nationalism was not so pragmatic as that of the men of the southwest. Instead, he was drawn to the various neo-Slav tendencies that had attracted interest even among the Kadets. Among other leading party

---

88. *Novoe Vremia*, March 17, 1913; *Kievlianin*, December 28, 1912, March 28 and April 22, 1913; *Rech'*, June 6, 1913.

89. *Novoe Vremia*, May 5, September 23, November 16 and 28, 1913; *Rossiia*, May 8, 1913.

90. *Novoe Vremia*, November 2 and December 17, 1912; February 10, 17, May 18, and November 3, 1914; January 30, February 1, March 4, and May 9, 1914; *Rossiia*, May 22, 1913; *Okrainy Rossii*, November 24, 1912; *Rech'*, June 3, 1913; *Kievlianin*, December 20, 1912, and February 10, 1913.

figures, only Savenko was active in the Galicia-Russia Society. Otherwise, the somewhat limited membership (250–300 in Petersburg) was dominated by nationalistically inclined Petersburg intellectuals and public figures.[91] The work of the society blended into the broader chorus of nationalist and neo-Slav agitation in the immediate prewar years. Riding this current, it was able to maintain a high level of activity and visibility on the eve of the war. Yet, it would be a distortion to argue that its views, or even the views of Bobrinskii, in any way represented the thinking of most party members on these issues.

The Nationalists and Foreign Affairs

It is altogether surprising that, of the leading Nationalists, only Bobrinskii and Savenko displayed any continuing interest in Russia's international political position. Nationalist movements elsewhere had displayed enormous concern with the testing of national will and strength in the international arena. However, the Nationalists were not especially concerned with deflecting attention from internal antagonisms by focusing on external enemies. The party had emerged as a result of the perceived threat to the dominant Russian nationality from within the multinational Empire. Therefore, the Nationalists were not particularly jingoistic, nor were they easily caught up in the rebirth of pan-Slav sentiment that swept moderate public opinion in the prewar years.

The manipulation of national sentiment as a conservative counterforce to the growth of socialist parties in the mass political arenas of Western Europe was simply unnecessary in Russia, due to the restricted franchise after 1907. Therefore, in Russia, the liberal and moderate Duma parties adopted bellicose appeals to the unity of all Slav brothers.

The government and its supporters in society were far more timid, fearing the internal social consequences of a war for which Russia was ill prepared. The famous 1914 memorandum to the tsar, written by Stolypin's old nemesis, P. N. Durnovo, predicted that the masses would not support the state, the war would be lost, the state blamed, and anarchy and revolution would be the result.[92]

Therefore, it is not surprising that those Nationalists who participated in

91. *Novoe Vremia*, November 21, 1912, and May 15, 1913.
92. *Novoe Vremia*, May 12, October 28, and December 20, 1913; March 16, May 8, and June 7, 1914; *Kievlianin*, November 30, 1912; Hosking, *The Russian Constitutional Experiment*, p. 222.

the neo-Slav movement came from the party's left wing. Bobrinskii, in particular, had personal and political ties to liberals and moderate conservatives that went back to the days of the quasi-oppositional *Beseda* group before 1905. He had been perhaps the most independent Nationalist, and, in speaking on foreign affairs in the Duma, he often felt it necessary to point out that his views were personal and not those of the party. Nor did Bobrinskii work closely with Savenko who, having begun his involvement with international affairs only late in 1912, tended toward inconsistency and half-baked positions.

The neo-Slav movement had been singularly unsuccessful in dealing with the questions raised by the existence within the Empire of the Poles, who were Slavic but Catholic. Slavic Orthodox unity meant either totally repressing any possibility of Polish autonomy or working out some sort of compromise with the Poles. Because the former course was foredoomed to meet total Polish resistance, liberal and conservative elements among the neo-Slavs began to raise the possibility of Polish autonomy.[93] The Nationalists had been organized precisely to meet the tangible Polish threat in the western gubernias, and quite naturally, they were indifferent to appeals for cooperation with their Polish brothers. Only Bobrinskii, from Tula, possessed the independence to view the problem with a degree of national disinterest. Yet, even he often tripped up on this contradiction.

The Nationalists finally became active on questions of foreign affairs when Serbia, Greece, Bulgaria, and Montenegro declared war on Turkey in September 1912. Savenko was wildly enthusiastic in support of the southern Slavs.[94] The National Club contributed to Guchkov's Red Cross effort behind the lines of Turkey's enemies. The newly elected Nationalist Duma deputies from Kiev held a large public meeting early in November at which telegrams of solidarity were dispatched to the Bulgarian, Greek, and Serbian kings.[95] The Nationalists were obviously pleased by the quick Slav victory, but they did not join the chorus of indignation that greeted the actions of the hastily called London diplomatic conference that limited its fruits. Among leaders of the Duma parties, only Savenko and the Kadet leader, Paul Miliukov (long a voice of moderation), did not accuse the government of being party to a sellout.[96]

Turkey's defeat had been a blow to Austrian intentions in the Balkans. But Savenko was afraid that the tenuous unity of the victorious south Slavs might dissolve at any moment. He also worried that Austria's

93. Ibid., p. 223.
94. *Kievlianin*, November 4, 1912.
95. *Kievlianin*, November 6, 1912.
96. *Kievlianin*, December 13, 1912.

embarrassment might force it into a still firmer alliance with Germany with whom, thought Savenko, Russia had no quarrel.

> We have no reason for war with Germany. Austria, of course, is another matter.... Germany understands it cannot decide questions of world significance without Russia. We must agree that we cannot do likewise without Germany.[97]

The Second Balkan War of June 1913 totally smashed the hopes of Slavic unity. Bulgaria went to war with Serbia over Macedonia. The Bulgarians were quickly defeated by the armies of their former allies. Both Savenko, who had been pro-Bulgarian, and Bobrinskii, who sided with the Serbs, were primarily distressed by the irremediable damage that had been done to the Slavic cause. As Bobrinskii declared in the Duma, "We cannot be Serbophiles or Bulgarophiles, but Slavophiles."[98] But the damage had been done.

Bulgaria and Rumania now moved closer to Austria, and Russian pretensions in the Balkans, pretensions not shared by the autocracy itself, would have to be postponed. Bobrinskii warned that the nation must now fear Germany, which was using Austria to strangle Russia.[99] Savenko was not moved by these events to share Bobrinskii's view of Germany. Instead, he began to speak of English untrustworthiness and secret English dealings with Turkey.[100] With only two of its leaders expressing themselves on international issues, and both of them disagreeing with each other, the Nationalists were hardly in a position to influence either public opinion or the government on matters of foreign policy.

By 1914, Savenko had moved in a slightly more anti-German direction, but when the Sarajevo crisis burst upon Europe, none of the Nationalists urged anything but caution.[101] Just days before the declaration of war, editorials in *Kievlianin* asked "What is Serbia to us?" The paper devoted minimal attention to the Austrian ultimatum to the Serbs.[102] The Nationalists had pledged to defend the tsar and the fatherland, but they exhibited no euphoria at the great test of national fitness now confronting Russia.

Although foreign affairs seemed to be one area in which one could expect a nationalistic party to demonstrate concern and influence, the

97. *Kievlianin*, January 17 and March 20, 1913.
98. Sten. ot., 4.1.3.1087.
99. Ibid., 1079–1092; Hosking, *The Russian Constitutional Experiment*, p. 238.
100. *Kievlianin*, June 2, July 11 and 28, 1913.
101. *Kievlianin*, March 6, 1914.
102. *Kievlianin*, June 12, July 3, 9, 10, 13, 15, and 16, 1914; *Novoe Vremia*, May 11, 1914.

Russian Nationalist Party approached international politics with surprising confusion and silence. Savenko made some attempt to explain the party's apparent disinterest in these matters. Addressing the Duma in the aftermath of the London conference, Savenko characterized neo-Slavism as expansionist and therefore imperialist. The Nationalists, threatened by non-Russian nationalities, had always given their first loyalty to Russia rather than to the multinational Empire.

> Now we are told imperialism is a higher notion than nationalism. Yet, gentlemen, if it's true that imperialism is placed above nationalism because an empire is wider, larger, and greater than a people, then if we follow that logic, the world is above empire. Therefore, cosmopolitanism should be placed above imperialism. But we will not follow that logic. We have never and will never understand Russian patriotism without Russian nationalism. ... The imperial idea is that ideological cement by which the various national parts of the state are bound into one permanent body. We must emphasize that any such imperial idea can only be the Russian national idea.[103]

It is possible to dismiss Savenko's speech as the kind of post hoc word juggling that he had used on other occasions to justify defeat. But the Nationalists had been suspicious of their chances within the Empire after the western zemstvo crisis, when Witte and others had opposed the national curiae on the grounds that they could undermine the solidity of the multination state. Therefore, the party once again found itself caught between the government, which was not doing enough to defend Russian interests, and the Duma parties, which were doing too much to involve the nation in dangerous and threatening adventures. Again the Nationalists found themselves isolated and impotent. The result was even greater apathy and still deeper pessimism.

Gloom and Doom on the Eve of War

At the end of January 1914, Nicholas, under pressure from reactionaries at court, dismissed Kokovtsov. If Kokovtsov's thoroughly self-serving memoirs can be believed, his ouster was the first of the ministerial changes orchestrated by the "dark forces" surrounding the overcelebrated friend

103. Sten. ot., 4.1.1.414.

of the tsar and tsarina, the "holy man" Grigory Rasputin.[104] In fact, in dismissing Kokovtsov, Nicholas was attempting to take a new approach to the presidency of the Council of Ministers. Previously, the president of the council had also held one of the two most important ministries, either Interior or Finance. Especially under Stolypin, that situation had given the president of the council too much real power for Nicholas's taste. The new president, Ivan Logginovich Goremykin, who was brought out of retirement, was to have no portfolio. Instead, he was to serve as a messenger between the tsar and his ministers. The tsar and his reactionary supporters hoped that such a figure could not pose a threat to the powers of the autocrat. Thus, Kokovtsov's removal was marked not only by a diminution of the competence of the head of government; it also resulted in a reduction in the importance and cohesion of the Council of Ministers.

The Nationalists were ecstatic with Kokovtsov's removal. In their great enthusiasm, they even hailed the appointment of the aging, barely competent, and reactionary Goremykin, who had been replaced by Stolypin in 1906.[105] Goremykin, almost literally brought back from the dead, was hardly a figure to arouse much optimism among even the most conservative circles of public opinion, but the Nationalists, thoroughly despondent, met any change with favor.[106] Nationalist deputies even began to talk about reviving the center majority and were soon speaking positively in the press about the mistrusted left-wing Octobrists and even the despised Kadets.[107] Their joy was short-lived. Nothing came of the hopes for a new majority, and, under Goremykin, the government drifted into a state of paralysis that sent the Nationalists into still deeper despair.

The party's national convention, held at the National Club in February, reflected this mood. While attendance was comparable to previous meetings, the actual proceedings were a "pale reflection" of the past.[108] In fact, Balashev's opening remarks specifically harked back to the good old days of Stolypin. By comparison, he said, the present political situation was unclear: The government had characterized its and the Duma's do-nothing attitude as a proper response to the achievement of social peace in the countryside. Although peasant disturbances had subsided, Balashev

104. Kokovtsov, *Iz moego proshlogo*, Vol. 2, pp. 33–41; Hosking, *The Russian Constitutional Experiment*, pp. 208–213; Raymond Pearson, *The Russian Moderates and the Crisis of Tsarism, 1914–1917* (London, 1977), p. 12

105. PRO, FO 371.2091.8009 (February 23, 1914); *Kievlianin*, February 23, 1914.

106. *Kievlianin*, January 16, 19, and 30, 1914.

107. *Rech'*, February 1 and 4, 1914; *Kievlianin*, April 24 and 30, 1914; *Novoe Vremia*, May 21, 1914.

108. *Novoe Vremia*, February 3 and 4, 1914.

noted that this fact constituted no assurance that the peasants might not rise in the future.[109] The rest of the convention had something of a perfunctory character with neither wing of the party making an attempt to gain control.[110]

During April, Demchenko challenged what many deputies thought was the government's campaign to limit the Duma's right to reject the budget. He combined this criticism with a thoroughgoing attack on the state's economic and fiscal policies.[111] *Rech'* went so far as to characterize the speech as oppositional, and the right-wing Nationalist deputy A. A. Motovilov moved to have the fraction censure Demchenko.[112] Mistrust of the government was so profound within the party, however, that Demchenko was supported by a vote of 50 to 4.[113]

This surface agreement did not lead to any unanimity on tactics. Many Nationalists were willing to criticize the government, but few could bring themselves to oppose openly the state and tsar whom that government served. The result was political paralysis. In April, Savenko wrote his wife:

> Those of us who are loyal cannot oppose the government, but to support the present government is impossible. We must go off to the side and be silent. This is the tragedy of Russian life.[114]

Savenko's words were not figurative. The Nationalists literally fell silent in the fourth Duma. With the exception of Demchenko's controversial address on the budget, no Nationalist deputy delivered a major speech in the second session.

This silence came at a moment of increasing political instability. As the social crisis grew, the government increased its attacks on the Duma. It sought to prosecute the Georgian Menshevik deputy, Chkheidze, for advocating the creation of a republic at a Duma session. At the same time, Maklakov and his allies in the Council of Ministers initiated a campaign to end the deputies' freedom of speech and immunity from prosecution.

These questions enflamed the Duma, but they paralyzed the Nationalists. The party made no attempt to express their views on these matters,

109. *Kievlianin*, February 6 and 8, 1914.
110. *Novoe Vremia*, February 4, 1914; TsGAOR 102 (1914) 265.981.1. Menshikov, Tsarskoe Selo, to D. N. Kuznetsov, Odessa (January 1, 1914). Ibid., 986.580; *Kievlianin*, April 13, 1914.
111. Sten. ot. 4.2.4.1006–1021.
112. *Kievlianin*, April 29, 1914.
113. *Kievlianin*, May 4, 1914.
114. TsGAOR 102 (1914) 265.987.600. Savenko, St. Petersburg, to N. K. Savenko, Kiev (April 28, 1914).

because quite simply, they had no clear views. Not surprisingly, when the Duma decided on responses to these challenges, the Nationalists split their votes.[115] It fell to Shulgin to express the party's uncertainty in the only speech by a Nationalist on a series of issues that had thoroughly engaged the rest of the Duma. He spoke on a bill that had been introduced in order to preserve the deputies' freedom of speech in the Duma. Shulgin claimed that the meaning of the proposal was "unclear," and he urged further discussion. Forced to make a decision, he chose reluctantly to support the bill, "as the lesser of two evils." He did not wish to see socialists using the Duma as a tribune, but he thought it more important "to resist government pressure."[116] Shulgin's speech reflected his new position as a spokesman for the left-wing Nationalists. However, the rest of the fraction was not swayed by his weak arguments and voted against the proposal.

If the Nationalists had no clear sense of their own political future on the eve of the war, they were equally unclear about what might be in store for Russia. Their impotence and apathy left them divided on how the state should deal with the rising and increasingly militant workers' strike movement, which by the spring of 1914 was almost as widespread as it had been in 1905. Still worse, the Nationalists could not even agree on the meaning and seriousness of the strikes, which were far more political and consciously revolutionary than they had been in 1905. Savenko was not convinced that the nation faced any serious revolutionary situation,[117] but others, like Father N. Sirovkin, a local party activist from Podol'e, were terrified.

> At the present moment, everyone is dissatisfied with everything. While this dissatisfaction is inchoate, it is growing. . . . I fear that we will again have a revolution, not now but in 1915. Certainly no later than 1916, but now it will be a truly horrible revolution.[118]

Predictably, the left wing of the party was less distressed by the labor agitation than the right wing was. Early in the spring, the party was unanimous in urging concessions to the strikers.[119] As agrarians, they clearly did not feel directly threatened.

However, the Sarajevo crisis and the much more threatening Petersburg general strike of early July forced the Nationalists to abandon this

115. Chermenskii, *IV-aia Duma*, p. 65.

116. Sten. ot. 4.2.4.95.1709.

117. *Kievlianin*, January 2, 1914.

118. TsGAOR 102 (1914) 265.437. Father N. Sirovkin, Podol'e, to N. G. Vysotskii, Moscow (March 26, 1914).

119. *Kievlianin*, April 16 and June 20, 1914.

moderation. On July 12, the Kiev Club, which represented the party's left wing, sent Goremykin a telegram, calling for the "harshest of repressive measures" and accusing workers, who had struck at a moment of national peril, of treason.[120] Thus, on the eve of the war, the party found itself thrust back into the arms of the state by the threat of revolution. It was in no position to ride the wave of opposition in order to extract concessions from a government it now despised. The Nationalists correctly perceived the strike movement to be a threat not only to their property but to the traditional structure of authority. That traditional authority—the autocracy and its bureaucracy—had been the original source of the wealth and position enjoyed by those landowners represented by the Nationalist Party. Although they had been uncomfortable with the state since the 1890s, many of them found it exceedingly difficult forthrightly to oppose the government of the tsar in a moment of such peril.

Instead, all the Nationalists could do, in Savenko's words, was to "go off to the side and be silent." In the third Duma, the Nationalists had been direct participants in the major events of the day. In the fourth Duma, they found themselves perplexed and troubled spectators, unsure of the course of events and incapable of influencing them. With the system collapsing around them, the Nationalists saw no way out of the crisis. When war finally came, it only postponed the solution of problems that had been plaguing Russia and the Nationalists since the first days of the fourth Duma.

In 1907, the government had enjoyed the support of the largest and most important Duma party, the Octobrists. By 1914, the Octobrists had passed into the opposition. Most Nationalists had given up on the government, and even many pravye were openly criticizing the course of state policy. There was no Duma party that was unanimous in its support for the autocracy. Accordingly, it is difficult to imagine who Nicholas and his advisers thought their allies were among the deputies in the lower house. In fact, the state had all but given up on the Duma. Only fear of massive disturbances and the adverse financial impact of international reaction kept the tsar from taking the final step. In 1907, there was hope that a constitutional system could take root, if it were based on cooperation between the state and the reliable social elements in the new Duma. By 1914, those hopes had been smashed.

For these reasons, one must agree with such Western historians as Geoffrey Hosking and Leopold Haimson that the "constitutional experiment" was a failure. On the eve of the war, Russia had not assimilated the

---

120. *Kievlianin,* July 13, 1914.

lessons of its brief parliamentary experience. The progress of the early years had been wiped out by 1914. Such scholars as Alexander Gerschenkron and Bernard Pares have held that the swift growth of Russian capitalism created conditions that enhanced the political stability of tsarism. But, if anything, the social groups and political parties called into being by the forces of modernization (of which the Nationalist Party was only one example) were actually undermining the social equilibrium and political cohesion of Russia's propertied classes at a moment when they were severely threatened by the increasingly revolutionary situation in Russia's cities.

Accordingly, it is difficult to agree with the traditional Soviet view, most recently advanced by E. D. Chermenskii, that fear of revolution forced the autocracy, the gentry, and the entire bourgeoisie into an uncomfortable but decisive alliance. This view (aimed especially at attacking the credibility of the Kadet party) places great stress on the ultimately antirevolutionary role played by all these groups. But recent Soviet scholarship seems closer to the mark in emphasizing the tensions among Russia's various elites during the prerevolutionary years. Iu. B. Soloviev's research on the government and the gentry, along with studies of the various elements of the bourgeoisie offered by V. S. Diakin and V. Ia. Laverychev, place greater emphasis on the lack of unanimity at the heights (*verkhi*) of Russian society.[121] This is a crucial difference. No less an authority than Lenin had argued in 1914 that the collapse of the unity of the ruling classes was the first phase of any revolutionary situation. Although Lenin was writing in exile and could not see it happening, that process was already well advanced by the eve of the First World War.

121. Iu. B. Soloviev, *Samoderzhavie i dvorianstvo v kontse XIX veka*; V. S. Diakin, *Russkaia burzhuaziia i tsarizm v gody pervoi mirovoi voiny*; V. Ia. Laverychev, *Po tu storonu barrikad: Iz istorii bor'by Moskovskoi burzhuazii s revoliutsii* (Moscow, 1967).

VII

The War Years:
An Epilog

The First Months of the War

The outbreak of World War I in July 1914 had a unifying effect on the political figures and parties in the Duma. Rallying around the tsar in the moment of national peril, the deputies quickly forgot their internal disagreements and their equally profound dissatisfaction with the government. A truce was declared between state and society. The Russian people were swept up in the patriotic fervor of the first days of war, and political attitudes were dramatically, if not fundamentally, revised. The Nationalists called off their internal bickering and offered to cooperate with the other parties. On July 21, 1914, a heavily attended meeting of the National Club passed a resolution that proclaimed what came to be called the "internal peace." "There are no more political parties in Russia. There is just one great unified Russian people."[1] At the Duma session of July 26, which was summoned expressly to vote war credits and demonstrate popular support, Balashev affirmed the Nationalists' abandonment of partisanship for the duration of the war.[2]

Other parties made similar pledges of nonpartisanship, but the Nationalists took perhaps the greatest political risk in making such a commitment. After this point, they ceased to function as a national political party. (In

1. *Novoe Vremia,* July 22, 1914. Two days before Savenko had made a similar declaration in his column in *Kievlianin,* July 20, 1914.
2. *Rech',* July 27, 1914; *Kievlianin,* July 28, 1914.

fact, of the major Duma groups, only the Kadets succeeded in maintaining even a semblance of their organizational structure during the war years.) Local Nationalist groups continued to exist, but most party members submerged themselves in the support work of the zemstvos and engaged in little that could be called party politics. With the proroguing of the legislative chambers after July 26, 1914, the Duma fraction found itself hard-pressed to serve as a center. Thus, the close coordination between national and local politics, which had characterized the Nationalists' activity even during their disintegration, now had to be abandoned. Even when the political honeymoon between state and society had ended with the crisis of the summer of 1915, the Nationalists did not revive their organization, despite the reactivation of the Duma. In fact, after 1915, the split in the party ranks made any such revival impossible.

The decision to forego partisanship proved dangerous for the Nationalists. Their genesis had been the result of the intense national and class antagonisms of the western borderland. Throughout their existence, they had refused to compromise the interest of those social groups they claimed to represent. Indeed, what political success they had achieved had been based on their ability to operate more like a modern representative political party of gentry interest than had either the Octobrists or the pravye. The Nationalists were the product of a period of interparty struggle, and they possessed a clear, if somewhat narrow, constituency whose needs did not always harmonize with those of the rest of society. Now, harmony was a political necessity, but the habits and attitudes that had evolved since 1907 were inappropriate to the new wartime demands of supraclass, supranational, and nonparty politics; their contentiousness was ill suited to the demands of the internal peace that characterized the first months of the war.

While the Octobrists, Progressisty, and Kadets were ostentatiously involved in organizing nongovernment support for the war effort, Nationalists from both wings found themselves standing off to the side. In the first weeks of the war, the zemstvos and city dumas had formed national organizations. The All-Russian Zemstvo Union, which had furnished aid to the wounded during the Russo-Japanese War, was revived under the leadership of Prince G. E. Lvov, a Kadet from Tver. The Union of Towns, of which the Kadet mayor of Moscow, M. V. Chelnokov, was president, engaged in the same kind of medical assistance.[3] Eventually, as govern-

3. V. S. Diakin, *Russkaia burzhuaziia i tsarizm v gody pervoi mirovoi voiny*, pp. 67–70; William Gleason, "The All-Russian Union of Towns and the Politics of Urban Reform in Tsarist Russia," *Russian Review* (July 1976): 290–292.

ment failures of supply and administration mounted, these groups—which came to be called the Voluntary Organizations—assumed far broader responsibilities and grew in their political pretensions.[4]

The Voluntary Organizations were supposed to be nonpolitical, and specific party labels came to have little meaning in their daily operation. In a sense, this phenomenon represented something of a revival of the earlier "nonpolitical" spirit of the zemstvos. Thus, it is significant that the two unions were dominated by the two parties, the Kadets and Octobrists, that had emerged from the zemstvo congresses of 1904 to 1906. However, all wings of the constitutionalist camp mistrusted the government. This mistrust was only temporarily submerged in the first months of the war. Once the Duma ceased to meet, the Voluntary Organizations became the main vehicle for the expression of the political aims of progressive, educated, and propertied society. Their work represented an opportunity for these forces to demonstrate that they were more capable of organizing Russia's war effort than the government was.[5]

The Nationalists, although eager to work for the nation's cause, did not immediately involve themselves in the efforts of the Voluntary Organizations. The Volynia, Kiev, and Podol'e zemstvos actually refused to join the Zemstvo Union and instead coordinated their own efforts in support of the troops.[6] This step in no way signified an unwillingness to render the kind of assistance that the national organizations were offering. Large sums were allocated for medical and relief aid.[7] The Kiev Club turned its building into a small hospital,[8] and such leading party figures as Shulgin and V. A. Bobrinskii volunteered to serve as medical aides at the front, where both were wounded.[9]

Problems cropped up immediately. The three southwest zemtvos were unable to offer any aid in the harvest, which was impeded by even the first mobilizations. By September, there were already serious shortages of medical supplies.[10] Most significantly, the Volynia, Kiev, and Podol'e zemstvos found their financial resources inadequate to support their

4. George Katkov, *Russia, 1917*, pp. 3–8.

5. Ibid., pp. 9–11.

6. Diakin, *Russkaia burzhuaziia*, p. 68.

7. *Rech'*, August 7 and 25, September 7, and November 4, 1914; *Kievlianin*, September 17, 1914.

8. *Kievlianin*, September 21, 1914.

9. *Rech'*, September 4 and 19, 1914; *Kievlianin*, September 18, 1914.

10. TsGAOR 102 (1914) 265.992.1136. N. N. Flinge, St. Petersburg, to B. A. Bulgakov, Kiev (August 2, 1914); *Kievlianin*, November 3, 1914.

independent efforts.[11] Kiev began to experience serious inflation as early as November, and so the southwest zemstvo organization had to ally with the All-Russian Zemstvo Union in order to have access to the funds that that group had been getting from the government.[12] By the spring, with fuel and other shortages already becoming serious in the west, the zemstvos of the southwest were working in relative harmony with the Zemstvo Union.[13]

Concentrating their efforts on consciously nonpartisan activity was only one reason for the Nationalists' virtual disappearance from the political scene in the first months of the war. To compound their difficulties, they now represented a potential ideological stumbling block to Russian hopes. The party had been the most visible and consistent anti-Polish force in Russian politics during the prewar years. It was now clear that much of the war would be fought on what had been Polish soil. The struggle for the loyalty of the Poles living under the Russian Empire, not to mention those in German and Austrian territory, would be crucial to military success. Therefore, the Nationalist Party represented an embarrassment. Many Poles hoped that autonomy would be the minimum reward for their cooperation in the war against Germany and Austria.[14] The Nationalists realized that this was not the moment to oppose Polish aspirations. As a result, they remained silent and kept their fears, which remained intense, to themselves.[15] Instead, they found other outlets for nationalist emotions.

The first months of the war had brought defeat at German hands in the north, but Russian armies experienced great success against the Austrians, capturing the city of Lvov and much of Galicia, located just west of the southwest gubernias. This success was a dream come true for the Galicia-Russian Society, which quickly sprang into action in support of the Russian occupation. Meetings became more frequent (as many as three a month), and in six months the budget had risen from 5,000 to 165,000 rubles.[16] The Russian administration, headed by Count G. A. Bobrinskii (a distant relative of the Nationalist V. A. Bobrinskii), soon embarked on a

11. TsGAOR 102 (1914) 265.992.1188. Lozinskii, Podol'e, to S. O. Lozinskii, Odessa (August 8, 1914).

12. *Kievlianin,* February 6, 14, and 24, May 9, 1915, and January 30, 1916.

13. *Novoe Vremia,* February 19, June 27, July 6 and 30, 1915.

14. TsGAOR 102 (1914) 265.992.1153. A. Strazhevskii, Odessa, to B. M. Romeiko-Gurko, Warsaw (August 4, 1914).

15. Ibid., 1194. Prof. Yu. A. Kulakovskii, Kiev, to E. P. Kulavokskii, Pushkino (August 8, 1914); *Kievlianin,* July 29, 1914.

16. *Novoe Vremia,* February 27 and May 5, 1915.

policy of harsh Russification.[17] Archbishop Evlogii and the society published propaganda leaflets and sent instructors to propagandize the Russian cause.[18] The heavy-handedness of these policies, coupled with widespread reports of atrocities committed by Russian troops, turned the Galician occupation into a political disaster.[19] The Galicians turned against the Russians and refused to cooperate with them. Worse yet, other Slavs living under Austrian rule could no longer be confident that liberation by the Russian army would bring them happiness and freedom. When the liberal press attacked the Russian administration in Galicia, the society made some attempt to defend the government. But the worst abuses planted doubts in the minds of such previously loyal men as V. A. Bobrinskii, who began to wonder about the state's ability to conduct the war successfully.

The Summer Crisis in the Nation and in the Party

The internal political peace was shattered by the disastrous retreats that began in May 1915 and continued until the end of August. Russian armies were forced out of Galicia. Grodno and Brest were abandoned without resistance. When the military situation finally restabilized, Russia had lost 15 percent of its land, 20 percent of its population was in occupied territory, and 30 percent of its industry was in enemy hands.[20] The decisive cause of the debacle was the calamitous shortage of shells and rifles. General headquarters was forced to limit artillery commanders to sixty shells a month per piece.[21] The army had been forced to retreat rapidly. The result was disorder among the troops and chaos in the rear as the country was flooded by 2,500,000 refugees from the war zones. The army found itself virtually defenseless, and the state's inability to supply adequate weapons was seen by much of society as the cause.

17. Daniel Graf, "Military Rule behind the Russian Front, 1914–1917: The Political Ramifications, *Jahrbücher für Geschichte Osteuropas*, No. 3 (1974):397.

18. TsGAOR 102 (1914) 265.992.1130. M. Glushkevich, Kiev, to V. A. Bobrinskii, St. Petersburg (August 2, 1914); *Rech'*, September 15 and 26, 1914; *Novoe Vremia*, April 5, 1915.

19. TsGAOR, 102 (1914) 265. 1019. 790. S. Kondaruzhkin, St. Petersburg, to editors of *Russkie Vedemosti* (April 25, 1915).

20. Michael Hamm, *The Progressive Bloc of Russia's Fourth State Duma*, p. 1.

21. Diakin, *Russkaia burzhuaziia*, p. 72; V. I. Gurko, *Features and Figures of the Past*, p. 549.

The Voluntary Organizations and the social forces they claimed to represent were incensed. Despite their lack of administrative experience, they considered themselves well equipped to organize production and supply. Moreover, they had now become convinced that the autocracy, which did not want their help, could not do the job. It was at this point that war industry committees were set up under the leadership of Moscow industrialists. Patriotic disinterest played a role in the creation of these groups, but they were also meant to help in stimulating profitable state orders while forestalling nationalization. As a result of the defeats, the tsar was powerless to stop the organization of the committees. He was even forced to accept Guchkov, whom he hated and feared, as president of the Central War Industry Committee. In early June, the government proposed a Special Council for Defense. This new group was to include representatives from the Voluntary Organizations, the Duma, and State Council as well as the various responsible ministries. It was to be headed by the war minister, V. A. Sukhomlinov, who had been so thoroughly discredited by the ineptness of his administration that society's representatives on the council refused to serve until he was removed. In late June, Sukhomlinov, under the cloud of treason, was finally dismissed.[22]

The Voluntary Organizations were not the only force working for a role for society in the war effort. Within the Council of Ministers, a conspiracy had been hatched to obtain the dismissals of the most reactionary and incompetent ministers in order to lay the groundwork for establishing government cooperation with the Duma and the Voluntary Organizations. It was widely assumed that these plans centered around a former follower of Stolypin, the Minister of Agriculture, A. V. Krivoshein, who was seen as sympathetic to the Octobrists and who nurtured hopes of replacing Goremykin as head of a new government that would then work with Russian *obshchestvennost'* (roughly translated, the public).

In June, a group of ministers friendly to Krivoshein presented Nicholas with an ultimatum. They threatened to resign unless certain archreactionary, unpopular figures were dismissed from their posts. These included the Minister of Interior, N. A. Maklakov; the Minister of Justice, I. G. Shcheglovitov; the Ober-Procurator of the Holy Synod, V. K. Sabler; and Sukhomlinov. The tsar had been urged by Grand Duke Nikolai Nikolaevich, the Supreme Commander, to dismiss these men. Despite the resistance of the tsarina, who warned of Rasputin's displeasure, Nicholas made the changes. A. A. Khvostov, a friend of Goremykin, became Minister of

22. Katkov, *Russia, 1917*, p. 133. Raymond Pearson, *The Russian Moderates and the Crisis of Tsarism, 1914-1917* (London, 1977), pp. 44–46.

Interior. A. D. Samarin, from the famous noble family of Moscow Slavophiles, was a popular choice for the Holy Synod. But the nomination of A. A. Polivanov to replace Sukhomlinov was shocking: Polivanov was closely associated with the despised Guchkov, and he was known to be sympathetic to an expansion of the tasks and responsibilities of the Voluntary Organizations.[23] There was no doubt that the choices represented a move toward cooperating with the educated public, but by retaining Goremykin, who was the liaison between the emperor and the ministers, Nicholas was able to minimize any real effects the changes might have. Accordingly, Krivoshein's group now set itself the task of effecting Goremykin's removal.

This maneuvering was carried out against a background of rising social discontent. Strikes and other labor disturbances had begun that spring and were continuing. At this point, these disorders were still not extensive, but their potential was not lost on the leaders of the Kadets and Progressisty, who, with the added stimulus of the army's retreats, began a public campaign for the convocation of a lengthy Duma session. This demand soon found support among the other Duma groups, including even the pravye. The parties shared a belief that the war had so sharply changed political attitudes that the earlier impotence and drift of the fourth Duma would not be repeated. In fact, something of a consensus had emerged on the necessity for broadening society's participation in the war effort. In May, *Rech'* quoted an unnamed Nationalist deputy (probably Shulgin or Bobrinskii):

> Under the influence of current events, many of our views have been subject to serious reconsideration. Facts, all too clearly, force us to adopt new slogans. Personally, I, and many of my colleagues, believe that the present situation has clearly proved the necessity for the participation of the representatives of society in the resolution of the urgent problems facing the country.... This is too important a question to be subjected to party considerations.[24]

When the Duma session was announced for July 19, the crisis atmosphere was, if anything, exacerbated by the possibility of renewed political conflict between the government and the Duma parties. Military failure had put an end to the "internal peace," and a sense of panic and doom affected the propertied classes along with the rest of the educated public.

On the eve of the Duma session, Polivanov, in what became a famous speech to the Council of Ministers on the military situation, proclaimed the fatherland to be in danger.[25] His picture of the extreme precariousness of Russia's position sent the ministers into complete panic. The more liberal ministers were now prepared to strike some political bargain with the representatives of society in order to revive Russia's hopes. Thus, the stage was set for the last attempt before the 1917 Revolution to achieve some degree of harmony between the state and Russian society.

The Formation of the Progressive Bloc

The public campaign during May for a lengthy and serious Duma session revived all the old tensions within the Nationalist Party. In mid-May, Rodzianko and other leaders of the Duma's central fractions assumed privately that Balashev and the Nationalists, along with the rest of the right, opposed a session.[26] However, significant elements among both the Nationalists and the pravye strongly favored an immediate calling of the Duma. On May 29, Balashev organized a private meeting at which the question was discussed among seven Nationalist Duma deputies, two sympathetic State Council members, and two members of the National Union's council (all unidentified). Balashev did not adopt any clear position, and although the majority of participants favored calling the Duma, the group reached no decision.[27] Most party leaders did not know of this gathering, and D. N. Chikhachev actually proclaimed Nationalist support for a lengthy and serious session at a meeting of the Duma's Council of Elders on June 16.[28] Therefore, both men were shocked to learn from Rodzianko that, at a conference with Goremykin, Rodzianko had been shown a "journal" of a Nationalist meeting at which the party had supposedly opposed calling the Duma.[29] The left wing of the party, led by Savenko, was incensed and called a meeting of the fraction's council for the next day.[30]

Balashev avoided that meeting by staying away from the capital.[31] He finally appeared at a session of the Council of Elders on June 23 and proclaimed himself in favor of a session. He denied that he had sent any

25. Diakin, *Russkaia burzhuaziia*, p. 96.
26. TsGAOR 102 (1915) 307a.20.
27. *Novoe Vremia*, June 18, 1915.
28. Ibid.
29. *Rech'*, June 17, 1915.
30. TsGAOR 102 (1915) 307a.78.
31. *Rech'*, June 19, 1915; *Novoe Vremia*, June 19, 1915.

"journal" to Goremykin. Balashev then demanded to know if Rodzianko had actually seen such a document or if Goremykin had mentioned Balashev's name.[32] Rodzianko was forced to admit he had not seen or heard any proof of the charges against Balashev.[33] While indecisive, the episode revived the left-wing Nationalists' mistrust of Balashev; and the intraparty tensions that had existed before the war reemerged with greater intensity than ever in the new crisis atmosphere.

On the eve of the Duma session, the Nationalist fraction was able to agree only on a very general resolution that supported the opening of the Duma and called for the reelection of the present presidium.[34] However, the entire fraction was not able to reach any decision about the appropriate duration of the session, and members were permitted to adopt their personal views on this question.[35] On the eve of events that would lead to the party's disintegration, the Nationalists were already thoroughly disunited. Any serious issue could have provoked a crisis in their ranks. That moment came with the formation of the fourth Duma's first solid working majority, the Progressive Bloc.

Even before the Duma met, the left wing of the Nationalists stood ready to forego long-standing party demands in order to find an answer to the crisis. In meetings of the Council of Elders and at private gatherings, some party members found themselves speaking in the same tones as members of the opposition. War and defeat had forced many Nationalists to think beyond the interests of those they had always represented. Shulgin recalled in his memoirs that, after he returned from the front, "I came to Petrograd no longer feeling like a representative of one of the southwest provinces. I felt I was a representative of the army." Immediately upon his arrival in Petrograd, he went straight to the office of the Kadets' leader, Paul Miliukov. Shulgin had never had any personal relationship with Miliukov but he asked him directly, "Are we friends?" Miliukov hesitatingly replied that he thought so, whereupon Shulgin declared his new respect for the patriotism that the Kadets had demonstrated in the nation's hour of peril. The two men quickly grew to respect each other, and the rapprochement between the Kadets and the left Nationalists soon became public.[36]

Bobrinskii's opening-day Duma speech reaffirmed the abandonment of

32. TsGAOR 102 (1915) 307a.81.2; *Rech'*, June 24, 1915; *Novoe Vremia*, June 24, 1915.
33. *Rech'*, June 25, 1912.
34. TsGAOR, 102 (1915) 307a.1.113; *Novoe Vremia*, July 17, 1915.
35. *Rech'*, July 19, 1915.
36. V. V. Shulgin, *Dni*, pp. 60–63; Paul Miliukov, *Political Memoirs*, (Ann Arbor, 1971), p. 321; Bernard Pares, *The Fall of the Russian Monarchy* (London, 1939), p. 258.

traditional party demands and the new desire to work with former enemies.

> The sincere desire of the Nationalists, and all those fractions with which we have talked, is that there should be no differences of party among us. We will eschew all that divides us. On matters concerning the war, we are of one mind, and if we have private differences, we will modify them in order to reach fraternal agreements. We will achieve this so that our enemy will know that he has united all of us.[37]

The liberal press was effusive in its praise for Bobrinskii's speech.[38] *Rech'*, in particular, began to talk of the "reasonableness" of Shulgin, Savenko, and Bobrinskii. The Nationalists gained Kadet support for a Duma resolution that called for a ministry enjoying the confidence of the country. Zemstvo Octobrists and Center Group members combined to pass this formula over a more radical version introduced by the Progressisty. A new spirit of cooperation had emerged in the Duma that extended from the Kadets into the ranks of the Nationalists.[39]

The left Nationalists began to return the compliments they had received from the Kadets. *Kievlianin* carried Miliukov's portrait side by side with that of Bobrinskii.[40] Savenko now hailed the patriotism and nonpartisanship of the Kadets.[41] A few days later, he was positively rapturous about the election of the leading Kadet, A. I. Shingarev, to the presidency of the Duma committee on defense. Initially, Shulgin had been chosen to fill the position, but he dramatically refused the post and urged the committee to support Shingarev.[42] By the end of July, Shulgin was announcing the emergence of a new majority.[43]

It was not long before Duma members began to talk more seriously about formalizing the new climate of cooperation that had arisen in response to the nation's crisis. The Duma's old social director, P. N. Krupenskii, organized the first dinner devoted to solidifying the new majority on August 6.[44] This event led to a series of meetings in the next few days that involved both Duma and State Council members. They were

37. Sten. ot., 4.4.1.70.

38. A. A. Kornilov, *Parlamentskii blok* (Moscow, 1915), p. 10; *Novoe Vremia*, July 20, 1915.

39. Diakin, *Russkaia burzhuaziia*, p. 90; Pearson, *The Russian Moderates*, p. 48.

40. *Kievlianin*, July 29, 1915.

41. *Kievlianin*, July 23, 1915.

42. *Kievlianin*, July 30, 1915.

43. *Kievlianin*, July 29, 1915.

44. Gurko, *Features and Figures of the Past*, p. 572.

surprised to find that they had broad areas of agreement, particularly on the question of a ministry enjoying the confidence of the country.

Their deliberations were given added urgency on August 9. A group of right-wing deputies from the State Council and Duma met at the apartment of P. N. Durnovo. Balashev and D. N. Chikhachev participated in this meeting, which voted to set up what these men called "an information bureau" to coordinate their work. Immediately, the liberal press branded this new group the "Black Bloc" and claimed that it was organized to oppose the newly emerging Progressive Bloc. At the end of the gathering at Durnovo's apartment, Balashev and Chikhachev went over to the progressives' meeting at Rodzianko's quarters. They made a last appeal for the more conservative deputies (Octobrist, Center, and Nationalist) to join them in a new right-wing majority. At this point, Savenko rose and denounced them.[45] This exchange only intensified the urgency of the liberal group. They then agreed to set up a formal alliance and elaborate a common program.[46]

On August 13, the split in the party was formalized. Shulgin announced that a group of Nationalists would enter the new Progressive Bloc. Initially, he was joined by Bobrinskii, Savenko, Demchenko, and twenty-four others. Later this fraction, called the Progressive Nationalists, grew to thirty-six members. Balashev continued to lead the majority of the fraction that stayed outside the new Duma group. Thus, the divisions that had been brewing since the first days of the fourth Duma now became an actual schism.[47] The Nationalist Party was reduced to two warring parliamentary groups and several local organizations that, because of the war, were no longer engaged in political activity. From this point on, individual Nationalists would play significant political roles, but the notion of a unified and effective national party was a dead letter.

On August 14, the leading figures of the bloc began the task of drawing up a program, though this was a secondary issue for the Progressive Nationalists. Their primary interest was in replacing Goremykin's cabinet. For them, a government that had the confidence of the nation was the central issue, and they were gratified that the Kadets chose to forego their traditional demand for a government formally responsible to the Duma.[48] Shulgin was willing to go along with more specific appeals for a canton-level (*volost'*) zemstvo and for the introduction of zemstvos into Siberia

45. *Rech'*, August 13, 1915.
46. TsGAOR 102 (1915) 307a.130; *Novoe Vremia*, August 13, 1915.
47. TsGIA, 1276.12.1799.79–80.
48. Diakin, *Russkaia burzhuaziia*, pp. 108–109; Hamm, *The Progressive Bloc*, p. 8; *Kievlianin*, August 23, 1915.

and the Caucasus because he considered such ideas "empty" in wartime.[49]

Those Nationalists who joined the Progressive Bloc were attempting to reach a compromise with "responsible" members of the opposition in order to head off more revolutionary disturbances. Shulgin described the Progressive Bloc as an attempt to stand between the streets and the government.[50] Specific questions of program were secondary matters. The Progressive Nationalists emphasized repeatedly that the bloc was a temporary agreement among parliamentary groups. In no way did it establish broad national alliances between political parties.[51]

It was, therefore, not surprising that on matters that involved their most immediate concerns, even the most cooperative Progressive Nationalists proved to be hard bargainers.[52] Despite all the talk of abandoning regional interest, Shulgin and Savenko, who were both involved in the actual deliberations on the program, conceded little on matters of direct concern to the west Russian gentry. The question of restrictions on Poles in the borderland was hotly debated. Savenko was willing to compromise on the designation of Polish as an official language, and he was ready to lift restrictions on Catholics. He was also prepared to allow Poles to accept state service roles, and he accepted, as he had not in 1911, the need to extend zemstvos to the three northwest gubernias (Kovno, Vilna, and Grodno) where they would have been dominated by Poles. However, he did oppose ending restrictions on Polish landholding. In particular, prohibitions against Polish landlords buying land from Russians had to remain. Savenko was supported by Stolypin's old assistant, V. I. Gurko, now a nonparty member of the State Council. Gurko was blunt and direct in clarifying the limits of the Nationalists' willingness to compromise. "Restrictions on language are senseless. Religious constraints are a remnant of the past, but landownership gives political power."[53] Ultimately, the bloc reached a meaningless compromise that did not threaten the Nationalists' land. Thus, for the Progressive Nationalists, joining the Progressive Bloc was to be a political compromise, an example of sound tactical judgment, a way to prevent still further drift to the left. In no way did their participation represent an economic understanding between the agrarian interests the Nationalists had always represented and the industrial and professional circles who made up the core of the bloc's support.[54]

49. Shulgin, *Dni*, pp. 63–66.
50. Ibid., p. 134.
51. Kornilov, *Parlamentskii Blok*, p. 20.
52. S. I. Shidlovskii, *Vospominania*, Vol. 2, p. 46.
53. *Krasnyi Arkhiv*, Vols. 50–51, (1932), p. 131.
54. Diakin, *Russkaia burzhuaziia*, p. 107.

The most difficult issue to resolve involved the treatment of Jews. Nothing had happened since the war to diminish the Nationalists' anti-Semitism. The matter was particularly touchy because much of the territory that had been lost that summer was part of the Pale of Settlement, the region along the western border to which Jews were restricted. Thousands of Jewish refugees were forced to flee into areas where they had previously not been allowed to live. Their reception had been hostile. Savenko and Shulgin, both of whom were convinced that Jews engaged in spying at the front, resisted any extension of civil liberties to Jews. This step had always been a central part of Kadet programs, and it was with reluctance that the Kadets accepted compromise language that called only for "taking steps toward" relieving the problem.[55] But this weak resolution proved too much for some Progressive Nationalists, and twelve of them refused to support this section of the program. Despite this, Savenko and Shulgin were especially grateful to the Kadets who, they claimed, had made the most significant compromises and given up more than any other party in order to achieve an agreement on a program.[56]

The Progressive Nationalists had been willing to support a number of reforms that they considered meaningless in time of war. In return, they had succeeded in limiting the program's language on questions of direct concern to them, that is, the nature of a new ministry, the rights of Poles in the borderland, and the so-called Jewish question. But the impact that the long-awaited fourth Duma majority would have on the tsar and the Council of Ministers was much more important than the specific content of the program. The program of the Progressive Bloc, with the demand for a government enjoying the confidence of the nation, leaked out to the press on August 26, but long before that the government had begun to feel the pressure created by the negotiations that preceded the bloc's emergence.

Throughout August, another more dramatic factor dominated the deliberations of the ministers: Through the good offices of the tsarina and Goremykin, Rasputin had spent five days with Nicholas persuading him to take supreme command of the army.[57] Nicholas had been contemplating this step for some time, and even progressive figures had been urging the creation of a powerful central authority at the head of the army. At the same time, the incompetent and dictatorial General Ianushkevich was to

55. *Krasnyi Arkhiv*, Vols. 50–51, p. 129.

56. Shulgin, "Glavy iz knigi gody," *Istoria SSSR*, No. 6 (1967):124; Shulgin, *Dni*, p. 65; *Novoe Vremia*, August 22 and 29, 1915; *Kievlianin*, September 3, 1915.

57. Diakin, *Russkaia burzhuaziia*, p. 113; Gurko, *Features and Figures of the Past*, pp. 566–567.

be replaced as chief of staff by General M. V. Alekseev, who enjoyed a reputation of competence and respect for civilian authority. Nicholas decided to assume command, and, on August 6, Polivanov announced the change to a stunned Council of Ministers. The Grand Duke Nikolai Nikolaevich, whom Nicholas replaced, had been thought to be a friend of the Voluntary Organizations and a supporter of those ministers, centered, it was thought, around Krivoshein, who were seeking Goremykin's removal. This step was a blow to their plans, but they were also genuinely distressed that the tsar, who had no military experience or competence, was taking a grave personal and political risk in assuming command at such a desperate moment. Much of the panic was unnecessary, because the role of supreme commander was largely symbolic. But, with Nicholas at the front, much power in the capital would fall into the hands of the tsarina who had a willing ally in Goremykin. Krivoshein, who still enjoyed the confidence of the tsar, accordingly began to agitate for a reversal of Nicholas's decision and for the removal of Goremykin.[58]

At the same time, the liberal ministers had been encouraged by the rallying of public opinion signified by the formation of the Progressive Bloc. In order to blunt this pressure, Goremykin invited Shulgin to an audience that included representatives of all Duma parties from the left Octobrists to the pravye. Goremykin urged them to form a new right majority; S. I. Shidlovskii and Shulgin not only rebuffed him, but Shulgin demanded that he resign.[59] Six days later, the liberal ministers sent the tsar a letter, begging him to reconsider his decision and demanding the dismissal of Goremykin. They threatened to resign if Goremykin did not go. The next day, Nicholas attended the first session of the Special Council of Defense and left for the front. The ministers then turned to the Progressive Bloc. On August 27, one day after its program appeared in the press, the State Controller, P. A. Kharitonov, arranged a meeting between four ministers and the bloc's leaders. The purpose of the gathering was described as purely informational. Nevertheless, it must have made a considerable impression on Goremykin's ministerial foes. The next day, the Council of Ministers met to discuss the question of proroguing the Duma. All the ministers were in favor of ending the session. It was impossible to use the special powers of Article 87 when the Duma was in session, and most of them felt constrained in their efforts without the emergency powers.[60] The group of liberal ministers who were disposed

58. Katkov, *Russia, 1917*, pp. 136–142; Pearson, *The Russian Moderates*, p. 56.
59. Shidlovskii, *Vospominania*, pp. 37–40.
60. Diakin, *Russkaia burzhuaziia*, p. 109.

toward cooperation with the public wanted some conciliatory gesture toward the Duma. They also demanded that Goremykin resign and that he inform the tsar that they would quit if he were not replaced. Goremykin agreed to transmit their desires to Nicholas, but in his audience with the tsar he sought and got an immediate prorogue of the Duma.

The bloc's leaders were far more fearful of the consequences of closing the session. Along with several of the ministers, some feared street disturbances if the Duma were required to disperse. *Kievlianin's* editorial for September 1 was explicit about this danger. "For victory we need time; ... to make use of that time, we need internal peace."[61] Despite the fears and public pressure, Goremykin informed the council of the tsar's decision on September 2: The Duma was to cease work the next day, and all ministers were to remain in their places. The ministers predicted disaster. Goremykin said that the fear of disturbances by urban workers was groundless. He argued, correctly, that the Duma had no special meaning to the proletariat. In fact, demonstrations, especially in Moscow, did occur, but these frightened rather than encouraged the bloc members. The closing of the Duma was severely condemned among educated and propertied society. The leaders of the Progressive Bloc were full of dire predictions,[62] while Shulgin and Savenko were simply bitter. As Savenko wrote in his column, "For a whole year the government demanded unity in the Duma. When finally, in the face of grave danger to the fatherland, this was done, the government dissolved the Duma."[63] *Kievlianin's* editorial expressed similar disgust. "There is nothing to add. The government has assumed a terrible responsibility."[64]

The bloc's hope of using the Duma as an overseer and critic of government activity had been dashed. Despite this fact, none of these respectable gentlemen was prepared to take what would have been the revolutionary step of remaining in session in defiance of the tsar. Nicholas had clearly changed his mind about cooperation with society. Later that fall, the ministers who most strongly favored cooperation with the public— Krivoshein, Shcherbatov, Samarin, and Kharitonov—either resigned or were dismissed from their posts.[65]

When the crisis had begun that spring, nearly all elements of society had expected that the government would welcome the support offered it by both the Duma and the Voluntary Organizations. Even many conser-

61. *Kievlianin,* September 1, 1915.
62. *Krasnyi Arkhiv,* Vols. 50–51, 115; Gurko, *Features and Figures of the Past,* p. 577.
63. *Kievlianin,* September 6, 1915.
64. *Kievlianin,* September 9, 1915.
65. Katkov, *Russia, 1917,* p. 132.

vative figures came to embrace the program of the bloc in order to alter the government's course. By September, any hopes for significant change had been smashed. The autocracy had rejected society. The processes that it had set in motion completely eroded what little support it retained among the educated public. While the nation's social and economic crisis deepened, the autocracy drew away from the rest of Russia. At the same time, its own internal behavior became increasingly idiosyncratic.

The Schism in the Nationalists' Ranks

The prewar divisions among the Nationalists had reemerged in May 1915 during the debate over the calling of the Duma. After the summer session began, those tensions were exacerbated by the growing personal and political friendship between the party's left wing and the Kadets. However, the formation of the Progressive Bloc touched off the crisis in the party ranks that led to the eventual split.

On August 7, the party's council, led by Balashev and dominated by the party's right wing, suggested participating in the formation of a bureau that would be formed by representatives of the pravye and Nationalists in the Duma and by the right and center groups in the State Council.[66] On the morning of August 9, the entire fraction voted to accept this "suggestion," and Balashev then took off for the meeting at P. N. Durnovo's quarters, secure in the belief that he had the support of the majority of the party.[67] Balashev's subsequent attempt to pry the left-wing Nationalists away from the Progressive Bloc had had just the opposite effect, and Savenko denounced him at the bloc's meeting.[68] The rumors about the so-called Black Bloc were the final blow for Savenko, Shulgin, Bobrinskii, and their allies.[69] They now gave themselves over to the Progressive Bloc.

However, Balashev claimed that the Nationalists had been committed to no group, and, in fact, no formal arrangement among the right-wing groups was ever worked out.[70] Nevertheless, on August 13, the left-wing Nationalists sent the party's council formal notice of their resignation.[71] The talks with the pravye were given as the immediate cause of the

---

66. *Kievlianin*, September 10, 1915.
67. *Kievlianin*, September 23, 1915.
68. *Novoe Vremia*, August 10 and 11, 1915.
69. *Kievlianin*, September 10, 1915.
70. *Novoe Vremia*, August 13, 1915; *Kievlianin*, September 22, 1915.
71. TsGAOR 102 (1915) 307a.137.

walkout, but they made it clear that their dissatisfaction dated back to the first days of the fourth Duma.[72] Those who quit the fraction, numbering twenty-eight at this point, then met and dubbed themselves the Progressive Nationalists. Bobrinskii was elected president of the new group; Shulgin became vice-president.[73]

Their letter to the Nationalists' party council stressed that the war had simply emphasized long-standing differences within the party. Shulgin, Savenko, Demchenko, Bobrinskii, and the other signers accused Balashev and his allies of fearing internal change more than Russia's defeat. By contrast, the Progressives demanded a strengthening of ties to the "broad Russian public."[74] Savenko made it clear that the question of political alliances and support for the war effort were the Progressives' primary concerns. No attempt was made to revise the party program. "Our program" said Savenko, "remains unchanged. It is the program of the All-Russian National Union."[75] However, the state's handling of the war effort had discredited the traditional authorities that he and other conservatives had always defended.[76] Speaking to the Duma on August 28, Savenko repeated this point.

> In 1906 I headed a rightist party in Kiev [the short-lived *partiia pravogo poriadka*]. Since that time, I have espoused rightist principles.... The war, however, opened the eyes of many. The horrors we are enduring led us in one way or another to a reconsideration of values.... Woe to those who have not seen this during the war ... who continue to push our fatherland into the abyss, to the brink of which the old bureaucratic regime and its functionaries have led our homeland.

Under these circumstances, society and its representatives had to be entrusted with greater powers to aid the war effort. Conservatives were in no position to argue. If this development meant a leftward shift of the political center of gravity, that was too bad. "Better a small list to the left now," argued Savenko, "than a huge list to the left after the war."[77]

In responding to the criticisms of what became known as the *Balashev-tsy*, the Progressive Nationalists took great pains to point out that the moderate forces with which they were now cooperating had considerably modified their politics under the impact of the war. Before 1914, the

72. Ibid., 141.
73. Ibid., 139.
74. *Kievlianin*, August 17, 1915; *Novoe Vremia*, August 14, 1915.
75. *Novoe Vremia*, August 16, 1915; *Rech'*, August 16, 1915; *Kievlianin*, August 20, 1915.
76. Hamm, *The Progressive Bloc*, p. 39.
77. Ibid., p. 28.

Nationalists had always mistrusted the Octobrists because of their willing-ness to cooperate with the "revolutionary" and "Jew-loving" Kadets. Now, in Shulgin's words, the Kadets had demonstrated their patriotism "with open hearts."[78] Savenko, on the Duma floor, noted the irony of a situation that had forced him to abandon his sense of the meaning of party labels.

> Before the war I considered that, while in many ways the pravye were in error, nonetheless, they were patriots. The war has revealed that there was no real patriotism among the leaders of the pravye. On the contrary, I saw much sincere, passionate patriotism among the leaders of the Constitutional Democratic Party.... They knew how to place the needs of the state above the interests of their party.[79]

The war and the formation of the Progressive Bloc had changed the terms of reference in political discourse. Before the war, party differences within society had been of great significance. There had been a multiplicity of political participants with a variety of views. Some represented specific social groups; others represented no one but themselves and their ideas. In that context, the Nationalists could do battle with other political groups and still maintain a correct, if somewhat critical, relationship toward the autocracy. By 1915, however, the meaningful political alternatives had been reduced to two—the state or society. Indeed, there had been clear signs of such a polarization even before the war. Party squabbling within society had been temporarily suspended since 1914. The demands of the Progressive Bloc had been calculated to be acceptable to some elements within the government and even to the tsar himself. But the prehistory of the bloc, the prewar backgrounds of its leaders, and the moment of its creation made it clear to all participants that they were asking the tsar and the government to make a decisive break with the traditional autocratic practices that had been challenged in 1905 but never abandoned.

Once the state refused to deal with these demands, Russian politicians were forced to choose between the two forces. There was nothing in the Nationalists' program or practice that had prepared them to make this choice, nothing that predisposed them in one direction or another. Moreover, they were now operating in a political context fundamentally different from that in which they had emerged. In a certain limited sense, political analysts were describing the present situation in tones and words similar to those used in the years preceeding the Revolution of 1905. In 1915, as in 1905, one read about a large and amorphous agglomeration of

78. *Kievlianin*, August 31, 1915.
79. Sten. ot, 4.4.1.2583–2584.

various well-meaning liberal and moderate conservatives who saw themselves as a good "us" pitted against an unremittingly evil and militarily
incompetent "them" (the autocracy and its bureaucracy). The Nationalists
had begun political activity at a time when those broad categories had lost
their meaning. They had never divided reality in terms of categories like
good and evil. Significantly, the two parties that emerged from the
zemstvo congresses of 1904 and 1905—the Kadets and Octobrists—were
most at home within the Progressive Bloc. The two parties that had been
formed after 1907—the Progressisty and the Nationalists—were far less
comfortable with the bloc's spirit of cooperation and its nonpartisan
character. Significantly, ideas and principles played a large role in the
views of the Kadets and Octobrists. The Nationalists and Progressisty were
more clearly based on interests, not ideas, and those interests had often
come into conflict.

The Progressive Nationalists adhered to the bloc because they saw the
necessity of adjusting to the changes the war had brought about. Yet,
sound tactical judgment or a desire to head off a more serious drift to the
left were only part of the reason for joining the bloc. Membership in the
Progressive Bloc implied, even if it did not formally require, a cutting of
ties with the bases of traditional authority from which most Nationalists
had derived their privileged social and economic positions. This choice
was one that traditional conservatives invariably had to make in the face
of growing modernizing forces. It was the Nationalists' tragedy that they
had to resolve this problem when an acute national crisis made a
compromise solution impossible.

However, the necessity of making such a choice begs the question of
why some Nationalists chose to join the new majority coalition, while
others refused to make the break with the state. Twenty-eight deputies
initially joined the Progressive Nationalists. By the end of 1915, the
fraction had grown to thirty-six. Balashev's group, the regular Nationalists,
had forty-nine members. On the surface, there would appear no firm
social basis for predicting the course chosen by specific individuals. Even if
one were to accept the Nationalists' firm commitment to self-interest—an
assumption that can no longer be made for all party members after
1915—a good economic and political argument could be made for either
course. Therefore, individual choices were probably based largely on
psychological and ideological considerations. Nevertheless, an examination of the backgrounds of the deputies who joined each of the groups
does reveal several differences that provide a better understanding, if not
a complete explanation, of the split.

There had been a slight turnover of Nationalist deputies since 1912,

engaged in activity that was atypical of the average west Russian noble landlord. He had built a fortune as a civil engineer and businessman working in the city of Kiev. That wealth and visibility provided the basis for a career in local government that led eventually to Duma membership. Once he arrived in Petersburg, Demchenko proved extremely energetic, and he, too, spoke often and with great precision in the Duma.

Thus, each of the Progressive Nationalist leaders had, in his own way, some personal or professional experience that made the personal styles and attitudes of the lawyers and professors among their new allies, the Kadets, less alien. The Progressive Bloc embodied many of the political attitudes of educated society in the capitals from which the Kadets and even some Octobrists had emerged. Because of their backgrounds, the leaders of the Progressive Nationalists found the political style and approach of this milieu less threatening and unfamiliar than the regulars did. It is therefore revealing that the left Octobrist, S. I. Shidlovskii, who became the chairman of the Progressive Bloc, explained Shulgin's adherence to the bloc by the fact that Shulgin was "smarter" than Balashev[80]. Similarly, Shulgin wrote to friends later in 1915, "how pleasant it would be if the stupid right wingers were as smart as the Kadets."[81] A political world in which the intelligence of individuals was a basis for cooperation and respect was alien to the regular Nationalists, who had grown up outside Moscow and Petersburg society. Shulgin, Savenko, Demchenko, and Bobrinskii, on the other hand, were comparatively more comfortable in that world.

By contrast, the leadership of the regular Nationalists could have held meetings at a hypothetical "old boys" club in Podol'e. This is not altogether surprising, considering Balashev's influence in the province. With the exception of P. A. Safonov, who was a landlord and marshal of nobility from Grodno, all the leading regulars were from Podol'e. D. N. Chikhachev, A. A. Pototskii, A. S. Gizhitskii, and N. N. Mozhaiskii, the most active of the right-wing Nationalists, were all residents of Podol'e. Other members of Balashev's group simply became invisible after 1915. These six men (Safonov included) comprised an extraordinarily homogeneous group. All were enormously wealthy landlords. All had been marshals of nobility. All had left state service in the late 1890s to work their farms, and all (except Safonov) were members of the new zemstvos. They were thoroughly typical products of their milieu. They did what was expected of

80. Shidlovskii, *Vospominania*, Vol. 1, p. 211; *Rech'*, September 5, 1915.
81. TsGAOR 102 (1915) 265.1040.2209. Shulgin, St. Petersburg, to "E. G.," in Kiev (December 11, 1915).

them and offered no surprises. The regulars simply accepted their situation without question and chose to defend it. They expected the state, whose service they had so recently left, to help them. This bred a certain passivity that was reflected in the regulars' virtual silence in the Duma. Only one of the *Balashevtsy,* Sergei Mikhailovich Bogdanov of Kiev, continued to speak out, but Balashev, Gizhitskii, and the other men from Podol'e tended to ignore him.

The Progressive Bloc was a political alliance among parliamentary representatives. It was not a compromise among social classes to submerge potentially conflicting interests in support of the war effort. As a result, the Nationalists, in debating the meaning of the bloc, dealt mainly with political and institutional questions. Was the state or were the representative institutions to assume political ascendancy? The Progressive Nationalists proposed timely compromises on these issues to preserve what had not already been lost, but they did not propose to sacrifice the welfare of the agrarian sector of the economy.

The regular Nationalists were unwilling to compromise even on the political issues, fraught as they were with disquieting precedents and new ways of conducting politics. The core of the Nationalist Party remained unwilling to change on these questions. Up to the very end, they remained loyal to the autocracy. Those nonnoble elements that had been attracted to the party in the days of its growth now spun off under the impact of the political crisis engendered by the war. The split reemphasized the partial transition of the Nationalist Party into the modern world. The same factors that had made their emergence possible in 1909 now made their disintegration inevitable. After the summer of 1915, all that was left of the party was two increasingly hostile Duma groups and a few thousand local members who worked with the zemstvos.

The Nationalists
Divided and Helpless

With the end of the summer crisis, the tsar and the revised Council of Ministers abandoned any desire to formulate a new relationship with the Duma or the Voluntary Organizations. From this point, the government, despite a certain stabilizing at the front, appears to have lost all ability to carry on the war effort in a coherent manner. The dismissals of the liberal ministers in October 1915 began what Purishkevich called the game of "ministerial leapfrog." Three of the ministries remained untouched by the chaos (Bark in Finance, Grigorovich at the Navy, and Prince Shakhovskoi in Trade and Industry stayed on until the end). However, before the February revolution, some twenty-seven changes were made in the ten other positions. In January 1916, Goremykin was replaced by B. V. Shturmer. Ten months later, A. F. Trepov took over; he lasted a month. Prince N. D. Golytsin presided over the final death rattle of the autocracy. The crucial Ministry of Interior changed hands four times.

Rasputin, working through the empress, was widely believed to have convinced Nicholas to make the rapid changes. Worse yet, Rasputin was assumed to be merely the tool of what came to be called "dark forces" surrounding the tsar.[82] These elements were supposed to be plotting a "shameful" separate peace with Germany in order to save the autocracy from further erosion. Rumors of treason in high places, centering around that "German woman," the tsarina, were given wide credence in liberal and moderate circles. However, no less a confirmed reactionary than Purishkevich also came to accept them as true.[83]

Neither wing of the Nationalists paid much attention to the rumors about Rasputin. The regulars, although committed to the slogan of a victorious war, had no desire to embarrass the autocracy. Accordingly, they never publicly mentioned either Rasputin or the possibility of a sellout to the Germans. The Progressive Nationalists, most notably Shulgin, gave little credence to what they dismissed as gossip. Therefore, the whole question of Rasputin and his influence had little impact on any of the Nationalists at a time when, in the opinion of many, the celebrated friend of Nicholas and Alexandra was dragging the state closer to the abyss.[84]

The decay of the government's highest spheres took place against the background of the steadily growing provisioning crisis. As early as the fall of 1915, it had become difficult to supply the towns with produce.[85] Kiev had been reporting shortages of food and fuel since the spring.[86] The

---

82. Miliukov, *Political Memoirs*, pp. 361–388; M. V. Rodzianko, *The Reign of Rasputin* (London, 1927), pp. 147–242.

83. Katkov, *Russia, 1917*, pp. 153–162. See also, S. P. Melgunov, *Legenda o separatnom mire* (Paris, 1957). Even in emigration, belief in Rasputin's influence and that of a so-called German party pervaded the memoirs of such men as Miliukov and Rodzianko. Since that time, Professors Melgunov and Katkov have disproven the separate peace allegations. Rasputin, however, was another matter.

84. Shulgin, *Dni*, pp. 82–83, 120. Purishkevich came to Shulgin secretly and confided to him the plan for the assassination of Rasputin. Shulgin urged Purishkevich to abandon the project. "I don't believe in Rasputin's influence. He doesn't affect the choice of ministers. . . . Kill him and nothing will change."

85. Diakin, *Russkaia burzhuaziia*, p. 132.

86. *Kievlianin*, October 30, 1916.

breakdown of transport had been the fundamental cause of a catastrophe that had spread hunger at the front and in the rear.[87] Russian railroads had been inadequate before the war, and their confused and disorderly administration during the war had led to a near collapse of the network. Some localities had large reserves of grain, while other regions starved. There was often no way to move food to where it was needed. Shortages naturally led to steadily mounting inflation. The breakdown of normal trade relations created an orgy of speculation and black marketeering.

The provisioning crisis had reached what seemed to be its peak in November 1916, just as the Duma was meeting for its fifth and final session. The government's insensitivity to the gravity of the situation reduced the deputies to total despair. Legislation had now become meaningless. New laws wouldn't put food on empty plates. The deputies could only decry the situation and criticize the government as peasant disturbances, workers' strikes, and food riots became ever more frequent, intense, and militant.[88] In these last months of the Russian autocracy, the two Nationalist Duma fractions adopted divergent approaches to the crisis. Those differences reveal still more about the basis of the party's disintegration and its long-term prospects, if any, for survival.

The Regular Nationalists

In response to the rumors of a separate peace, bloc members and many others had made the waging of "war to a victorious conclusion" an explicit political demand. Right-wing circles tended to avoid the slogan, but both Nationalist fractions embraced it because a separate peace would have meant the permanent loss of their homes and estates along the western border. Accordingly, the regulars were just as strong as the Progressives in urging that the war not be stopped.[89] This position forced the Balashevtsy to adopt an extremely unclear and hesitant attitude toward the government. They had to draw the line between criticizing and opposing the authority of the state. As a result, the right-wing Nationalists did not feel comfortable either criticizing or defending the government. As each new prime minister presented himself to the Duma, the reactions of the regulars were always guarded and unclear. More often than not, they abstained from commenting on each new minister's official declaration to

87. Hamm, *The Progressive Bloc*, p. 217.

88. A. M. Anfimov, *Rossisskaia derevnia, v gody pervoi mirovoi voiny* (Moscow, 1962), pp. 354–364.

89. See L. V. Polovtsov's Duma speech of February 10, 1916. Sten. ot., 4.3.2. 1285–1292.

the Duma.[90] This silence proved demoralizing to the fraction members, many of whom simply abandoned the Duma and returned to their homes to work with the zemstvos or the Red Cross.[91] The Duma lost all political meaning for many of the right-wing Nationalists.

If the regulars' attitude toward the government was ambiguous, their extremely hostile feelings toward the Progressive Bloc were clear. In the press and on the Duma floor, they repeatedly charged that the bloc sought a ministry responsible to the Duma and a full parliamentary system.[92] For the regulars, these demands constituted the most threatening kind of attack on the traditional notion of the autocracy. They had believed in representative institutions but not in parliamentarism. The Balashev group also claimed, in pointed criticism of the Progressive Nationalists, that the bloc sought equal rights for Jews.[93] But the regular Nationalists' criticisms of the Progressive Bloc took a back seat to the more dramatic and visible attacks of the pravye, especially those of N. E. Markov.[94] On most issues, the regular Nationalists deferred to their allies on the right. When they did state positions, more often than not only nuances distinguished their views from those of Markov and his colleagues.[95]

Balashev's willingness to let the pravye speak for his fraction was not the result of any formal policy of cooperation. The "Black Bloc," to which the liberal press alluded constantly, did not exist in any formal sense. On many occasions, the *Balashevtsy* found it necessary to distance themselves from their neighbors to the right. These disagreements usually concerned calling the Duma into session. Balashev's group nearly always favored long Duma sessions, which were opposed by the pravye, except for Purishkevich.[96] In fact, by the fall of 1916 Purishkevich had split from the official pravye fraction, taking sixteen other deputies, primarily peasants and priests, with him.[97] At the same time, conservative support for the state eroded still further when the long-silent Congress of United Nobility passed a resolution denouncing the "irresponsible dark forces" and announcing its lack of confidence in the government.[98]

90. *Rech'*, January 28 and February 29, 1916.
91. *Rech'*, November 19, 1915.
92. *Rech'*, February 6 and 18, 1916.
93. *Rech'*, May 9, 1916.
94. *Novoe Vremia*, December 14, 1916; *Rech'*, December 14, 1916.
95. *Novoe Vremia*, June 8, 1916; *Rech'*, June 8 and 10, 1916.
96. TsGAOR 102 (1913) 14. 307b.93; *Kievlianin*, December 13 and 29, 1915; *Rech'*, February 23, 1916.
97. *Novoe Vremia*, November 17, 23, 24, and 25, 1916; *Kievlianin*, November 22, 1916; *Rech'*, November 26, 1916.
98. *Rech'*, December 2, 1916; *Kievlianin*, December 5, 1916.

Throughout the growing crisis, the regulars had been silent and invisible. As a result, Balashev's declaration at the opening of the fifth session on November 1, 1916, shocked many observers. His speech was overshad-* owed by Miliukov's broadside against the government, which became famous for its rhetorical repetition of the question "Is this treason or folly?" Nevertheless, the significance of Balashev's criticism was not lost. He attacked the government for ignoring the efforts of the zemstvos, for the ministerial leapfrog, and for contradictory, uncoordinated, and poorly conceived orders. Balashev repeated the call for a victorious conclusion to the war, and, for perhaps the first and certainly the last time in his career, he received the applause of the Duma's left wing.[99] But his words were too little too late. Very quickly after the split in the party, events passed the regular Nationalists by.

The Progressive Nationalists

In attacking the Progressive Bloc, the regulars reserved a special wrath for the Progressive Nationalists who, they claimed, had sold out the party's long-standing demands. The most sensitive issue was that of equal rights for Jews. As a result, the Progressives found themselves constantly defending their position. In fact, Shulgin's colleagues were painfully divided on matters pertaining to Jews, and, at a number of crucial moments, they divided their votes.[100] Shulgin and Savenko, both of whom emerged as leading public spokesmen for the bloc, stoutly defended the compromise formulation worked out in the bloc's program. Both of them claimed that it was the Kadets who had made the profound sacrifices.[101]

In March 1916, Shulgin summed up the Progressive Nationalists' reasons for their position on the so-called Jewish question. His reasoning, emphasizing sensible tactics in response to changes brought about by the war, could be taken as a general justification for the Progressive National- ists' participation in the bloc. His remarks were made in response to the attacks of Markov.

> You do have a strong position on this question. I agree with you. It is strong because the attitude toward Jews that you advance here, does have a real basis. ... But we say, "Yes we recognize this, but we think that it is a minus for victory." We think that any kind of constant oppression against our fellow

99. *Novoe Vremia*, November 2, 1916; *Rech'*, November 2, 1916.
100. *Rech'*, March 11, 1916.
101. Sten. ot., 4.4.2.2578–2582.

citizens, who, despite everything, fight alongside us, is a minus for victory, and we will seek to diminish that minus.[102]

Despite the failure of the bloc to attain any of its aims, the Progressive Nationalists remained committed participants and loyal allies. They hailed the sixth Kadet party congress and described it as "patriotic and free of party politics."[103] By the fifth session, Savenko was making speeches that, before the war, could have been made by a Kadet.

> We have before us the question of the rights of popular representation, of the strength of our Fundamental Laws. The government ignores the representatives of the people and acts without them. Billions of the people's wealth are spent without the participation of the legislative bodies.[104]

In the spring of 1916, Shulgin published a series of editorials in *Kievlianin* in which he sought to clarify his position toward the bloc. He admitted that little had been accomplished, but he had not really expected a great deal at the outset. Significantly, Shulgin sought to emphasize that, although the Progressive Nationalists felt loyalty to the bloc, their votes on any number of specific questions could not be taken for granted.[105]

The question of setting ceiling prices on bread and grain was the most difficult issue that confronted the Progessive Nationalists.[106] This question assumed decisive importance as the provisioning crisis grew more serious. In September 1916, Shulgin came out in favor of imposing limitations on the price of bread.[107] This stand was in direct opposition to the immediate economic interests of the landowning agrarians that the Nationalists had always represented.[108] Shulgin's position set off a debate within the fraction. By October, in budget committee sessions, he was forced to switch his position.[109] Yet, a few days later, after considerable personal pressure from Miliukov, Shulgin changed his mind again and accepted

---

102. Ibid., 2. 3023.

103. *Kievlianin*, February 26 and March 17, 1916. *Kievlianin*'s characterization conveniently ignored the sharp contention at the Kadet congress. Miliukov, who now shared a strong personal relationship with Shulgin, was challenged by leftist tendencies within his party which would have scared the Progressive Nationalists out of their wits. See Pearson, "Miliukov and the Sixth Kadet Congress," *Slavonic and East European Review* (April 1975): 210–229.

104. *Novoe Vremia*, December 10. 1916.

105. *Kievlianin*, April 13 and 15, 1916.

106. *Kievlianin*, February 4, 1916.

107. *Kievlianin*, August 3 and September 5, 1916.

108. *Kievlianin*, September 13, 1916.

109. *Rech'*, October 13, 1916.

fixed prices on grain.[110] Now, landowning interests back in Kiev were enraged. T. Lokot (the only visible Octobrist spokesman in Kiev before the war but now a member of the Kiev Club) wrote an editorial for *Kievlianin* in which he denounced the Progressive Bloc's demand for price limits on bread as an attack against landowners. Moreover, he characterized the attack as "class-based."

> It seems that, for our Russian liberals and radicals, the class and political interests of the bourgeoisie and intelligentsia are closer to those of commercial and industrial capital than they are to the interests of the agrarian classes.[111]

Finally, in December, Shulgin, under pressure, spoke out in defense of the agrarian sector against the demands of urban interests that sought to lower bread prices.[112]

Shulgin's ultimate refusal to compromise on bread prices revealed the nature of the Progressive Nationalists' cooperation with the bloc. The willingness to give lip service to what had been always characterized as bourgeois political demands did not signify a corresponding economic compromise between industrial and agricultural property. The Progressive Bloc did not represent a broad agreement that balanced conflicting economic interests between a modernizing, urban bourgeoisie and a traditional landowning gentry. In fact, by the fall of 1916, the Kadets were the main bourgeois element still in the bloc, and they were, properly speaking, a party of the intelligentsia and professional classes. The Progressisty, who were dominated by Moscow industrialists, had quit the bloc over the failure to press for a responsible ministry on the eve of the fifth and final session of the fourth Duma. Progressive Nationalist participation in the bloc was impermanent and shallow, based on temporary political agreements that made tactical sense to Shulgin and his allies but that could not be permitted to subvert fundamental interests. It is highly doubtful that, given the narrow basis of agreement in its program, the Progressive Bloc would have survived long after the war if conditions had been different.

The Progressive Nationalists joined in the chorus of doom with which the Duma greeted the crisis situation of the fall of 1916. Bobrinskii, elected (along with the Kadet Nekrasov) as one of the vice-presidents of the Duma, proclaimed that "the government is in a struggle with all social

110. Ibid.
111. Ibid.
112. *Kievlianin*, December 9, 1916; Shulgin, *Dni*, p. 141.

forces, including even the noble assemblies."[113] Savenko predicted doom: "The government fears revolution very much, but it has forgotten that the greatest cause of revolution in the country right now is the government itself."[114] But it remained for Shulgin to describe the seriousness of the situation with appropriate accuracy and drama: "If we now stand up in direct and open judgment of this state and struggle against its banner, it is because we have been truly pushed to the limit.... We can go no further."[115] Shulgin had prefaced his remarks by noting that he had never before practiced opposition to authority. But opposition to the autocracy came easier for him than it did for his former colleagues, the regular Nationalists. Shulgin, Savenko, Bobrinskii, and Demchenko had never been full or extensive participants in any level of state service. Thus, it was less difficult for them to withdraw support for a tsar they had never formally pledged to serve. Yet, even the Progressives could not make the final break until, in Shulgin's words, they had been "pushed to the limit."

The Party in the Provinces

The split among the Nationalists had its reflection in the local politics of the borderland. In March 1916, the Kiev branch of the Russian National Union accused Demchenko of profiteering on the boot and artillery shell factories he had organized.[116] The right-wing Nationalists' attack on Demchenko was interpreted as part of a broader campaign against the work of the zemstvos, and the two wings of the Nationalist Party became still more alienated from each other as a result of the accusations.[117]

In fact, both the Kiev Club and the local branch of the National Union had virtually ceased political activity. Those Nationalists who remained active now devoted their energies to the work of the zemstvos. Significantly, the close coordination of the work of the Podol'e and Kiev zemstvos came to an end. Podol'e was thoroughly dominated by the regular Nationalists. Balashev, Gizhitskii, Pototskii, and D. N. Chikhachev were still members. Rakovich, their close ally, retained his titles of gubernia zemstvo president and gubernia marshal of nobility. In 1916, he was

113. *Rech'*, November 6 and 21, 1916; *Novoe Vremia*, November 10, 1916; *Kievlianin*, November 10, 1916.

114. *Novoe Vremia*, December 17, 1916.

115. *Rech'*, November 4, 1916; *Novoe Vremia*, November 4, 1916; *Kievlianin*, December 2, 1916.

116. *Rech'*, March 17 and 24, 1916.

117. *Novoe Vremia*, March 10, 1916; *Kievlianin*, July 6, 1916.

elected by the zemstvo to the State Council. Political loyalties in the Kiev gubernia zemstvo were more divided, but there the left was stronger. F. N. Bezak, who was associated with the regulars, was defeated for the State Council seat by the Progressive Nationalist, K. E. Suvchinskii; the vote was 37 to 19.[118]

Absenteeism was extensive at the 1916 winter session of the Podol'e gubernia zemstvo. Of the Duma deputies, only Gizhitskii bothered to appear. Little attention was given to support for the army. When the members dealt with the war, their primary concern was the refugee problem.[119]

By contrast, the Kiev zemstvo was far more concerned and active. In addition, the gubernia zemstvo assembly became an arena in which the different tendencies within the party came into direct conflict. The last session of the Kiev gubernia zemstvo before the February revolution dramatically illustrated the divisions in what had always been the Nationalist Party's strongest area of support. The president of the zemstvo board, M. A. Sukovkin, an ally of the Progressives, opened the session on January 28, 1917, with an extremely pessimistic speech in which he obliquely criticized the government for interfering in the work of the zemstvos.[120] In the next few days, speakers graphically detailed the extent of Russia's crisis. The meat and bread shortages in Kiev were decried. The collapse of transport in what had been a great center of railroading was noted with great bitterness. Several speakers described what they called the "collapse" of agriculture in the borderland, and others lamented the sorry state of the zemstvo's finances.[121] Each description of a problem set off harsh exchanges and mutual accusations among the members.

Finally, on February 3, 1917, Sukovkin rose to give the final address. Bezak, in his capacity as zemstvo assembly president, was presiding. Sukovkin declared that the zemstvos could not remain silent in the face of the current crisis. He urged the members to oppose government attempts to discredit the zemstvos. When he mentioned the word "government," Bezak interrupted him.

Bezak: I will not allow politics here.
A voice: It's not politics. Let him go on.

118. *Kievlianin*, September 8, 1916.
119. Podol'skoe zemskoe sobranie, *Stenograficheskie otchety*, (February 24, 1916), pp. 18, 56–60; *Zhurnaly Podol'skogo gubernskogo zemstva* (Kamenets, 1916), February 22–28, 1916, pp. 3–5.
120. *Kievskaia Mysl'*, January 28, 1917.
121. *Kievskaia Mysl'*, January 29, 30, and 31, 1917; *Kievlianin*, February 2, 1917.

Sukovkin: We are not granted the possibility of working.

Bezak: Again, that's politics.

K. P. Grigorovich-Barskii [the regular Nationalist Duma deputy]: I have always thought zemstvo meetings were no place for politics, but these are different times. Because of the actions of the government, economic questions have become political.

Bezak: The law does not allow politics. Otherwise I would allow it.

Yu. A. Kistiakovskii [a Progressive sympathizer]: Sukovkin said we can no longer live this way, if we are true to the economic interests of the population.

The meeting broke down into a shouting match.[122] To avert chaos, Sukovkin rose to declare that all could agree that only a strong and just state could lead Russia to victory. The members then voted unanimously to send the tsar the now-traditional telegram of loyalty, and the meeting broke up.

This final exchange between Sukovkin and Bezak displayed the problem the Nationalist Party was never to resolve. Under the impact of the final crisis, Sukovkin and even such right-wing Nationalists as K. P. Grigorovich-Barskii had recognized the necessity of challenging an authority that not only had led Russia to the brink of disaster but that had stifled their honest efforts to save the nation. Bezak, on the other hand, in order to cut off a threatening political exchange, could only revert to empty traditional notions of authority and law. Ironically, the Nationalists had always scoffed at the distinction between "economics" and "politics" in the zemstvos. Yet, faced with a rebellious meeting, Bezak reverted to the traditional and the familiar in order to avoid embarrassment. Much the same can be said for the majority of Nationalists who, despite all their criticisms and difficulties, remained loyal to the autocracy right up to the end.

When the end finally came for the Russian autocracy, the Progressive Nationalists readily joined in the Duma's efforts to establish the first Provisional Government. Shulgin, who had accepted the tsar's abdication along with Guchkov, was on the Executive Committee of the Duma.[123] *Kievlianin* urged its readers to remain calm and support the new republic.[124] However, after the celebrated April crisis, Shulgin, Shidlovskii, Guchkov, Miliukov, and their allies were removed from the political scene. More liberal and some socialist figures entered the Provisional Government. However, the conservatives continued to meet, along with Balashev,

122. *Kievskaia Mysl'*, February 3, 1917.
123. *Russkie Vedemosti*, March 2, 1917.
124. *Kievlianin*, March 4, 1917.

Purishkevich, and other Duma members, in a series of private sessions during the spring and summer of 1917. Discredited and demoralized, they spent the months before the Bolshevik Revolution lamenting the death of noble landholding and preparing for the worst.[125]

125. A. K. Drezen, *Burzhuaziia i pomeshchiki v 1917* (Moscow-Leningrad, 1932). These are stenographic records of the private meetings of Duma deputies. These meetings began in May 1917 and lasted until mid-July.

Selected
Bibliography

In the absence of any secondary literature on the Nationalist Party, this study has been based primarily on archival sources, Duma records, and newspaper articles. Along with the primary sources, I have listed only those secondary sources that bear directly on the Nationalists. Exhaustive bibliographies on the Duma and Russian politics can be found in the following two volumes: Geoffrey Hosking, *The Russian Constitutional Experiment* (Cambridge, 1973), for the years 1907–1914; and Raymond Pearson, *The Russian Moderates and the Crisis of Tsarism, 1914–1917* (London, 1977). As its title suggests, this excellent, perceptive, and original study covers the war years. Although Pearson's work concentrates on the Kadets, Octobrists, and Progressisty, his bibliography contains the few major works on Russian conservatism during the war.

Unpublished Sources

I. Archives

Tsentral'nyi Gosudarstvennyi Arkhiv Oktiabrskoi Revoliutsii (Moscow)
Fond 102: Department of Police
Fourth Division (*4-oe deloproizvodstvo*)
Special Branch (*Osoboe otdelenie*)
Collection of Intercepted and Inspected Letters (*Fond perliustratsii*)

Fond 115:   The Union of October 17th
Fond 434:   Council of the United Nobility
Tsentral'nyi Gosudarstvennyi Istoricheskii Arkhiv v Leningrade
Fond 1276:   The Council of Ministers
Fond 1278:   The Duma
Fond 1288:   The Department of Local Government of the Ministry of Interior
Fond 1327:   The Special Division for Elections of the Ministry of Interior
Fond 1629:   I. Ia. Gurliand
Fond 1662:   P. A. Stolypin
British Public Records Office (London)
Foreign Office Series 371 (Russia), 1905–1917

II. Dissertations

Brainard, Michael. *The Union of October 17 and Russian Society, 1905–1914*. Ph.D. dissertation, Columbia University, 1976.

Chermenskii, E. D. *Borba klassov i partii v IV-oi Gosudarstvennoi dume*. Doctoral dissertation, Moscow University, 1948.

Hamm, Michael. *The Progressive Bloc of Russia's Fourth State Duma*. Ph. D. dissertation, Indiana University, 1971.

Hutchinson, John. *The Octobrists in Russian Politics, 1905–1917*. Ph.D. dissertation, University of London, 1966.

Manning, Roberta. *The Russian Nobility in Revolution and Counter-Revolution*. Ph.D. dissertation, Columbia University, 1974.

McNaughton, Ruth. *The Provincial Nobility and Political Trends in the Zemstvos, 1906–1910*. Master's essay, Columbia University, 1972.

Schaeffer, Mary. *The Political Policies of P. A. Stolypin*. Ph.D. dissertation, Indiana University, 1964.

Simmonds, George. *The Congress of Representatives of the Noble Associations: A Case Study of Russian Conservatism*. Ph.D. dissertation, Columbia University, 1964.

Vaisberg, I. D. *Sovet Ob'edinn'onogo Dvorianstva i ego vlianie na politiku samoderzhavia: 1906–1914*. Candidate's dissertation, Moscow University, 1956.

Published Sources

I. Newspapers and Periodicals (all dailies, except as otherwise noted)

Golos Moskvy, 1908–1914
Kievlianin, 1907–1917

Kievskaia Mysl', 1909–1912
Kievskie Vesti, 1910–1911
Minskii Golos, 1911
Minskoe Slovo, 1911
Mogilevskii Vestnik, 1911–1914
Novoe Vremia, 1907–1917
Okrainy Rossii (weekly), 1907–1913
Pis'ma k Blyzhnym, (bimonthly), 1908–1912
Podolianin, 1910–1911
Podolskie Izvestia, 1911–1912
Rech', 1907–1917
Rossiia, 1907–1915
Russkie Vedemosti, 1909–1912
Volyn', 1911
Individual issues of other dailies, including *Birzhevie Vedemosti*, *Moskovskie Vedemosti*, *Slovo*, and *Utro Rossii*

II. Published Documents

Drezen, A. K. *Burzhuaziia i pomeshchiki v 1917*. Moscow-Leningrad, 1932.

Gosudarstvennaia Duma, *Stenograficheskie otchety*, St. Petersburg, 1907–1917, 3–ii sozyv, 1907–1912, 4–ii sozyv, 1912–1917.

Kievskoe gubernskoe zemskoe sobranie, *Stenograficheskie otchety*. Kiev, 1913.

Krasnyi Arkhiv, 106 vols. Moscow, 1923–1941.

Lado, *Sbornik obshchestvennogo postiashchenii narozhdaiushchei Russkoi Natsional-Demokratii*. St. Petersburg, 1912.

Materialy po agrarno-ekonomicheskie issledovania iugo-zapadnogo kraia. Gaisin, 1908.

Ministry of Agriculture, *Kratkie spravochnye svedenia o nekotorikh Russkikh khoziaistvakh*. St. Petersburg, 1901.

Obzor deiatel'nosti Vserossiskogo Natsional'nogo Soiuza. St. Petersburg, 1910–1913.

Olshanskii, N. N. *Gosudarstvennaia duma, portrety, biografii, avtografii*, 3–ii, i 4–ii sozyvy. Moscow, 1910 and 1913.

Osoboe deloproizvodstvo po vyboram, *Vybory v tret'iu Gosudarstvennuiu dumu*. St. Petersburg, 1911.

Podol'skoe gubernskoe zemstvo, *Stenograficheskie otchety gubernskogo zemskogo sobrania*. Kamenets-Podolsk, 1912–1914; *Zhurnaly Podol'skogo gubernskogo zemstva*. Kamenets-Podolsk, 1912–1914.

Sbornik kluba Russkikh natsionalistov. Kiev, 1909, 1910, 1911, 1914.

Shchegolev, P. E., ed. *Padenie tsarskogo rezhima*, 7 vols. Moscow-Leningrad, 1925–1927.

Ustav Vserossiskogo Natsional'nogo Soiuza. St. Petersburg, 1909.

Ves' iugo-zapadnogo kraia. Kiev, 1907.

Vol'noe Ekonomicheskoe Obshchestvo, *Agrarnoe dvizhenie v Rossii, 1905-1906 gg.*, 2 vols. St. Petersburg, 1908.

III. Memoirs

Gurko, V. I. *Features and Figures of the Past.* Palo Alto, 1939.
Kokovtsev, V. N., *Iz moego proshlogo*, 2 vols. Paris, 1933.
Kryzhanovskii, S. E. *Vospominania, iz bumag S. E. Kryzhanovskogo, poslednogo gosudarstvennogo sekretaria Rossiskoi Imperii.* Berlin, n.d.
Naumov, A. N. *Iz utselevshikh vospominania*, 2 vols. New York, 1954–1955.
Nikonovich, F. *Iz dnevnika chlena Gosudarstvennoi Dumy ot Vitebskoi gubernii.* Vitebsk, 1912.
Shidlovskii, S. I. *Vospominania*, 2 vols. Berlin, 1923.
Shulgin, V. V. *Dni.* Belgrade, 1927.
Shulgin, V. V. "Glavy iz knigi 'Gody'," *Istoriia SSSR*, No. 6 (1967).

IV. Books and Articles

Anfimov, A. M. *Krupnoe pomeshchich'e khoziaistvo Evropeiskoi Rossii.* Moscow, 1969.
Avrekh, A. Ia. "Raskol fraktsii Oktiabristov v IV-oi dume," *Istoriia SSSR*, No. 4 (1978): 115–127.
Avrekh, A. Ia. *Stolypin i tret'ia duma.* Moscow, 1968.
Avrekh, A. Ia. "Tret'eiunskaia monarkhiia i obrazovanie tret'edumskogo pomeshchich'e-burzhuaznogo bloka," *Vestnik Moskovskogo Universiteta* (Istoriko-filologicheskaia seriia), No. 1 (1956):3–70.
Avrekh, A. Ia. "Tret'ia duma i nachalo krizisa tret'eiunskoi sistemy," *Istoricheskie Zapiski*, Vol. 53 (1955): 50–109.
Avrekh, A. Ia. *Tsarizm i tret'eiunskaia sistema.* Moscow, 1966.
Avrekh, A. Ia. "Vopros o zapadnom zemstve i bankrovstvo Stolypina," *Istoricheskie Zapiski*, Vol. 70, (1961): 61–112.
Chermenskii, E. D. *IV-aia Gosudarstvennaia duma i sverzhenie tsarizma v Rossii.* Moscow, 1976.
Chmielewski, E. "Stolypin and the Russian Ministerial Crisis of 1909," *California Slavic Studies*, Vol. 4 (1967): 1–38.
Chmielewski, E. "Stolypin's Last Crisis," *California Slavic Studies*, Vol. 3 (1964): 95–126.
Chmielewski, E. *The Polish Question in the Russian State Duma.* Knoxville, 1970.
Conroy, Mary Schaeffer. *Peter Arkadevich Stolypin: Practical Politics in Tsarist Russia.* Boulder, 1976.
Diakin, V. S. *Russkaia burzhuaziia i tsarizm v gody pervoi mirovoi voiny.* Leningrad, 1967.

Diakin, V. S. *Samoderzhavie, Burzhuaziia i dvorianstvo, v 1907-1911 gg.* Leningrad, 1978.

Doctorow, Gilbert. "The Fundamental State Laws of 23 April 1906," *Russian Review* (April 1975): 32-52.

Doctorow, Gilbert. "The Russian Gentry and the Coup d'Etat of June 3, 1907," *Cahiers du Monde Russe et Soviétique*, No. 1 (1976): 43-51.

Emmons, Terence. "The Russian Landed Gentry and Politics," *Russian Review*, (July 1974): 269-283.

Emmons, Terence. *The Russian Landed Gentry and the Peasant Emancipation of 1861.* Cambridge, 1966.

Haimson, Leopold, ed. *The Politics of Rural Russia, 1905-1914.* Bloomington, 1979.

Harper, Samuel. *The New Electoral Law for the Russian Duma.* Chicago, 1908.

Iaroshevich, A. I. *Ocherki ekonomicheskoi zhizni iugo-zapadnogo kraia.* Kiev, 1908.

Iurskii, G. *Pravye v tret'-ei Gosudarstvennoi dume.* Kharkov, 1912.

Izgoev, A. S. *P. A. Stolypin.* Moscow, 1912.

Katkov, George. *Russia, 1917.* London, 1967.

Korelin, A. P. "Dvorianstvo v poreformennoi Rossii," *Istoricheskie Zapiski*, Vol. 87 (1971): 91-173.

Kovalchenko, I. D., and L. V. Milov. *Vserossiskoi agrarnyi rynok.* Moscow, 1974.

Kovalevskii, P. I. *Osnovy Russkago natsionalizma.* St. Petersburg, 1912.

Kovalevskii, P. I. *Psikhologia Russkoi natsii.* Petrograd, 1915.

Kovalevskii, P. I. *Russkii natsionalizm i natsional'noe vospitanie.* St. Petersburg, 1912.

Leshchenko, M. N. *Selianskii rukh na pravoberezhnoi Ukraini v period revoliutsii 1905-1907 rr.* Kiev, 1955.

Levin, Alfred. "The Reactionary Tradition in the Elections to the Third Duma," *Oklahoma State University Occasional Papers.* Stillwater, 1962.

Levin, Alfred. "The Russian Voter in the Elections to the Third Duma," *Slavic Review* (December 1962): 660-677.

Levin, Alfred. *The Second Duma.* Hamden, Conn., 1966.

Levin, Alfred. *The Third Duma: Elections and Profile.* Hamden, Conn., 1975.

Minarik, L. P. *Ekonomicheskaia kharakteristika krupneishikh zemel'nykh sobstvennikov Rossii kontsa XIX-nachala XX veka.* Moscow, 1974.

Natsionalisty v 3-ei Gosudarstvennoi Dume. St. Petersburg, 1912.

Perrie, Maureen. "The Russian Peasant Movement of 1905-1907: Its Social Composition and Revolutionary Significance," *Past and Present* (November 1972): 123-155.

Pershin, P. N. *Agrarnaia revoliutsia v Rossii*, 2 vols. Moscow, 1966.

Pinchuk, B. *The Octobrists in the Third Duma, 1907-1912.* Seattle, 1974.

Proskuriakova, N. A. "Razmeshchenie i struktura dvorianskogo zemlevladenia evropeiskoi Rossii v kontse XIX-nachale XX veka," *Istoria SSSR*, No. 1 (1973): 55-76.

Rogger, Hans. "The Beilis Case," *Slavic Review* (December, 1966).

Rogger, Hans. "The Formation of the Russian Right," *California Slavic Studies,* Vol. 4 (1964).

Rogger, Hans. "Was There a Russian Fascism? The Union of Russian People," *Journal of Modern History,* No. 5 (1964).

Shulgin, V. V. *Vybornoe zemstvo v iugo-zapadnom kraie.* Kiev, 1909.

Sikorskii, I. A. *O Psykhologicheskikh osnovakh natsionalizma.* Kiev, 1910.

Soloviev, Iu. B. *Samoderzhavie i dvorianstvo v kontse XIX veka.* Leningrad, 1973.

Telichuk, P. P. *Ekonomichni osnovi agrarnoi revoliutsii na Ukraini.* Kiev, 1971.

Veselovskii, B. B. *Istoria zemstva za sorok let,* 4 vols. St. Petersburg, 1909.

Viazigin, A. S. *Gololobovskii intsident.* Kharkov, 1909.

Zaslavskii, D. O. *Rytsar' chernoi sotni V. V. Shulgin.* Leningrad, 1925.

Index

Absenteeism
    in Duma, 174
    of Russian landlords, 52, 135, 159
    in zemstvos, 190–191, 232
Agrarian capitalism, 54, 55, 59
Agrarian reform, 27–28, 142
Agriculture
    defense of interests in, 174, 175
    industrialization and, 11
    nobles and, 3, 15–18
        political activity and, 20–21
    structure of, in west borderland, 52–55
    sugar beets and, 53, 57–58, 60
    Ukrainian, 56
    war shortages and, 229–230
    wartime collapse of, 232
Akimov, M. G., 80, 81, 117
Alekseev, General M. V., 215
Alekseev, S. N., 144
Alexandra Feodorovna (Tsarina), 207, 215, 225
All-Russian National Club, 168
    analyzed, 191–192
    formation of, 97–99
    growth of Nationalists and, 113
    Kholm question and, 111, 112–113
    zemstvo bill and, 108, 117
All-Russian National Union, 84, 103, 106, 114, 133, 135, 145, 218

All-Russian National Union (*continued*)
    activity of, ends, 231
    creation of, 70, 71–72, 93–99
    government assistance and, 149–150
    National Club and, 97–99
All-Russian Zemstvo Union, 203, 204, 205
Anchinnikov, V. A., 158
Anti-Semitism, 112. *See also* Jews
    Balashev's opposition to, 141
    Beilis affair, Shulgin and, 187–188
    Kadet opposition to, 214
    Nationalists and, 94, 97
    political party support and, 25–26
    pravye and, 35, 36
Antsiferov, N. N., 133
Army, 232. *See also* Military reform
    early success of, 205
    Nicholas and, 214–215
    retreat of, 206
Article 87. *See* Fundamental Laws
Assimilation policy, Independent National-ists, 125
Austria, 194–195, 205
Avrekh, A. Ia., 34, 73n27

Balashev, Peter Nikolaevich, 37, 42, 85, 125, 134, 137, 145, 148, 157, 158, 188, 202, 223, 231, 233

Balashev, Peter Nikolaevich (*continued*)
  estate of, farming and, 20
  fourth Duma and, 167, 168, 170, 171, 173, 177, 180
  Kutaisov affair and, 151–152
  moderate right and, 68, 75–76, 77
  national convention and, 197–198
  vs. Progressive Bloc, 212, 217, 218–221, 226–228
  replacement of Guchkov by, 91
  Russian National fraction and, 94–95, 96, 97
  secret conference and, 209–210
  sense of self-importance, Kokovtsov and, 141
  zemstvo bill and, 106–107, 108
Balashevtsy (Nationalist group during World War I), 218, 220, 221, 223, 226–228
Baliasnyi, Mikhail, 147, 148
Balkans. *See* War, in Balkans
Bariatinskii, A. N., 107
Beilis, Mendel, 187
Bensidoun, Sylvain, 14
Bezak, F. N., 37, 42, 77, 137, 150, 167, 174, 185, 232–233
Bielorussia, 56, 58, 59, 61, 136
Black Bloc. *See Balashevtsy*
Black Hundreds (archreactionary groups), 26
Bloody Sunday (1905), 12
Bobrinskii, A. A., 23, 46
Bobrinskii, Lev, 46
Bobrinskii, Vladimir Alekseevich, 20–21, 41, 42, 111, 114, 132, 141, 144, 168, 180, 192, 204, 206
  Congress of United Nobility and, 23
  cooperation in Duma and, 210–211
  foreign affairs and, 193–195
  government assistance and, 149–150
  moderate right and, 67–68, 77
  as a Nationalist, 46
  as organizer of Galicia-Russia Society, 144, 192
  profile of, 221, 223
  Progressive Bloc and, 212, 217–218, 230, 231
Bogdanov, Sergei Mikhailovich, 42, 69, 85, 109, 126, 137, 167, 224

Bogdanov, Sergei Mikhailovich (*continued*)
  Kiev Club split and, 181–183, 185, 186
  Nationalist party fractions and, 72
  Octobrist coalition suggested by, 76, 78–79
  Octobrist ideology and, 92
  tension in Duma and, 172–173, 180
Bogrov, Dmitri (Stolypin's assassin), 140
Borderlands. *See* Western Russia (borderlands)
Bourgeoisie, 30, 172, 174, 201. *See also* Industrialization
  landed, 17
  Progressive Bloc and, 230
Bureaucracy, 3, 4, 86, 92, 93, 98, 104. *See also* Government
  assistance to Nationalists and, 157–158, 160
  formation of, 15
  Nationalists and, 127–128, 148–152
  petitioning of, by gentry, 6, 8

Capitalism. *See also* Agrarian capitalism
  impact of, on nobles, 14, 18
  industrial, social values and, 9
  social unrest and, 201
Catherine the Great, 14
Center Group (led by Krupenskii), 168–169, 173, 191
Central Russia, 42
  election of fourth Duma in, 162–165
Chelnokov, M. V., 203
Cherkassov, Baron, 82, 93, 94
Chernov, Professor V. E., 57, 70, 107, 128, 131, 137, 139, 181
  zemstvo bill and, 117, 119–120
Chikhachev, D. N., 37, 42, 70, 134, 135, 137, 157, 159, 167, 180, 209, 223, 231
  Progressive Bloc and, 212
  zemstvo bill and, 107, 108–109
Chikhachev, N. N., 167, 186
Chkheidze (Georgian Menshevik deputy), 198
Cities, 3. *See also* Urban sector
  agricultural surplus for, nobles and, 16
  discontent and disturbances in, 11
  election of 1912 and, 161

Cities (*continued*)
  electoral divisions of, 31
  electors in, 47, 48
Congress of the United Nobility, 28, 227
  formation of, 22–23
Conservatives. *See also* Nationalists; Octo-
    brists; Pravye
  basic conflict of, 5
  groups of, 1905–1907, 22–27
  ideology and, 8–9
  zemstvos and, 21–22
Constitutional Democratic Party. *See* Ka-
    dets (Constitutional Democratic Party)
Constitutional question, 68–69, 73, 96, 200
  ministerial crisis and, 81–82
Constitutionalism vs. anticonstitutionalism,
    46, 79
Council for Local Economy, 92
Council of Ministers, 112, 171, 173, 197,
    215
  ministerial crisis and, 80, 81
  ministerial "leapfrog" in, 224–225
  reorganization of, 13
  restrictions on Duma and, 176–178, 198
Countryside. *See* Rural sector

Demchenko, Vsevolod Iakovlevich, 117,
    131, 137, 153, 154, 167, 183, 184
  challenge to Duma and, 198
  profile of, 223
  Progressive Bloc and, 212, 218, 231
  tension in Duma and, 172–173, 179–180,
    185
Dmitriev, P. P., 189
Dorrer, Count V. F., 23
Dribintsev, V. S., 161
Duma (lower house of parliament)
  campaign for serious session in, 209–210
  challenge to, 198–199
  closing of, 215–216
  creation of, 1, 12–13
  the fourth, elections to
    background to, 142–143
    government-Nationalist relationship
      and, 148–152
    ideology of Nationalists and, 146–148

Duma (*continued*)
    Nationalist Party restructuring and,
      143–146
  results of, by region, 152–165
  the fourth, sessions of
    background to, 166–167
    first, composition and working of, 167–
      176
    new zemstvos and, 189–191
    second, division in, 176–181
    split in Kiev and, 181–189
  the government and first two, 27–29
  importance of, to Nationalists, 7–8
  influence of government and, 5–6
  Nationalists' linkage to local politics and,
    6–7, 62–63, 71, 77, 114–115, 143–
    144, 152, 173
  restrictions on, 176–178, 198–199
  right fraction in third, 26
  the third (1907)
    electors and, 43–49
    makeup of, overview, 65–67
    moderate right in, 67–72
    Nationalists and, 49–64
    new electoral law and, 31–33
    realignment of forces in, 73–79
Durnovo, P. N., 80, 117, 120, 193
  Progressive Bloc and, 212, 217
Duverger, Maurice, 6
Dvoriantsvo. *See* Nobles

Eiler, A. A., 134, 135
Elections
  fourth Duma (1912)
    background to, 142–143
    preparations for, 143–152
    results of, 152–165
  to Nationalist Party council, 145
  president of Kiev Club, 181–182, 184–
    185
  presidium, fourth Duma, 170
  third Duma (1907)
    electors and, 43–49
    makeup of, 31–42
    Nationalists and, 49–64
    new electoral law and, 31–33

Elections (*continued*)
zemstvo, 19, 86–89
first in borderland, 128–130
results and aftermath of, 136–141
Electoral law, 77
manipulation of, 5, 28–29
restrictive, third Duma, 1, 26
third Duma election and, 31–33
Electoral process, structure of, 4–5
Electors, 31
of third Duma, 43–49
Evlogii, Archbishop, 144, 206
Kholm question and, 111–112

Famine of 1891, 19
Finland, the National campaign and, 102–106
France, Radicals in, 10
Fundamental Laws
Article 87 in, 13, 28, 122, 215
Article 96 in, 80
issuance of, 12–13

Galicia-Russia Society, 144, 192–193, 205–206
Gentry. *See also* Landlords; Landowners; Nobles
changing position of, 2–6
election of 1912 and, 156–157
electoral law and, 31–33
party organization and, 154
reliance of, on state, 63–64
transformation of, after 1905, 13–19
west Russian, zemstvos and, 69–70
zemstvos and, 19–22, 109
Gerbel', S. N., 130, 133, 134, 150
Germans, 105, 125
Germany, 9, 195, 205
radicals in, 10
Girs, A. A., 128, 130, 135, 150
Gizhitskii, Alexander Stepanovich, 20, 37, 77, 132, 134, 135, 137, 158, 167, 189, 223, 231
Glebov II (Octobrist member of Duma), 69
Gololobov, Ia. G., 75, 82, 93, 94
Golos Moskvy (Octobrist newspaper), 34
Golytsin, N. D., 225

Goremykin, Ivan Logginovich, 25, 27, 197, 200, 207
as emperor's liaison, 208
Progressive Bloc and, 215–216
replacement of, 225
serious Duma session and, 209–210
Government. *See also* Bureaucracy; Zemstvos
ambiguousness toward, Nationalists and, 148–152, 171–172, 173, 200–201
conservatives and, conflict between, 5, 8–9
Duma restrictions and, 176–177, 198–199
first two Dumas and, 27–29
Nationalist party structure and, 77–78
nobles' role and, 3–4
reliance of gentry on, 63–64
service to tsar, nobles and, 2, 3, 15, 16–18, 20, 185–186, 221, 231
zemstvo elections and, 130–131, 133
Grigorovich-Barskii, D. N., 154
Grigorovich-Barskii, K. P., 137, 156, 184, 185, 233
Grodno (province), 162
Guchkov, Alexander, 21, 38, 74, 144, 163, 167, 194, 221, 233
Octobrist split and, 178
Octobrists and, 23, 24, 67
political attack on, 74–75
replaced by Balashev, 91
resigns presidency of Duma, 123, 124
Russian National fraction and, 94, 95–96, 100
Stolypin and, 73, 79, 81–82, 91, 122
trade union support of, 74–75
Gurko, V. I., 213

Haimson, Leopold, 200
Henderson, Neville, 38–39
Hosking, Geoffrey, 200

Ianushkevich, General, 214
Iasnopolskii, M., 17
Ideology
conservative, Nationalists and, 8–9
Nationalist, revised, 146–148
Octobrist, 92

Ignatiev (Governor of Podol'e), 158
Independent Nationalist Party, 125, 126
Industrialization (modernization), 201
    agrarian interests and, 230
    in Kiev, 60
    nobility's position and, 2, 4, 5, 6, 16, 19
    political parties and, 172, 174–175
    Revolution of 1905 and, 10–12
Ivanov, S. I., 154

Japan, War of 1904 and, 12
Jews, 47, 48, 70, 89, 97, 105, 125, 160. *See also* Anti-Semitism
    Balashev's group and, 227
    Nationalists' attitude toward, 10
    opposition to tsarism and, 51
    Progressive Bloc and, 228–229
    restriction of (Pale of Settlement), 51, 214
    in western provinces, 50, 55
    zemstvos and, 106

Kadets (Constitutional Democratic Party), 7, 10, 28, 68, 75, 76, 78, 82, 110, 129, 136, 148, 183
    anti-Semitism and, 214
    cooperation with Nationalists, 210, 211
    domination of Duma by, 27
    formation of, 21
    in fourth Duma, 154, 163, 171, 175, 178
    nationalism and, 146–147
    Progressive Bloc and, 212, 214, 219, 220, 223, 228–229, 230
    World War I and, 203, 208
Kazan, 163–164
Kharitonov, P. A., 215, 216
Kholm, question of, 102, 110–113
Khomiakov, N. A., 39
Khvostov, A. A., 207
Kiev (city)
    election of fourth Duma in, 153–154
    election of 1909 in, 89
    influence of, on Nationalists, 60–63
    population of, 60
Kiev (gubernia or province) 52, 56, 125, 204
    bread prices and, 230

Kiev (*continued*)
    election of fourth Duma in, 155–157
    Nationalist split in, 181–189
    political organization in, 130–132
    population growth in, 60
    wartime politics in, 231, 232
    zemstvo finances in, 190
    zemstvo election results in, 137
Kiev Club of Russian Nationalists, 83, 90, 103, 113, 114, 128, 134, 155, 172, 200, 204, 231
    creation of, 70–71
    election of 1909 and, 89
    split in, 181–189
    zemstvo bill and, 117, 119, 120
Kievlianin (Nationalist newspaper), 70, 83, 91–92, 126, 136, 183, 216
    Beilis affair and, 187–188
Kokovtsov, V. N., 128, 140–141, 144
    dismissal of, 196–197
    as enemy of Nationalists, 148–149
    fourth Duma and, 171, 173, 176–177
Konovalov, A. I., 174
Kovalevskii, P. I., 104, 105, 146–147, 148
Krivoshein, A. V., 207, 208, 215, 216
Krupenskii family, 41
Krupenskii, Pavel Nikolaevich, 21, 42, 79, 126, 163
    forms Independent Nationalists, 125–126
    fourth Duma and, 168–169
    moderate right group and, 68, 75, 77
    National Club resignation of, 191
    Progressive Bloc and, 211
    Russian National fraction and, 97
    zemstvo bill reaction and, 124–125
Kryzhanovskii, S. E., 28, 108, 128
    Kholm and, 111, 112
    zemstvos and, 70
Kulakovskii, Professor, 182
Kutaisov, A. P., 135, 136, 159
    government assistance and, 150–152

Labor, 29. *See also* Strikes; Trade unions
    discontent of, 11
    disturbances of, 199–200, 208, 226
    movement revived, 142, 166
Lado (Baliasnyi), 147

Ladomirskii, N. N., 37, 114, 161
  National Group and, 69
Land. *See also* Landlords; Landowners
  holding of, in west borderland, 56–57
  nobility's position and, 2
  noble-owned, 14–15
  non-Russians and, 125
  owned by Poles and Russians in border-
    lands, 52
  value of, 55
Landlords. *See also* Gentry; Landowners
  dealings of, with Jews and Poles, 48
  electoral law and, 31–33
  lack of agricultural knowledge among, 15
  land lost by nobles, in Ukraine, 56
  land retained by, 57, 58
  new class consciousness of, 63
  peasant demand for land and, 58–59
  Polish vs. Russian, in borderland, 49–52,
    55, 57, 118, 213
  Pikhno proposal and, 83–86
Landowners, 47. *See also* Gentry; Land-
    lords
  election of 1912 and, 156, 158, 160, 162
  electoral law and, 31–33
  Nationalist, 221
  Octobrist, 42
  social isolation of, 61
La Polambara, Joseph, 100 n104
Lena massacre, 30, 142
Lenin, V. I., 201
Liberals, 29. *See also* Kadets (Constitutional
    Democratic Party)
  nationalism and, 147
  zemstvos and, 11, 19–20, 21, 38
Liubinskii, A. S., 62
Local government, organs of. *See* Zemstvos
Lokot, T., 230
Lublin (province), 110
Lvov, G. E., 203

Makarov, A. A., 149–150, 151, 157
Maklakov, N. A., 176, 177, 198, 207
Maklakov, V. A., 187
Manifesto of October 17, 21, 30
  issuance of, 12–13
Markevich, V. N., 129, 134, 137

Markov II, N. E., 23, 34, 67, 176–177, 227,
    228
Marxist Social Democrats, 11, 28, 74, 164
Melnikov, M. A., 159
Menshikov, M. O., 47, 71, 84, 105, 114, 123
  Russian National fraction and, 97, 98
Michels, Robert, 4
Military reform, 79–80, 81. *See also* Army
Miliukov, Paul, 194, 210, 211, 221, 233
Ministerial boycott (1913), 177
Ministerial crisis (1909), 73, 79–82
Ministry of Interior, 127, 176
  appointive zemstvos and, 52
  election information (1907) of, 33
  Finland question and, 103
  petitioning of, by gentry, 6
Minsk, 61
  election of fourth Duma in, 159–160
  political organization in, 132–134
Mitrofan, Bishop, 160–161
Modernization. *See* Industrialization
Mogilev (province), 150
  election of fourth Duma in, 160–161
Mozhaiskii, N. N., 158, 223

Namier, Lewis, 40
Nationalism, 82, 101, 102
  conservative camp and, 9–10
  imperialism and, 196
  Nationalist conception of, 9–10, 48, 89,
    104, 146–147, 168–169
  party variants of, 146–147
  psychological aspects of, 104–105
  Russian National fraction and, 97, 98
  Union of Russian People and, 25
  west Russian landlords and, 50, 51
  "zoological," 94
Nationalists (Russian Nationalist Party), 6,
    33
  borderland and, 49–64
  borderland interests of, 48–49
  class orientation of, 18
  constituency of, 8
  Duma (national) and provincial (local)
    linkage of, 6–7, 62–63, 71, 77,
    114–115, 143–144, 152, 173
    policy abandoned, 203

Nationalists (*continued*)
    zemstvo lack and, 79
  early growth of, 113–116
  educational level of electors of, 47
  election to party council of, 145
  establishment of, 1–2
    and formation of National Union, 93–100
    and rural shift to right, 91–93
    Stolypin's position and, 91–93
  foreign affairs and, 193–196
  in fourth Duma
    division of, 176–181
    factions of, 167–176
    ministerial boycott and, 176–177
      new zemstvos and, 189–191
      split in Kiev and, 181–189
  fourth Duma elections and
    background of, 142–143
    the government and, 148–152
    ideological revisions and, 146–148
    restructured organization and, 143–146
    results of, by region, 152–165
  future (pre-party)
    absence of zemstvos and, 20
    constitutional question and, 68–69
    in third Duma, 36–37, 39–42, 43–47, 48–49
  geographical background of, 41–42
  ideology and, 8–9, 146–148
  importance of Duma to, 7–8
  influence of Kiev (city) on, 60–63
  landholding patterns and, 57–58
  local government and, 128
  meaning of, outside borderland, 162
  moderate right of, 34, 39, 69–72
    Octobrist split and, 74–79
    zemstvo elections and, 89–91
  modernization of organizational stucture of, 100
    fourth Duma elections and, 154, 157, 161–162
    in west Russia, 127–136
  national campaign of
    Finnish question and, 102–106
    Kholm question and, 110–113
    zemstvo bill and, 106–110

Nationalists (*continued*)
  national convention (1914) of, 197–198
  National Group and, 34, 39, 69, 70, 71–72, 75
  nationalism and, 9–10, 48, 89, 104, 146–147, 168–169
  party platform (1912) of, 145–146
  personality profile of leaders of, 220–224
  power base of, 101–102
  and restrictions on Duma, 176–179, 198–199
  rise of
    ministerial crisis and, 73, 79–82
    moderate right party creation, 74–79
    Octobrist position and, 67–72
    overview of, 65–67
    Pikhno proposal and, 83–86
  social base of, 63, 77, 78, 95
  societies associated with, 191–193
  Stolypin's relationship with, 73, 81–82, 91–93, 100, 102, 115, 116
  stronghold of (borderland), 49–64
  World War I and
    first months of, 200–206
    psychological and ideological effect of, 220
    summer crisis of (1915)
      background to, 206–209
      division of regulars and progressives, 226–231
      politics in provinces, 231–234
      progressive bloc formed during, 209–217
      schism during, 217–224
  and zemstvos in the borderland, 45, 62, 115–116
  bill for
    crisis of, 116–127
    proposal of, 106–110
  early activity of, 189–191
  election of 1909, 89–91
  election of 1911, 136–141
  lack of, party development and, 79
  organization of, for elections, 127–136
  Pikhno proposal and, 83–86
  Shulgin on, 61, 62
Navy, 79, 80–81. *See also* Army
Neidgart, A. B., 80, 117

Nekrasov (Duma Kadet deputy), 230
Nicholas II, 8, 68, 112, 116, 166
  abdication of, 233
  Kokovtsov's dismissal and, 196–197
  manifesto of October 17 (1905) of, 12–13
  memorandum of 1914 and, 193
  Pikhno proposal and, 83–84
  Stolypin and, 27, 28, 66, 139
    faith in shaken, 121
    ministerial crisis and, 80–81
    zemstvo bill and, 117, 118–119, 120,
      121–122
  Union of Russian People and, 25
  war with Japan (1904) and, 12
  World War I and
    army command of, 214–215
    closing of Duma and, 216
    government changes and, 207–208,
      225
    war industry committees and, 207
Nikolaevich, Nikolai, 207, 215
Nobles. *See also* Gentry; Landlords; Land-
    owners
  agriculture and, 3, 15–18
  attitude of, toward
    peasants, 15–16
    state, 3–4, 5
  as country gentlemen, politics and, 40
  electoral law and, 31–33
  estates of, 14–15, 57, 58
    large, farming and, 17–18
    and Nationalist leaders, 20–21
  Kiev Club and, 89
  in moderate right group, 69
  Polish vs. Russian, 49–52, 55, 57, 118
    Pikhno proposal and, 83–86
  political party choices of, 46
  political party formation and, 4–6
  service to tsar and, 2, 3, 15, 185–186, 221
    transition to farming and, 16–18, 20
  transformation of noble estate, Revolu-
    tion of 1905 and, 13–19
  wealth of, differences in, 14
  zemstvo control and, 19–22, 126
  zemstvo election of 1909 and, 86–87

October 17 manifesto of Nicholas II. *See*
  Manifesto of October 17

Octobrists (Union of October 17), 7, 10, 28,
    33, 40, 141, 146, 183–184, 189
  All-Russian Union formation and, 93–94,
    96, 97, 99, 100
  anti-German proposal and, 125
  areas of strength of, 56
  disintegration of, 73–74, 94–100
  distinguished from Nationalists, 41–42,
    49
  educational level of electors of, 47
  election of 1912 and, 144, 163, 164
  formation of, 21, 22, 23–25
  in fourth Duma, 167, 168, 169, 170–171,
    173, 174, 175–176
    split of, 178–179
  geographical distribution of, 60
  local and Duma linkage and, 62
  Pikhno proposal and, 84–85
  Progressive Bloc and, 220, 223
  social base of, 37–38
  split of moderate right from, 74–79
  Stolypin's relationship with, 25, 66, 73,
    79, 81–82, 91–92, 117, 120
  in third Duma, 34, 36, 37–39, 43–46, 47,
    65–66
  World War I and, 207
  zemstvos and, 38, 72
  zemstvos bill and, 107, 109–110, 120,
    121, 122–124, 125, 126
Ofrosimov, Ia. N., 84, 150

Pan-Slavism, 9–10, 144, 146, 192–194, 196
Pares, Bernard, 40, 201
Parliamentary system, 4, 5
Party of Peaceful Renovation, 24
Patriotic bloc, 153–154
Pavlovsky, G. P., 14
Peasants, 19, 22, 29, 90, 95, 101, 143, 148,
    162, 197–198
  as agricultural workers, 53
  categorized, 58
  electoral law and, 31, 32–33
  fourth Duma elections and, 155–156,
    158, 160, 163, 164, 165
  lack of land for, 58–59, 165
  market economy and, 55
  Nationalist, 40

Peasants (*continued*)
  nobles' psychological block concerning, 15–16
  renting to, by nobles, 17
  Stolypin's attitude toward, 28
  strikes by, 59
  violent disturbances of, 11, 21, 36, 50, 226
  west borderland landlords and, 50–51
  Witte's political judgment of, 25
  zemstvos, fear of, 106, 109, 117, 118, 127, 139
  zemstvos elections and, 137, 138
Peter the Great, 13, 15
Pikhno, D. I., 70, 136, 180
  zemstvo proposal of, 83–86
Pilts (Governor of Mogilev), 160–161
Podol'e, 52, 56, 57, 125, 204
  election of fourth Duma in, 157–159
  new zemstvo in, Nationalists and, 189–190
  political organization in, 134–135
  wartime politics in, 231–232
  zemstvo election results in, 137–138
Poland. *See also* Poles
  Kholm question and, 110–113
  western borderland history and, 49
Poles, 48, 70, 105, 125, 141, 205, 214. *See also* Poland
  election of 1912 and, 158, 160
  as landlords, vs. Russian landlords, 49–52, 55, 57, 118, 213
  landowning and, 57
  Nationalists' attitude toward, 10
  neo-Slav movement and, 194
  Pikhno proposal and, 83, 85, 86
  restricting of, 69
  Savenko on, 213
  western zemstvo bill and, 106, 107, 108, 109
  zemstvo election and, 128, 136, 137–138, 139
Political labels, imprecision of, 33–35, 87, 158, 163
Political opinion. *See* Conservatives; Pravye; Liberals
Political parties. *See also specific political parties*
  gentry and, 3, 4–5, 6
  industrialization and, 172, 174–175

Political parties (*continued*)
  liberation movement and, 11–12
  nobles' choice of, 46–47
  nobles' prejudice against, 40
  World War I and, 202–203
Polivanov, A. A., 208–209, 215
Polovstov, L. V., 114
Pomestie (landed estate). *See* Nobles, estates of
Pototskii, A. A., 57, 59, 77, 107, 125, 134, 137, 158, 186, 223, 231
Pravye (extreme right), 33, 40, 68, 79, 90, 97, 100, 110, 136, 183, 184, 189, 200, 209, 217, 219
  in fourth Duma, 158, 159, 160, 163, 169, 175, 179
  split in, 227
  in third Duma, 34–35, 36
Priests, 47, 143
  domination of peasants by, 31
  electoral law and, 33
  as electors, 44, 45
  fourth Duma elections and, 155, 156, 157, 158, 160–161, 164
  Nationalist, 40
  zemstvos and, 106, 107, 108, 110
Progressive Bloc
  formation of, 209–217
  personality profile of leaders in, 221–223
  political position of, 228–231
  separation of, from Nationalists, 217, 221
Progressives, 110, 129, 162, 163, 169, 174, 178, 182, 204, 208
  use of term, 87
Proletariat (working class). *See* Labor
Pskov (province), 163, 164
Purishkevich, V. M., 23, 34, 67, 224, 234
  pravye split and, 227

Railroads
  Nationalist Party development and, 7
  role of, in Kiev's growth, 60
  workers of, in Kiev Club, 89
  during World War I, 226, 232
Rakovich, I. A., 83, 89, 106, 117, 134, 150, 186, 189, 231
Rasputin, Grigori Efimovich, 207, 214, 225

Reva, I. M., 131, 137
    zemstvo's finances and, 190
Revolution of 1905, 21
    background of, 10–19
Right, the. *See* Conservatives; Pravye
Robinson, Geroid, 14–15
Rodzevich, O. V., 133
Rodzianko, M. V., 122, 124, 170, 177, 180, 183
    charges against Balashev and, 209–210
    Progressive Bloc and, 212
Roshko, E. K., 186
Rubach, M. A., 14, 56
Rukhlov, S. V., 71, 72, 111
    Kiev Club members and, 89
Rural sector, 3
    fourth Duma election in, 155–156
    shift to right in, 86–91
    split among Nationalists and, 231–234
Russia. *See* Central Russia; Western Russia (borderlands)
Russian Nationalist Party. *See* Nationalists (Russian Nationalist Party)

Sabler, V. K., 207
Safonov, P. A., 223
Samarin, A. D., 208, 216
Savenko, Anatoly Ivanovich, 70, 95, 125, 130, 137, 139, 141, 145, 167, 193, 198, 199, 200
    class struggle and, 147–148
    closing of Duma and, 216
    election of 1912 and, 153, 154, 155, 156
    foreign affairs and, 193–196
    Kiev Club and, 89
    Kiev Club split and, 181–186
    Kutaisov affair and, 150–152
    National Club and, 98–99, 191
    nationalism and, 104, 105, 107
    Octobrist position and, 99–100
    profile of, 221–222, 223
    Progressive Bloc and, 209, 211, 212, 213, 214, 217–219, 228–229, 231
    tension in Duma and, 172–173, 174–175, 177, 179–180
    zemstvo bill and, 92–93
Sazonov, N. D., 144
Sazonovich, P. V., 161

Sazonovich, S. P., 90
Serbia, 194, 195
Serfs, emancipation of, 15, 49. *See also* Peasants
Service to tsar. *See* Government, service to tsar, nobles and
Seymour, Richard, 39
Shcheglovitov, I. G., 176, 207
Shcherbatov (Council of Ministers member), 216
Shidlovskii, S. I., 179, 215, 233
Shingarev, A. I., 211
Shipov, D. N., 21
    Octobrists and, 23–24
Shteiger, Baron, 156, 185
Shturmer, B. V., 225
Shulgin, Vasillii Vitalevich, 71, 136, 167, 199, 204, 225, 233
    bread prices and, 229–230
    closing of Duma and, 216
    isolation of landowners and, 61
    Kadets and, 210, 211, 212, 214, 219, 223, 228
    Kiev Club split and, 183–184, 187–188
    Kutaisov affair and, 150–151
    profile of, 222–223
    Progressive Bloc and, 212–213, 214, 215, 217, 218, 228–229, 231
    zemstvo issue and, 61, 107, 109
Shvindt (Mayor of Berdichev), 150
Sidorov, A. A., 70
Siedlice (province), 110
Sikorskii, A. I., 104
Sinadino, P. V., 68
Sirovkin, N., 199
Skrynchenko, D. V., 132, 133
Slovo (liberal newspaper), 74, 76
Social classes. *See also specific social classes*
    capitalism and, 201
    class struggle and, 147–148
    discontent among all, 11
    emergence of modern, 2–3
    Stolypin and, 171
Social Democrats. *See* Marxist Social Democrats
Socialist Revolutionaries, 12, 140, 164
State, the. *See* Bureaucracy; Government
State Council, 106, 110, 113
    Pikhno proposal and, 83, 86

State Council (*continued*)
 zemstvo bill and, 117–119, 120–121, 122,
  123
Stolypin, Peter Arkadevich, 1, 7, 73, 76, 101,
  128, 134, 144, 162, 165, 166, 171
 agrarian reform of, 27–28, 142
 appointment of, 27
 assassination of, 140
 declares martial law, 24
 Finland and, 102–103
 franchise restriction and, 28–29
 Guchkov and, 73, 79, 81–82, 91, 122
 Kholm question and, 110, 112
 mental state of, 121
 Nationalists and, 73, 81–82, 91–93, 100,
  102, 115, 116, 148
 Nicholas II and, 27, 28, 66, 139
  faith in shaken, 121
  ministerial crisis and, 80–81
  zemstvo bill and, 117, 118–119, 120,
   121–122
 Octobrists and, 25, 66, 73, 79, 81–82, 88,
  91, 117, 120
 political base of, ministerial crisis and, 79–
  82
 replacement of, by Kokovtsov, 140–141
 social peace and, 30
 zemstvos in borderland and, 41, 70, 93,
  108, 109
  bill for, political cost to, 116–127, 130,
   139
  Pikhno proposal and, 83–86
Strikes, 11, 60, 166, 208, 226. *See also*
 Labor
 Bloody Sunday and, 12
 Lena massacre and, 30, 142
 Nationalists and, 199–200
 peasant, 59
Struve, Peter, 146
Suffrage, 4, 20. *See also* Electoral law
Sugar beets. *See* Agriculture, sugar beets and
Sukhomlinov, V. A., 207, 208
Sukovkin, M. A., 232, 233
Suvchinskii, K. E., 125, 126, 137, 186

Taxation, 175, 190
Terms (political). *See* Political labels, imprecision of

Third Element, 19
Towns. *See* Cities; Urban sector
Trade unions, 74–75. *See also* Labor
Trepov, F. F., 83, 134, 150, 151, 185
Trepov, V. F., 80, 117, 118–119, 120
Tsar. *See* Nicholas II
Tsarina. *See* Alexandra Feodorovna (Tsar-
 ina)
Turkey, 194, 195

Ukraine, 56
Ukrainian nationalist movement, 51
Union of Liberation, 12, 20
Union of October 17. *See* Octobrists (Union
 of October 17)
Union of Russian Nationalists, 113
 formation of, 89
 Podol'e branch of, 113, 114, 134, 135,
  189–190
Union of Russian People, 22, 146, 162
 formation of, 25–27
 in third Duma, 35–36
Union of Towns, 203
Urban sector. *See also* Cities
 election of 1909 and, 88
 influence of, on Nationalists, 60–63
 tension in Duma and, 175
Urusov, Alexander Petrovich, 23, 41, 71, 98
 as leader of National Group, 69, 71–72
 as a Nationalist, 46

Vasilchikov, B. A., 98, 99
Viatka Monarchist Party, 114
Vishnevskii, G. A., 156
Vitebsk (province), 150
 election of fourth Duma in, 160
Volkonskii, Vladimir Mikhailovich, 21, 177
Voluntary Organizations, 204, 207, 208,
 215, 216, 224
Volynia, 52, 56, 125, 150, 204
 election of fourth Duma in, 159
 political organization in, 135–136
 zemstvos election results in, 136
Von Gubbenet, N. K., 37, 161
 National Group and, 69
Vyborshchiki. *See* Electors

War. *See also* Revolution of 1905; World War I
  in Balkans
    First (1912), 194
    Second (1913), 195
  with Japan (1904), 12
War Industry Committees, 207
Weiss, John, 9
West Russian Meeting, 90–91, 92, 93
Western Russia (borderlands). *See also* Western zemstvo bill; Zemstvos
  election of fourth Duma in, 153–162
  electors in, 47
  as Nationalist deputies' homeland, 41–42
  as Nationalist stronghold, 49–64
  Nationalists stress protection of, 72
  political organization in, 127–136
  population composition in, 50
  railroads, Nationalist Party and, 7
Western zemstvo bill, 49, 82, 103, 106, 161. *See also* Nationalists, and zemstvos in the borderland; Zemstvos (local government institutions)
  analyzed, 106–110
  crisis of, 116–127
  effects of, on fourth Duma, 168
West-Russia Society, 144, 192
Witte, Sergei, 3, 12, 19, 23, 27, 80, 90, 196
  industrialization and, 6, 10–11
  peasants and, 25
  zemstvo bill and, 117, 118
World War I
  army in, 205, 206, 214–215, 232
  bread prices and, 229–230
  first months of, 200–206
  food riots and, 226
  shortages during, 225–226, 229, 232
  summer crisis of 1915 and
    background to, 206–209
    division of Nationalists and, 226–231
    Progressive Bloc formed during, 209–217

World War I (*continued*)
  provinces during, 231–234
  schism in Nationalist ranks and, 217–224

Zamysloviskii, G. G., 34
Zamyslovskii, A. A., 187
Zemstvo congress, 20, 28, 220
Zemstvos (local government institutions). *See also* Nationalists, and zemstvos in the borderland; Western zemstvo bill
  appointive in borderlands, 52, 69, 71
  in Caucasus and Siberia, 212–213
  elections
    first in borderlands, 127–130
    of 1909, 86–89
    nobility control and, 19
    political organization and, 130–136
    results and aftermath, 136–141
  financial concerns of, 190, 204–205
  gentry concern with, 19–22
  Kadets expelled from, 40
  lack of, Nationalist Party development and, 79
  law of 1890 and, 52
  normalization of, in west, 69–70
  Octobrists and, 38, 72
  plan to introduce, in borderlands, 41, 61, 62, 90–91, 99
    conservative argument against, 90
    Pikhno proposal and, 83–86
    Savenko's plan for, 92–93
    Stolypin and, 41, 70, 93, 108–109, 116–127
  political shifts in, 21–22, 24–25, 86–89
  reform of 1864 and, 52
  resentment of central government and, 11
  during World War I, 232–233
Zhilin, N. A., 156